Growing up
Māori

He kākano e ruia mai i Rangiātea,
E kore e ngaro

I am a seed from Rangiātea,
I will not be lost

Growing up
Māori

EDITED BY
WITI IHIMAERA

TANDEM PRESS

First published in 1998 by
TANDEM PRESS
2 Rugby Road, Birkenhead, Auckland 10
New Zealand

ISBN 1 877178 16 0

Cover and text design by Christine Hansen
Front cover photographs (clockwise from top):
Patricia Grace and family; Apirana Taylor; Joanna Paul (left);
Tainui Stephens and father; Phil Kawana.
Back cover photograph:
Witi Ihimaera with his grandmother.
Typesetting by Graeme Leather
Printed in New Zealand by Publishing Press Limited

Ngā tīpuna ki mua,

Ko tātou kei muri.

The ancestors in front,

We are behind.

ACKNOWLEDGEMENTS

Grateful acknowledgement is made to the following for permission to reprint previously published material:

Auckland University Press for Makereti's 'The Way it Used to Be', p. 19
Iranui Haig for 'Titiro, Moko! Whakarongo, Moko!', p. 40
Margie Hohepa, Makere Harawira and the editors of *Te Pua* for the pieces 'Us Kids' and 'Fair-skinned, Blue-eyed', pp. 58 and 202, respectively
Ngahuia Te Awekotuku for 'He Whare Tangata: He Whare Kura? What's Happening to Our Māori Girls?', p. 72
Mihi Edwards and Penguin Books (NZ) for 'My Beginnings', p. 98
Hodder Moa Beckett for 'Dad, Mum and Ruatāhuna' by Sir Howard Morrison, p. 133
Donna Awatere Huata for 'First Things First', p. 141
Ngā Tauira Māori for the cartoon on p. 189
Oxford University Press, Australia for the quote by Eruera Stirling, from *Eruera: The Teachings of a Māori Elder* © Oxford University Press, on p. 295

Thanks also to Bob Ross, whose idea it was to collect the stories about growing up Māori, our editors, Sara Haddad and Ross Calman. The University of Auckland and Merimeri Penfold provided research and language assistance. Jessica Ihimaera Smiler and Olivia Ihimaera Smiler, as always, were a constant inspiration.

The publishers have made every attempt to contact the copyright holders of all previously published material. We apologise if there have been any omissions and would be pleased to hear from anyone not duly acknowledged.

CONTENTS

PART TWO: POST-MODERN MĀORI

Tīhei mauriora!
Tīhei uriuri, tīhei nakonako
Ka tau, ha, whakatau ko te rangi i runga nei
Ka tau, ha, whakatau ko te papa i raro nei
Ka tau, ha, whakatau ko Te Matuku mai i Rarotonga
Koia i rukuhia manawa pou roto
Koia i rukuhia manawa pou waho
Whakatina kia tina, Te More i Hawaiki
E pupū ana hoki e wāwau ana hoki
Tārewa tū ki te rangi
Aua kia eke, eke panuku, eke Tangaroa
Hui ē! Tāiki ē!

INTRODUCTION

1.

I OFTEN have a laugh with myself when friends whom I ask to help me on some matter or to come with me to a meeting answer with, 'Sorry, I'm too busy.' *Busy?* Nobody can be busier than a Māori. In March and April, when I was putting *Growing Up Māori* together, here's what some of the invited contributors were doing for the iwi.

Winston Peters was flat out as Deputy Prime Minister. Sandra Lee was making impassioned speeches during the presentation of the Ngāi Tahu settlement bill. I was able to briefly hongi John Tamihere during the opening of Robyn Kahukiwa's exhibition in Auckland – John was fighting in the High Court to have urban iwi included in the fisheries settlement. Deirdre Nehua was at the exhibition with Syd Jackson – Deirdre had just flown back from Christchurch.

The next day I bumped into Te Kui (Merimeri Penfold) on her way back from the High Court. I caught a glimpse of Sir Hugh Kawharu walking on his way to present evidence. Mike Smith was on the television news, supporting the urban iwi, haranguing Sir Tipene O'Regan on television: 'Come on, Tipene, let us in.' I heard that Syd and June Mead were also at the hearing.

On my way down to Wellington (the sixth time in the month) I had a quick exchange with John Turei who was in the capital for the day – 'The word iwi was never around in my time,' he said. I got a telephone call from Jenny Te Paa, back from a meeting in Tonga, saying she hoped to meet the deadline. Judge Mick Brown said he just couldn't do it. Then, in Gisborne, where I went on business (and a tangi for my uncle John Kaua), I tried to get in touch with Tame Iti. But he was still busy on the Waikaremoana Claim.

Mika, the hit of the Edinburgh Fringe Festival, was preparing to go overseas again. Merata Mita was making a documentary on a million black men marching on Washington. Alan Duff was in the middle of writing columns, signing a new film contract for *What Becomes of the Broken Hearted?* and making a speech to the Children's Book Foundation. Adam Parore was playing cricket. Tawera Nikau was in Sydney proving he's one of the best league players in the business (even if he wasn't selected for the New Zealand team).

Phew, and that's not the half of it.

2.

Growing Up Māori is, therefore, not a poll on the question. So if you're looking for a representative and thematically consistent cross-section of Māori on the question of growing up Māori – forget it. Most of the contributors who appear in the following pages are there because, somehow or other, they were able to take a few minutes to respond to the kaupapa. To support them, the experiences of other contributors have been extracted from their biographies or other publications. In all cases, the words of the contributors are their own.

Another point of caution: most Māori offer subjective experience and they write as they talk. White hot. Straight for the jugular. What comes to the mind is what gets put down on the page. Thus, what the contributors have written about and the way it has been written has been their choice for that moment. Each writer has given a particular response on a particular day prompted by a particular memory. But, on another day, the response may have been different.

To be frank, although this collection *is* entitled *Growing Up Māori*, that very notion is problematic. It frames Māori identity the same way as the opening shot of the film adaptation of Alan Duff's novel, *Once Were Warriors*. In the film we see a Māori meeting house in a rural landscape. Then the director, Lee Tamahori, cunningly has the camera pull back from the meeting house – and we see that it is only a billboard above an Auckland motorway and, in the background, is the reality of South Auckland. In many respects the title is like that billboard. But rather than change it, the decision was made to retain it as an ironic context, an iconic representation of reader expectations that they will find stories that show that the way Māori were is still the way Māori *are*. Well, sorry, folks, but things are not as simple as that.

The oldest witness featured in this book is Aunty Ada Haig, born in 1913, and one could arguably say that this book provides a window on growing up Māori over some 85 years. But pull the camera back and what we have instead is the other, real, story of how Māori have responded to Pākehā colonisation since the signing of the Treaty of Waitangi in 1840. Even for those other writers who were born before 1920, like Tom Smiler Junior and Mihi Edwards, one of the great themes of their lives was their engagement with Pākehā. Waka Vercoe, Te Kui, Patricia Grace, J.C. Sturm and Howard Morrison carry the story on during the inter-war years, and one gets the impression of accommodation of Pākehā within a Māori framework – though not necessarily vice versa.

Then come the years of the Second World War and their aftermath. Already stripped of political and economic power, and a minority in a country in which they were the tangata whenua, Māori also began to be driven by economics from their rural hearths to settle among Pākehā . The stories begin to change, as the balance of power changes, and we can trace the changes in the work of Irihapeti Ramsden, Sir Paul Reeves and Waerete Norman, among others.

The post-war years accelerated this great rural to urban drift and the accompanying discontinuity in transmission of Māori family histories and culture across time and space. By the 1950s, at least fifty percent of Māori lived in urban areas. By far the greatest challenges to Māori have been in how they have managed the journey. Some, like Deirdre Nehua, Donna Awatere, Alan Duff and Moana Jackson, reveal how the family has been the battleground upon which identity has had to be fought for – and how punitive the process has been. Others like Reina Whaitiri, Mike Smith and Riwia Brown reveal the playground and schoolroom as another significant arena of challenge where, pushed into corners, we had to come out fighting.

Then came the years of Māori protest, 1970 to 1990. By this point Māori were down to nine percent of the population. But as we can read from the work of the first and second generation of urban Māori like Tainui Stephens, Joanna Paul, Phil Kawana and Andrew Vercoe, resurgence of pride has meant reclamation of identity.

Thus, together, all the witnesses in *Growing Up Māori* attest to a truly epic story of survival, of resilience, of maintaining a sense of – if not the semblance of – tribal and personal sovereignty, and Māori identity, in the twentieth century. We no longer grow up *that* way. We grow up *this* way. And this *is* the Māori way, today, of growing up.

3.

With all the above in mind, *Growing Up Māori* has been devised so that its contributors can tell you in their own words their own stories. But as editor, I also wanted to make the collection interesting and entertaining. So we start with a prologue, in which the past is put before us, by way of two firsthand accounts of what it was like to grow up *before* Captain Cook discovered New Zealand for Britannia in 1769. Part One is entitled 'Māori Born, Pākehā World', and Part Two is entitled 'Post-modern Māori', so you have two books, really, for the price of one. A lot of crossovers occur between the two books but the main theme of both is how Māori identity continues to be constructed from the past *and* in the present.

The notion of Māori identity is, in fact, problematic. There is no racial or full-blood definition, and many of the contributors in *Growing Up Māori* can claim as much Pākehā ancestry as they can Māori ancestry or, at least, Pākehā influence in their years of growing up. Much of our identity has to do with whakapapa, with memory based not only on the bloodlines and physical landscapes we live in but also the emotional landscapes constructed by loving grandparents or whānau with aroha, manaakitanga and whanaungatanga.

So, another caution, and this has to do with any wish to look for answers to the question of what exactly defines a Māori and Māori identity. There's no one answer to that question. And the answers, collectively, are both explicitly and implicitly recounted in all the stories of the contributors. You'll find them if you want to. You won't if you don't look hard enough.

What *is* more to the point is that all the contributors are here because *they* identify themselves as being Māori. All have made a sovereignty choice, based on genealogy, belonging, upbringing, pride, politics or downright stubbornness that links them with the mana of our Māori forbears – the ancestors in front and we behind. Some of the contributors have grown up Māori because their cultural context was Māori. Others have grown up Māori because although their context was Pākehā, there

The Ihimaera family, circa 1940. My grandmother and father are at left back.

was a grandparent or parent who hooked them back into Māori identity. Yet others have grown up Māori because, well, they didn't want to be Pākehā. Still others have grown up Māori out of a sense of loss – and as we all know, a sense of loss is often the place from which one begins the journey to find one's self and one's tribe.

Growing up Māori has come to mean growing up and across the fractures in time and space within our culture as well as finding oneself and one's location in the pastiche that is the post-modern world.

We all now live in a universal reality. The original template came from Rangiātea, that's where the seeds were sown. I like to think that since then the process of maintaining our identity has been like the constantly changing patterns of a cat's cradle. The primary pattern of culture was created when Māori began to live with each other in Aotearoa, and traditions and histories were devised based on our tribal and family relationships. Then the Pākehā came and, increasingly, the tensions of maintaining that original pattern meant our ancestors had to weave more complicated designs over more empty spaces to ensure that the landscapes of the heart, if not the land, could be maintained.

Today, Māori identity has continued to be created within the spaces of the cat's cradle. More string has had to be utilised to keep the Māori template intact. Between the polarities of many hands are the tensions and stresses that have maintained the pattern in a state of constant transformation. Part of the purpose has been to catch and hold us, indeed, to cradle us. Another part of the purpose has been to allow us, in those spaces, to transform and continue the process of becoming.

The Māori today is not the same Māori as yesterday. Neither will be the same as the Māori of tomorrow. How Māori he or she will be will depend on the hands which create the patterns of the cat's cradle. If it is woven wisely, having within it the cradle of culture and the wisdom to enable, also, a *letting go*, Māori will surely reach goals that will take us all to places yet undreamed of. The potential is there and is evident in the work of Jacq Carter, among others. Jacq is the youngest of all the contributors and she blows all the fuses.

Finally, all the people who contributed to *Growing Up Māori* did so not because they wanted to write about themselves but because they wanted to leave the gifts of their histories and experiences to the mokopuna, the children who are to come. They wanted to tell the new generations that this is how we were in our own times, so that *they* will have a compass point by which they can chart their own directions in the future. And what are our dreams for the mokopuna? Keri Hulme said it something like this:

It doesn't matter if your heads are in the clouds –
You have stars for feet.

WITI IHIMAERA
AUCKLAND, OCTOBER 1998

PROLOGUE

I ngā rā o mua

Ka noho te iwi rā i Hawaiki. Ka mea ki te tārai waka mā rātou, hei rapu whenua hou mō rātou. Ka tāraia te waka, ka oti ... ka mānu ki te wai, ka utaina ... Kātahi ka rere mai te waka rā, ka whiti mai ki tēnei motu.

The people dwelt in Hawaiki. They planned to shape a canoe for themselves, in order to search for a new land of their own. That canoe was shaped. When it was finished ... it was launched and loaded up ... Then the canoe travelled forth, and made a crossing to this land.

– HOANI NAHE, NGĀTI MARU (1860)

The Way it Used to Be

MAKERETI

*We begin **Growing Up Māori** by putting the past before us: two pieces, the purpose of both being to show how we used to grow up traditionally and what came to change all that. The first piece is from Makereti's **The Old Time Māori**, the first comprehensive ethnology written by a Māori, and is an abridged version of the chapter on childhood.*

Makereti was born in Rotorua in 1872. She was also known as Maggie Papakura and was a very popular guide to the thermal wonders of Whakarewarewa. She went to England in 1912 and studied anthropology at Oxford University in the 1920s. She died in 1930. Her ethnography was first published in 1938.

When a marriage took place in the old days, one of the most important things in the minds of the couple was the children they would have. The Māori were anxious to have children, as many as they could have. Whether boys or girls, they were all welcomed, no matter to what class they belonged. If it happened that a wahine rangatira (woman of rank), who was married to a tangata rangatira (man of rank) became hapū (pregnant) with her first child, this important event was hailed with great rejoicing and ceremonial feasting. Gifts were brought and presented to the young mother, in the way of choice foods, so that she might feed her child that it might be born strong and healthy. If she longed for any kind of food, it was procured for her, no matter how difficult it was to get. Sometimes this meant expeditions to a distant part of the forest or country, and in the old days these expeditions were difficult, as there were no conveyances, and in many cases, no roads. These foods, although procured for the mother, were really for the child. If she lived by the sea, she might long for inland foods such as kererū (pigeon) or other birds, or inanga and other small fish from the lakes. This food not only helped to feed the child, but helped the mother to get plenty of milk in her breasts.

Generally whakawhānau or giving birth to a child was not a matter to worry over, and a Māori woman of the old days did not suffer or go through the same painful experience as the wahine Pākehā (European woman). She lived a natural life and generally went about doing her ordinary duties up to a few days before her confinement, when she left the kāinga to live in a small temporary place which was built for her. Here she would live with someone who saw to her wants in carrying food from the kāinga. The food would be brought halfway from the kāinga by someone who had cooked it, and the attendant would get the food from there. A woman was considered tapu (unclean) for a certain time before and after confinement, that is, until after the tua or tohi had taken place about seven or eight days after the birth of the child.

When the time came for the mother to whakamamae, have labour pains, her mother, grandmother, and other relatives were with her, especially if it were her first child. They would sit close to her as she knelt in front of the hunga whakawhānau i a ia, the one who was attending to her. The attendant sat on the ground of the whare (a temporary structure) with her knees up to her chin. The young mother knelt in front of her with her legs apart, while the attendant pressed her knees lightly on the upper part of the poho (abdomen) of the patient, thus helping to force the child downward. As each pain comes, the attendant puts her arms round the body of the patient, and pulls her forward gently against her knees. As the pains get stronger, she presses her knees in harder, encouraging her with the words 'Kia kaha e whae', Be brave, O mother. And the relatives looking on say the same. Not a murmur comes from the patient, no matter how great the pain, for what is pain but nothing, when she is giving her husband the son or daughter which he so desires? The presence of her mother and relatives close to her helps her greatly to bear the pain. She must be brave just as they were, and her forebears before her. And when the great moment comes and the child is born, she will say, 'He aha ai?' ('What is it?') But whether it is a boy or a girl, it is welcomed.

The infant is then shaken with its feet up and its head down to loosen the nanu (secretion) in its mouth and nose. The attendant or one of the relatives would then draw out any remaining nanu by placing her mouth over the nose or mouth of the infant, and taking a deep inward breath. This relieved the infant of all the thick fluid which might be in its nose and mouth, and prevented the child from having an ihu hupe or secretion in its nose, or from being whango (having a husky voice) when it grew up. If a child does not cry when it is born, it is shaken to make it cry. If anything was needed to soften the pito (cord), which sometimes looks sore, a piece of soft cloth was soaked in the oil from the kernel of the tītoki berry, and placed over the pito before wrapping the child in old pūeru cloth. The soft old cloth would be an old woven korowai or korohunga.

A Māori infant did not use the clothes which are needed for Pākehā children. Indeed there was only one garment used, and that was the one wrapped round his little body. The child was then placed on the whāriki, floor-mat, without mattress or pillow, and was quite happy and comfortable.

When the attendant has finished with the infant, she turns her attention again to the mother, who in the meantime has been waiting for the whenua, i.e. the placenta, to come away. During the short time that the attendant was spending with the child, one of the relatives would support the young mother until she was ready. Sometimes the afterbirth comes quickly, and in some cases takes a long time. When it comes away the whenua is taken by the mother, aunt, or other close relative to a secret place already chosen and ready to receive it. It is there buried. If the whenua does not come away as it should, the patient is sometimes taken to a running stream – she would walk herself – and here she would lie in shallow water, and the attendant would stand on her poho, first on one foot and then on the other till the whenua and all the parapara (blood) has come away. She would then walk back to the whare where her relatives were. After this she would be considered well enough to attend to the infant and to herself.

Her ū (breasts) which had received special attention during the months of her pregnancy would have the waiū (milk) flowing easily, and so the child is fed from the breast soon after it is born. In the old days the ū were mirimiri, massaged, and also the matamata, nipples, and a Māori mother never had the difficulty of the women who have come in contact with civilisation. When a woman became hapū, her breasts were attended to from three months right up to the birth of the child...

When an infant was seven or eight days old, or when the pito fell away, the tua or tohi took place. This was a cleansing ceremony, or taking away of the tapu from the mother and child, and was also a dedication of the infant to the care of the gods. The tohi was not a baptismal ceremony as used by Europeans at the christening of the child, although the naming of the child occurred at the end of the ceremony. Through this tohi ceremony a male child was made tapu, and this tapu was greater than the tapu of a female infant. The tohi for one was not the same as that for the other. Just as there was one whakatuputupu repeated over a male infant to make him grow strong, so was there a different whakatuputupu repeated for a female child. There was a karakia pure repeated over a male child, and a different pure was repeated over a female child. The tohi or tua repeated over a male child made him very tapu, as he was endowed with tapu and mana which came direct from the gods, and the many heavenly beings who dwelt in the heavens, and the many beings from above, from Tāwhirimātea, and from the many beings below, and from the many many beings in Hawaiki. This tapu prevented a man from doing many things which were only done by the women, a fact which caused many ignorant writers to say how lazy our men were, and how the women were made to work. The tua repeated over a female infant was different. She received only part of the mana from ngā atua, the gods, half from the heavenly beings in the heavens, and half from the many many beings in Hawaiki. A female infant was made noa, so that she was able to carry food on her back, to cook food, to gather shellfish from the sea sand, and to do many things which the men were unable to do on account of their tapu...

A Māori mother tends her baby from the day it is born, though she has many offers of help from relatives. She need never bring up any of her children, as the grandmothers and grandaunts always want to do it for her. If the mother died, the baby would be fed from the breast of a relative who also had a young baby. The mother, as I have said, suckles her infant on the breast, sometimes until it is a year or even two years old. When weaning it, she sometimes rubs her breasts with the sap of the kawakawa (*Somaria fluvialis*), a fern which has a bitter taste.

The head, arms, legs and body of the infant were massaged so that they would have a good shape, and the joints were massaged to make them supple. The fingers were bent backwards and forwards, and a female infant had the first joint of both thumbs pressed backwards, to make it easier for her to whatu, i.e. to weave clothing when she grew up. All Māori fingers have an upward turn from the palm, and are tapered and well shaped. The nose was pressed gently between the thumb and first finger from time to time to prevent the child being parehe (flat-nosed). The legs were bandaged together fairly tightly to prevent them from being crooked, and the body was bound in the pūeru (cloak) to keep the back straight. It was an unknown thing to see a round-shouldered or bow-legged Māori.

From a day old, the child is carried straight up on its mother's back. A pūeru is passed round the child and crossed in front of the mother, and the ends are tied at the back under the child's tou, so that he sits against them. Sometimes, if the mother is doing nothing, she will hold the ends of the cloak in front. This way of carrying the child is very comfortable for the child and for the mother, and enables the mother to carry on her work with the child on her back.

An infant was taught to be clean from its birth, when it would be held out by an attendant or by its mother. The child soon learnt what was expected of it.

A mother could not bear to hear her child cry, especially at night. She would take it up in her arms and croon over it, singing oriori, or lullaby songs, to soothe it. The Māori had many of these songs, and some mothers made up their own, some being very beautiful and poetic. Their oriori over their dead children are most heart-rending, expressing the intensity of the grief they feel for the loss of their little ones. Many such songs have been made up by fathers.

The first teaching is given when the child begins to crawl and walk. It will first try to get up by holding on to its mother's or grandmother's knee while she is sitting on the ground. The Māori always sat on the ground, the men tailor fashion, and the women with their knees up to their chins, or with the knees bent and almost touching the ground and their feet to the left underneath them, or with one knee up to the chin, and the other leg bent underneath. Sometimes a small enclosure with a rounded top was made in which the child might learn to use his limbs and to stand and walk, but this was seldom used.

A child would still be at its mother's breast when it began to walk, and sometimes for a long time afterwards. A woman first gives the child food when it is nine months or more old, unless she has not much milk, then earlier. But a mother nearly always had plenty of milk for her child. When she gives ordinary food to her baby she is careful of what she gives it, and masticates it well before giving it to the child, either straight from her own mouth to the child's, or taken from her mouth with the two first fingers and thumb, and so given to the child. This method might be used until the child was weaned, and sometimes afterwards. The mortality among children was not high in pre-Pākehā days. Only the weak ones perished, as the life the Māori led was a hard one.

The first word a baby would learn would be its mother's name, and then its father's. Each parent had his or her name, and the child had its own name. There were no surnames. Sometimes a child would be called by the same name as his father, but this was seldom done, unless the father died. A son might take the name on the death of his father, but this was not usual. For example, a son's name might be Wahiao and his father's Umukaria, and all his descendants would have their own names, but never the same as his or his father's until, probably many generations later, the name might reappear. Children never said 'mother', 'father', 'uncle', etc., like European children, but always addressed their relatives by their own names.

Māori children did not wear any clothes except the maro, an apron, which a boy wore from about the age of five or six or more, and a girl from about the age of five. They wore nothing on their feet or on their heads. An infant's hair was not cut. Its nails were not cut, but bitten off by its mother, and buried or hidden where no one else could get at them.

The Māori never beat their children, but were always kind to them, and this seemed to strengthen the bond of affection which remains among Māori throughout life. Between the ages of three and nine, children enjoy a great deal of freedom. A child is free to play when and where he likes, and always has companions on the marae in front of the whare (house). It is extraordinary how a Māori child knows the danger of fire or boiling water. Although he is free to wander where he likes, and even plays with fire and goes among the boiling pools, you will scarcely ever hear of a child being burnt or scalded. The children were fond of tākaro (play). They had few toys, yet they amused themselves making mud pies, playing hunahuna (hide and seek), punga, and many other games. It was a wonderful sight to see a little Māori child eating various kinds of foods with his fingers, and never making a mess or making his fingers dirty...

When girls are old enough to understand what is said to them, their mother begins to tell them how they should behave in the kāinga. She teaches them to take care of their good name, and speaks freely of the time when they will be mate wahine, or mate marama, so that they will know what to do when it happens. When a girl reached that age, she knew all about it, as it had been explained to her by her mother, grandmother, or other close relative. She knew just what to do for herself, although her mother might show her at first what to do. It was important for a girl to know, because when she was mate wahine there were many things which she must not do because she was tapu (unclean) in the eyes of the old Māori. During this period she used a whakaaupuru (diaper) of woven fibre, with soft moss on the inner side, and this was replaced from time to time, while the used moss was buried by the girl in a secret place where no one would ever find it. On no account could the moss of whakaaupuru be thrown anywhere. When a girl is in this condition she is careful not to step over a man who is lying down or over a man's sleeping place, not to sit where a man sleeps, especially where his head rests, and she must not get into a bathing pool where men bathe, and she must not dare to rinse anything she may have used in that water. Any of these things would desecrate the laws of tapu, and in the old days, she would not dream of desecrating such laws. No eyes but her own must look upon her whakaaupuru or anything else that she used. She could not prepare a hāngi (oven) or cook tawa berries. If she did, they would not be cooked. She would not gather shellfish, as this would make them all go to another part of the coast. Nor would she go on cultivated ground, as the crops would be a failure.

And she had to be careful in many ways too numerous to mention in this chapter. When she reached the age of mate wahine, she was supposed to be grown up and to have sense. A Māori girl matured earlier than a European, and was generally mate wahine at fourteen or fifteen, or even much earlier. It was seldom that she became ill at such a time. Her natural life prevented this. She went about as usual in the rain and did various work, other than that which she was prohibited from doing. A man would have nothing to do with his wife during this period. When the change of life came, a woman in the old days did not suffer at all. It all took its course in the natural way, without any laying up. She worked as usual on the things which she could do, such as getting flax and firewood, and preparing flax for, and making baskets, mats, etc.

There is much teaching to inculcate unselfishness. Where there is not much kīnaki (relish) at a meal, the little girl is asked to share hers, no matter how small it is, with other members of the family. Much of this was arranged by the mother to teach the little girl to be thoughtful for others. She was taught not to let the old people go to the spring to fetch water, but to bring it to them in calabashes. No child was ever ordered, but was always asked in a kindly way to help. I am sure that this is the reason why children looked on work as a pleasure in the old days.

She was quick to learn all the duties which her mother performed. By the age of eight or ten or more, she liked to show her parents what she could do, and would get up early to light the fire, getting the hot embers together with a stick and putting a few dry sticks on and scraping away the ashes, then blowing the embers with her breath until the fire burnt up and she could put on thicker pieces of wood. She would not be waked, or made to get up. A Māori child of eight looked as old as a European child of eleven or twelve.

Housework was not hard. There was no furniture. For the sleeping place in the whare, there was a quantity of rarauhe fern or raupō (bulrush), over which whāriki, or sleeping-mats, were spread. If the day was wet, the mats were rolled up towards the head of the bed against the wall. On other days, these floor-mats were taken out and put in the sun, and the bed was often remade of fresh fern.

She learned to waruwaru, i.e. to scrape kūmara and taro to prepare it for cooking in a hāngi. Little girls learn to prepare a hāngi when quite young, but do not actually prepare it themselves until they are grown up. They go to the forest with their mother and gather sticks for firewood, making them into kawenga, that is, bundles on their backs with ropes of fibre or flax fixed round them like braces at the back and front. The girl puts each arm through the brace in front of the kawenga, which rests on a mound, or even on the ground, and carries it home on her back. This is a very easy way of carrying large bundles or wood or baskets of kūmara, which often had to be carried several miles, for the plantations were often a long way from the kāinga, and the Māori often had to go a long way for aruhe (fern-root), or berries from the forest.

Girls soon learned how to clear away the weeds among the plants and between the rows, for weeding was generally done by women, and how to loosen the ground with a timo, an implement for grubbing. They helped their mothers to cut and carry bundles of flax to the kāinga, and how to prepare flax for making rourou, the baskets from which foods was eaten, taka, the mats on which kūmara and taro might be served when it was ready for eating, rough kete (baskets) for holding kūmara, taro, and other foods, whāriki, the floor-mats on which they slept, and tuwhara, the rough or more coarsely made mats which were put under the whāriki, and were also used for the kāuta or wharau (cooking-shed).

A little girl will carry the baby on her back to relieve her mother, and it is her ambition to grow up and be able to do all the things that her mother does. Girls join in all the games, swimming, running, poi dances, tītitorea, and matemate. The children, like all Māori, are very modest. They bathe together, yet never see anything, and many will sleep side by side along the sleeping side of a whare, and nothing wrong enters their mind. They went to bed at sunset, and rose at sunrise, and when they lay down on the whāriki, the children heard from their elders the history of their people, their folklore, and other stories, which delighted them until they fell asleep.

At about fourteen to eighteen, girls were taught to pūkana (roll the eyes), and walk with a parepare movement of the hips. This moving gait of the hips, which was so wonderful in the old Māori, is the same as that practised by the modern civilised girl, only more marked. They were taught to do the ordinary haka and to sing pao and waiata, though they learned the waiata later. Singing came naturally to the Māori. They nearly always sang when walking or working or paddling a canoe, or going through a bush or lonely road. Many of them have beautiful voices.

Boys were massaged on the head, face and limbs with the romiromi massage to get them into form so that they would be strong when they grew up to fight, to do the war dances, peruperu, and whakatūwaewae, i.e. dance with long pointed sticks before a battle. They were taught to use weapons of stone, greenstone, and wood, and especially the whakahoro or use of arms, and the art of karo, the parrying of weapons. Upoko-titi was a favourite game of children, played with both hands. Each one crooked his kōiti (little finger) over the next finger, and the same with the next, until all are bunched together.

From the age of six to that of fifteen or sixteen, the father undertook the boy's training, and the grandfather took a great part as well. They taught him to be hospitable and generous, and to share any delicacy he might be eating. A parent would ask for a portion so as to teach the boy unselfishness, though if there were only a little kīnaki, or relish, parents like to give it to their children, who ate with them. Parents did many things and devised many methods to teach children good habits and a generous nature. The boy was taught to see that everyone had kīnaki before eating his.

As he grew up, he was taught all the things that his father did. He accompanied him to the cultivations, and learned to use the kō in planting the kūmara, and the songs which accompanied the movements of the workers. He learned the planting of kūmara and taro, and how to build the whata, the open storehouse on posts, and the making of the pātaka (closed storehouse), and how to dig the rua, the pit in the ground for storing kūmara. He learned how to hunt and snare birds, of which there were more than 200 species, and how to make hīnaki, traps for eels, nets for sea fishing, and nets for catching inanga and pahore, the small fish in the lakes, and how to dive for kōura and kākahi, the crayfish and freshwater mussels. By the time he was eight or nine, he had learned a good deal about these and other methods of procuring food.

He accompanied his father and relatives to the forest, and watched them cutting down trees and preparing logs for the houses, or hewing them out for canoes, all laborious work which took a long time with their primitive implements, and learned how to choose trees for a canoe or house, and to cut them down and take them long distances to the kāinga, or to the river or lake. He learned how to cut timber for the whare (houses) and for building the pā, fortified villages.

He was taught the customs and arts of his people, whakatūwaewae, a war dance, with the taiaha or tewhatewha or pouwhenua, and koikoi. He learned how to hold himself up as a rangatira ought, and the use of the long, two-handed weapon, each with his own way of tripping and killing the enemy. He was taught to use a patu pounamu or short-handled stone weapon for close combat, which was most important for a warrior, as all their fighting was hand to hand. Beside this, he learned the haka, or war dances which occurred when they approached the enemy, with distorted faces, eyes pūkana (rolling), and arero whētero, tongue out to show defiance. He was trained in the use of all war weapons when quite young by the old men, and his training went on all through his life, at first with harmless sticks, and then with weapons...

Children slept all together in the same whare as their parents and sometimes their grandparents from the age of three until they were grown up. Going to rest was always a great joy to the children, especially to those who were with their grandparents. When they lay down on the whāriki (floor-mats, they had no pillows), their grandfather or grand-uncle, or whomever they might be with, would tell them stories of the brave deeds of some of their ancestors, the various battles they fought and won, the battles they lost, and the reasons for these wars. Probably a famous ancestor was killed and a party went and avenged his death. The old man would teach them their line of descent from that ancestor, and from other noted ancestors back to the time of the arrival of the great fleet of canoes in New Zealand about 600 years ago, repeating the genealogical tree from the different members of the canoe down to himself night after night until the child could say them from memory, and repeat them all by the time that he was ten years old. If an ancestor was mentioned, he would know how many generations back he had lived, and how he was related to his other descendants. From these old people, the children learn much in the way of folklore, legend, genealogy, and tradition.

The old people told them stories of the patupaiarehe, the fairies who moved past in the mist of early morning, or in the mist after the rain, the fairies who sometimes came down from their homes on the tops of historic mountains. They told the children how dear their home and lands were to them, and to their fathers before them, and tried to make the children feel the same. They taught them the names of the birds of the forest, and of the different trees and shrubs and plants, all the names of which the old people knew, and wonderful stories of the mountains, rivers, and streams, as though they were living human beings. They tried to impress on the childish mind the ways of the unknown which the Māori observed, for the old Māori was familiar with the stars and knew their names, Kōpū the morning star, and Matariki the Pleiades. They spoke of the comets and other signs which appeared as omens in the sky, those which were good and those which were not. Everything was personified to the Māori, as he was very near to Nature.

When Goblins Came to Whitianga

TE HORETA TE TANIWHA

*Captain James Cook sailed the **Endeavour** into Mercury Bay on 3 November 1769. On shore, and also a visitor to the bay, was a boy of twelve years or so named Te Horeta Te Taniwha. Eighty-three years later, Te Horeta's account of Cook's visit was written down. There are several versions of the account of this prominent Ngāti Whanaunga elder. The one reprinted here comes from J.C. Beaglehole's **The Discovery of New Zealand**.*

The arrival of the Pākehā brought the greatest threat of discontinuity to the Māori world that it has so far had to face.

When the goblins came, growing up was no longer the same for Māori.

In the days long past, when I was a very little boy, a vessel came to Whitianga. Our tribe was living there at that time. We did not live there as our permanent home, but were there according to our custom of living for some time on each of our blocks of land, to keep our claim to each, and that our fire might be kept alight on each block, so that it might not be taken from us by some other tribe.

We lived at Whitianga, and a vessel came there, and when our old men saw the ship they said it was a tupua, a god, and the people on board were strange beings. The ship came to anchor, and the boats pulled on shore. As our old men looked at the manner in which they came on shore, the rowers pulling with their backs to the bows of the boat, the old people said, 'Yes, it is so: these people are goblins, their eyes are at the back of their heads; they pull on shore with their backs to the land to which they are going.' When these goblins came on shore we (the children and women) took notice of them, but we ran away from them into the forest, and the warriors alone stayed in the presence of those goblins; but, as the goblins stayed some time, and did not do any evil to our braves, we came back one by one, and gazed at them, and we stroked their garments with our hands, and we were pleased with the whiteness of their skins and the blue eyes of some of them.

These goblins began to gather oysters, and we gave some kūmara, fish and fern-root to them. These they accepted, and we (the women and children) began to roast cockles for them; and as we saw that these goblins were eating kūmara, fish, and cockles, we were startled, and said 'Perhaps they are not goblins like the Māori goblins.' These goblins went into the forest, and also climbed up the hill to our pā at Whitianga. They collected grasses from the cliffs, and kept knocking at the stones on the beach, and we said, 'Why are these acts done by these goblins?' We and the women gathered stones and grass of all sorts, and gave them to the goblins. Some of the stones they liked, and put them into their bags, the rest they threw away, and when we gave them the grass and branches of trees they stood and talked to us, or they uttered the words of their language. Perhaps they were asking questions, and, as we did not know their language, we laughed, and these goblins also laughed, so we were pleased. The warriors and old men of our tribe sat in silence and gazed at these goblins. So these goblins ate the food we had presented to them, with some relish they had brought on shore with them, and then we went up the Whitianga River with them. Now, some of the goblins had walking-sticks which they carried about with them, and when we arrived at the bare dead trees where the shags roost at night and have their nests, the goblins lifted the walking-sticks up and pointed them at the birds, and in a short time thunder was heard to crash and a flash of lightning was seen, and a shag fell from their trees; and we children were terrified, and fled, and rushed into the forest, and left the goblins all alone. They laughed, and waved their hands to us, and in a short time the bravest of us went back to where the goblins were, and handled the bird, and saw that it was dead. But what had killed it? Our old people waited in suspicion, and went back to the settlement, as also did the goblins. We were now at quiet and peace with them, and they gave us some of the food they had brought on shore with them. Some of this food was very hard, but it was sweet. Some of our old people said it was pungapunga (pumice stone – it was ship's biscuits) from the land from which these goblins came. They gave us some fat food, which the same old people of our tribe said was the flesh of whales; but the saltness of this food nipped our throats, and we did not care for such fat food.

After the ship had been lying at anchor some time, some of our warriors went on board, and saw many things there. When they came on shore, they gave our people an account of what they had seen. This made many of us desirous to go and see the home of the goblins. I went with the others; but I was a very little fellow in those days, so some of us boys went in the company of the warriors. Some of my playmates were afraid, and stayed on shore. When we got on board the ship we were welcomed by the goblins, whom our warriors answered in our language. We sat on the deck of the ship, where we were looked at by the goblins, who with their hands stroked our mats (i.e. cloaks) and the hair of the heads of us children; at the same time they made much gabbling noise in talking, which we thought was questions regarding our mats and the sharks' teeth we wore in our ears, and the hei-tiki we wore suspended on our chests; but as we could not understand them we laughed, and they laughed also. They held some garments up and showed them to us, touching ours at the same time; so we gave our mats for their mats, to which some of our warriors said 'Ka pai', which words were repeated by some of the goblins, at which we laughed, and were joined in the laugh by the goblins.

There was some supreme man in that ship. We knew that he was the lord of the whole by his perfect gentlemanly and noble demeanour. He seldom spoke, but some of the goblins spoke much. But this man did not utter many words; all that he did was to handle our mats and hold our mere, spears, and wahaika, and touch the hair of our heads. He was a very good man, and came to us – the children – and patted our cheeks, and gently touched our heads. His language was a hissing sound, and the words he spoke were not understood by us in the least. We had not been long on board the ship before this lord of these goblins made a speech, and took some charcoal and made marks on the deck of the ship, and pointed to the shore and looked at our warriors. One of our aged men said to our people, 'He is asking for an outline of this land'; and that old man stood up, took the charcoal, and marked the outline of Te Ika a Māui. And the old chief spoke to that chief goblin, and explained the chart he had drawn. The other goblins and our people sat still and looked at the two who were engaged with the chart marked with charcoal on the deck. After some time the chief goblin took some white stuff, on which he made a copy of what the old chief had made on the deck, and then spoke to the old chief. The old chief explained the situation of the Rēinga at the North Cape; but, as the goblin chief did not appear to understand, the old chief lay down on the deck as if dead, and then pointed to the Rēinga as drawn by him in the plan. But the goblin chief turned and spoke to his companions, and, after they had talked for some time, they all looked at the map which the old chief had drawn on the deck; but the goblins did not appear to understand anything about the world of spirits spoken of by the old chief, so they scattered about the deck of the ship.

I and my two boy-companions did not walk about on board of the ship – we were afraid lest we should be bewitched by the goblins; and we sat still and looked at everything we saw at the home of these goblins. When the chief goblin had been away in that part of their ship which he occupied, he came up on deck again and came to where I and my two boy-companions were, and patted our heads with his hand, and he put his hand out towards me and spoke to us at the same time, holding a nail out towards us. My companions were afraid, and sat in silence; but I laughed, and he gave the nail to me. I took it into my hand and said 'Ka pai', and he repeated my words, and again patted our heads with his hand, and went away. My companions said, 'This is the leader of the ship, which is proved by his kindness to us; and also he is so very fond of children. A noble man – one of noble birth – cannot be lost in a crowd.' I took my nail, and kept it with great care, and carried it with me wherever I went, and made it fit to the point of my spear, and also used it to make holes in the side-boards of canoes, to bind them on to the canoe. I kept this nail till one day I was in a canoe and she capsized in the sea, and my god (i.e. the nail) was lost to me.

The goblin chief took some of his own things and went with them to our old chief, and gave him two handfuls of what we now know were seed-potatoes. At that time we thought they were parareka (fern), and we called them by this name, as the things he gave to the old man were not unlike the bulb of the parareka, or like the lower end of that fern, at the part where it holds to the stem of the fern-tree. The old chief took the gift and planted it, and we have partaken of potatoes every year since that time. These things were first planted at a place in the Wairoa called the Hunua, halfway between Drury and the Taupō settlement, east of the entrance of the river Wairoa, opposite the island of

Waiheke; and the old chief to whom the potatoes were given was of the Ngāti Pou tribe, who occupied the Drury district at that time.

After these parareka had been planted for three years, and there was a good quantity of them, a feast was given, at which some of the potatoes were eaten, and then a general distribution of seed parareka was made amongst the tribes of Waikato and Hauraki...

One of our tribe was killed by the goblins who first came to Whitianga. We – that is, our people – went again and again to that ship to sell fish, or mats, or anything that we Māori had to sell; and one day one of our canoes, in which were nine persons, paddled off to the ship; but one of that nine was a noted thief, and this man took a dogskin mat to sell to the goblins. There were five of them at the stern of the canoe and four in the bow, and this thief was with those in the stern. When they got alongside of the ship, the goblin who collected shells, flowers, tree-blossoms, and stones was looking over the side. He held up the end of a garment which he would give in exchange for the dogskin mat belonging to this noted thief; so the thief waved with his hand to the goblin to let some of it down into the canoe, which the goblin did; and, as the goblin let some of it down into the canoe, the thief kept pulling it towards him. When the thief had got a long length of the goblin's garment before him, the goblin cut his garment, and beckoned with his hand to the man to give the dogskin mat up to him; but the thief did not utter a word, and began to fold up the dogskin mat with the goblin's garment into one bundle, and told his companions to paddle to the shore. They paddled away. The goblin went down into the hold of the ship, but soon came up with a walking-stick in his hand, and pointed with it at the canoe which was paddling away. Thunder pealed and lightning flashed, but those in the canoe paddled on. When they landed eight rose to leave the canoe, but the thief sat still with his dogskin mat and the garment of the goblin under his feet. His companions called to him, but he did not answer. One of them went and shook him, and the thief fell back into the hold of the canoe, and blood was seen on his clothing and a hole in his back. He was carried to the settlement and a meeting of the people called to consult on the matter, at which his companions told the tale of the theft of the goblin's garment; and the people said, 'He was the cause of his own death, and it will not be right to avenge him. All the payment he will obtain for his death will be the goblin's garment which he has stolen, which shall be left to bind around his body where it is laid.' His body was taken and put into one of the ancient cave burial-places. Not any evil came from this death, and we again went to barter with the goblins of that ship, and the goblins came again and again on shore, nor was there one evil word spoken, or any act of transgression on our part for that death.

If you sign the Treaty of Waitangi

on the Queen's flag

your children will forever reside

in a crumbling rose of cobweb.

- APERAHAMA TAONUI

PART ONE

Māori Born, Pākehā World

E tipu e rea i ngā rā o tōu ao;
Ko tō ringaringa ki ngā rākau a te Pākehā
Hei oranga mō tō tinana;
Ko tō ngākau ki ngā taonga a ō tīpuna
Hei tikitiki mō tō māhuna;
Ko tō wairua ki te Atua
Nāna nei ngā mea katoa.

Grow, child, in the days of your world;
Grasp with your hand the tools of the Pākehā
as a means to support your body;
Keep in your heart the knowledge of your ancestors
as a topknot for your head;
And turn your spirit to the Lord
from whom all things come.

– APIRANA NGATA

NGĀ TOHU WHENUA

My tipuna is the third signatory on the Treaty. He drew a
spiral. Many of the marks, however, are Xs. I think a spiral
is the appropriate image. Not for the coiled energy flow, as
in a frond, or the whakairo delineations expressing the rank
of a person, spirals and patterns conveying the thoughts and
the spirit of the carver – bound to the ethos of his people –
but for the descent a spiral can emit, not blood,
but the spiral that leads to the pit: into a holding cell,
or the pit housing the tangata whenua. We have
gone from pito, our birthright under Tāne-nui-ā-rangi,
placentas punching out kauri and tōtara, to this, a pit.

X is inappropriate. X reduces one to a line on the page, a mark
collated and paraded to justify muskets with stiff bayonets,
speeches denouncing traitors and savagery, while brown ribs
jutt and ribs inside marae decay and fall away. At the Turnbull
I bought a poster of my village being bombed. The account
is in the microfilmed journals of the enemy. Our ancestors
cannot tell their story themselves. We are the mixed descendants,
the profit-and-loss inheritors, guilt scaled according to our descent.
You will read so far and the meaning will leave you,

by necessity. How did one continue, faced
with holocaust? Civilised savagely, the ancestor
eyes of extinguished lives, their photos in acid-free folders,
display cases, catalogues and tagged.
But where are their memorials?
on every point in the country, forever.

Robert Sullivan

Titiro, Moko! Whakarongo, Moko!

IRANUI TE AONOHORIU HAIG

Te Aonohoriu Haig, or Aunty Ada as she is affectionately known, was born in Tokomaru Bay in 1913. Her parents were Hirini Karaka-Waiti and Te Iwingaro Potae. She had six brothers and three sisters. Aunty Ada was raised at Waimā by her grandparents Wiremu Potae and Te Rina Waara. She was educated at the local native school at Tokomaru Bay and then attended Hukarere College.

Aunty Ada married Te Arani Sonny Haig in 1938 and had eleven children. Today she lives in Tokomaru Bay and has twenty-one grandchildren and nine great-grandchildren.

This piece is a transcript of an interview conducted on 3 January 1995 by Marie McCarthy – one of her family members.

Ko Hikurangi te maunga
Ko Waiapu te awa
Ko Ngāti Porou te iwi
Ko Te Whānau-a-Ruataupere te hapū

I was one of the lucky ones that grew up with the old people. I was brought up by my grandparents. Fortunately for me there were a lot of old nannies and koroua around and they always spoke Māori. They didn't understand English a lot of them. Even for myself, I learnt English from over the fence. The neighbours had five boys, and they spoke Māori and English. Sometimes they would forget themselves and would swear like anything, and an aunt of mine would say, 'Hey! Hey! Hey! Moko is at home, you speak nicely, so that she can speak good English.' That's how I picked up my English.

Now my grandfather didn't understand English but my step-grandmother did because she went away to secondary school, Hukarere College. However, she didn't speak English very often at all about the house, and very seldom did she say anything. But, when she did she always addressed me in Māori. So, by the time I went to school I spoke two languages, Māori and English.

Today my first language is Māori and English is my second. Because I am a Māori, anything Māori makes me feel good. Mind you I've got Pākehā blood in me, but the stronger side of me is my Māori side.

I used to spend a lot of time down the road with my old nannies, some of them were in their 80s and 90s, they were all old people. It was my job to walk them down the road and take them to the post office to pick up their pension. I'd just take them along the road and guide them along. I was a companion for them. They'd always turn around and speak to me in Māori and do different things for me. So honestly, I never had playmates. My playmates, my friends, were these old dears. When we were together they'd pat the ground for me to sit down, and the ladies, the women folks, would get up and do their thing.

In those days there was no such thing as action songs like they do today. They sang mōteatea and their body movements were always very graceful. They would always say to me, 'Moko, titiro! Moko, whakarongo!' I used to look, listen and wonder. But what ever for? It didn't click but I knew I had to obey them. When I look back I'm grateful for that sort of thing because they were teaching me how to do the body movement when singing.

The way womenfolk did it in those days is totally different from today. We lift our legs today but those old kuias didn't; it was just a body movement, a sway of the hips and it was graceful. These old dears would get up and do their thing when they were singing, dropping their eyes and doing a pūkana. Sometimes, when they did a pūkana, their bodies would go down too. This is why they'd say to me, 'Titiro, Moko! Whakarongo, Moko!' Those were the things that they were wanting me to copy, but I didn't click.

I learnt to say yes, never to say no to my old people, and that was what I was taught by my grandfather – accept what they have to say. I am grateful for that because they were trying to get me to maintain my Māoritanga, and that's how they did it.

I went away to Hukarere College as a young girl. What I remember most clearly was how I used to hear the girls talk about their mothers, fathers and nannies. It was all confusing to me as I grew up with my nannies and koroua and it made me begin to think about where my mum and dad were. It also made me start to wonder which of these nannies and koroua I had grown up with back home were my real ones? I remember one day returning home to my grandfather and his second wife who had brought me up, and asking where my mother was. All he said to me in Māori was, 'Ah, you ask.' So off we went.

Eventually we arrived at this house and there was this lady sitting on the verandah making a kete and in the garden a man weeding. I just sat. My grandfather went on his way and left us together so that we could get to know each other. I was often taken back to my mother and father after that incident and I used to stay there for a few days so that I would get used to them. I liked them both.

Of course as time went on I found out who my brothers were. These boys used to come back to Waimā and bring me chocolates. That was good! One time they came over and they brought me a doll. I couldn't make head or tail of it, because when I was young I was a tomboy. I went to school dressed as a boy. I had to saw and cut our wood and fill the box for my grandmother. I was to do these chores before I was allowed to go and play. Sometimes, the saw used to become crooked because I was trying so hard to hurry so that I could join the other children. My grandfather never used to say a thing but I soon realised from his look that the most important thing was not to worry about playing, but to finish my work properly. If I concentrated on my work and did it properly then I would get away to play a lot quicker. Those are some of the teachings that I got from my old people. Have patience. Don't rush through things quickly.

I'm now teaching the young people in the same way that the old people taught me, and teaching them about the things I was taught. I'm just passing things on to the younger generation of today. There are quite a few things that I show them and they tell me how much easier it is my way. I tell the young people that if you do it yourself, you'll know what it's like. When I go down to collect seafood, for instance, I teach people how to collect. Some people are used to just digging the food out. They would cut out the kina and pāua with a knife. Well I was taught differently. You suffocate them. You just put your hand over the kina and hold it. It's a game of patience, really, when I look back. Have patience. Don't hurry through things. Take your time so you can do it properly. Patience is a virtue, so they say.

As a child I didn't think of it that way, I didn't think about the way they had taught me to do these things. Now, I'm trying to teach my children, my moko, in this way. Like, for example, I tell them to wait, and they tell me that they want things now. In my day, our old people would just look at me without saying anything. They didn't give in to me. So I learnt to wait.

My role on the marae is the pōwhiri. Well, the community of Tokomaru Bay now know what is to be done, I've only got to look and they know what to do. I now realise the relevance of all the things I learnt. When I reached a certain stage in my growing up I was invited to pōwhiri the manuhiri.

One particular day something happened in Tokomaru Bay: a very popular man, a minister in the Anglican church from Tūpāroa, Ruatōria, died. Because my grandfather was a chief in Tokomaru Bay the telephone calls came through to him. They were bringing the body back and calling in to Waiparapara marae, where we were staying at the time. At ten o'clock, we were all there at the marae, the whole of Tokomaru Bay from Waimā right round. It is an experience that I will never forget. We were all waiting at the marae for the body to arrive. Then we got a message that there had been a delay. People from the different marae along the road had stopped the hearse and made the body call in.

So, by the time they got to Tokomaru Bay it was four o'clock. Of course by this time most of the people of Waiparapara who had waited and gathered had gone home because they were cold and also because the children were coming home from school. This left mainly the younger people and of course my grandfather. Just as everybody left, there was a change. At one end of the bay the sun was still shining and there was a lovely blue sky, at the other end of the bay it was really muggy looking, dark, with no blue sky. It was quite eerie. We all knew it was because of the occasion: somebody had died.

Unexpectedly, the hearse arrived; it came half-way up to Waiparapara marae. We scrambled around looking for the lady that usually did the pōwhiri on the marae at Waiparapara, but she couldn't be found. We had checked her home but she wasn't there, either. The people who had come with the hearse were up and down the beach, there were about twenty carloads of people. Of course we were all looking around in a panic for this lady to do the pōwhiri. It ended up that her daughter and I were told to do the karanga. They got the body out of the hearse and they started carrying it up, and the karanga, it just automatically came to me. So I called first and my mate carried on with the second karanga. By the time the locals returned to the marae, the pōwhiri had started, the karanga had gone out.

The funny thing about it is that when my grandfather enquired as to where the lady was who did the karanga, it was discovered that she really was at home and that she had purposely stayed away from the marae as it was time for us to karanga. That's how I first started to do the karanga. It was something that came automatically. Even today when I do the karanga, I don't remember afterwards the words I used. A lot of people come to me and ask me to write the words down. I tell them that they are to look and listen and it will be planted in them.

I am also expected to go with groups that leave the bay to karanga for us. At the moment none of the women here want to karanga. So I try to disappear – out of sight, out of mind – so that they'll pōwhiri. But if they see me there, that's it, they just move away. When they do see me I notice that they are listening to what I say. I tell them, that's what I want them to do, because then they can do it if I'm not around.

I used to be involved in the Te Ātaarangi method of teaching Māori. Ngoingoi used to work for the National Council of Adult Education, and both her and I used to teach Māori using Cuisenaire rods. Not only did mothers come along, but we also had quite a few old people attend. As Ngoi was a member of the National Council of Adult Education she looked at it this way: if we teach the parents first then they can teach their children. Of course kōhanga reo wasn't thought of at that time. The way we viewed things was that a Māori child is born Māori and needs her own language. She wasn't born a Pākehā. She was born a Māori. I just feel that they are Māori children and when you teach them their language you give them their wairua back. Their wairua is the language. If they can speak Māori, it means they are Māori. If they can't speak Māori, then what are they?

I look at it this way: well those children are Māori children, right? And they've got to have something to stand on, two legs to stand on. You need your own language to carry on. I have seen it with the little ones. When we push our children to learn their own language, they've got their two legs to stand on. They can back up what they do and what they want to say. Make them strong. It gives them confidence in themselves, which is good because some of those Māori children have got no confidence, they don't know their own language, they only know the English language. When some Māori children speak the Māori language, you see those others that don't understand, you see the lost look on their faces and in their eyes, and that's why we push for Māori to be spoken. As I always say to myself, when you go down the road it is English that is spoken. When you switch the TV on, what's the language? It's English. You see, that's why I keep going around telling parents, You speak Māori to your children. Because they are Māori children. Give them two legs to stand on. English is only easy to pick up because it is around them all the time. That's my experience travelling around.

Well, the sad part about all this is that none of my own children spoke Māori. I was too busy giving it and teaching it to other children, and other people, that I forgot about my family. They understand Māori, but it took me quite a while to realise how funny it was that my own children can't even speak Māori, and there am I going to and fro. They can join in the action songs and the hakas, they know it, but to speak it in a conversation, they can't. Now, because of te kōhanga reo their children are speaking the language, and now they are starting to learn to speak to their children. This is why I support kohanga reo, it can also help the parents in their language development.

We taught a lot of history with our language courses. I do that because other schools used to come here to Tokomaru Bay. Schools from Auckland used to spend a week here with us and we would teach them. This happened for about four or five years when one little local girl stood up and asked Ngoi why the local children hadn't been taught about Tokomaru. Ngoi looked at me and I looked at Ngoi and all the teachers we were looking at one another. And she was right. Before the week was up we had them here on the marae. We got all the parents together and we talked. Here we were inviting other people on to the marae, and teaching them about us and our own kids hadn't been taught. They are quite happy now.

It's very important for our children to know what Tokomaru is all about and about the people of this area. It's important for them to know because when they go to other areas and they hear people talking about their own language and history, they can therefore say they know about where they come from. You know, it gives them confidence in themselves. The result is that they listen more and they don't end up saying things that they shouldn't say when they are in a different area. They learn to respect other people; that's what it's all about, really.

This is a busy time in my life. It is more active in lots of ways. Your mind is more active. The only thing now is I can't get around as much as I used to and my mind slips a little bit. The older Māori of the bay meet and talk on the marae, that's our senior citizens' club. To me as a Māori I feel much warmer there on a marae, but you go to the Pākehā place, it's totally different. It doesn't have that wairua, that Māori way.

For myself, now, I still like to wander down the road to have a look. The kids always ask where I've been. I tell them it's lovely outside, there's fresh air. All they do is sit inside watching TV. They tell me they don't want to miss the TV programmes. I tell them there is plenty of programmes outside. You look at the waves, you look at the clouds, oh ... it's a southerly wind. That's how I learnt. I was the one that was sent out by my grandfather, at night, to look where the morning star was, and where the Milky Way was, and the shape of the moon and all that sort of thing. You've got all the signs there, whether it is going to be a fine day, a good day for fishing or what sort of weather we will have in the next two weeks.

One of the things that I learnt, you know, after all these years, is that when the nannies tell us to whakarongo and titiro, that's what one should be doing.

We need to look and listen, that's the way we learn.

Two Worlds

PATRICIA GRACE

*Patricia Grace was born in 1937. She is a writer of international renown and is one of New Zealand's leading novelists and short-story writers. She is also a well-known children's writer. Affiliated with Ngāti Raukawa, Ngāti Toa and Te Ātiawa, her award-winning fiction includes: **Waiariki** (short stories, 1975), **Mutuwhenua** (novel, 1978), **The Dream Sleepers** (short stories, 1980), **Wahine Toa** (with Robyn Kahukiwa, 1984), **Potiki** (novel, winner of the New Zealand Book Awards, 1986), **Electric City** (short stories, 1991), **Selected Stories** (1991), **Cousins** (novel, 1992), and **The Sky People** (short stories, 1994). Her novel, **Baby No-Eyes**, has just been published.*

*Patricia Grace has an Honorary Doctorate from Victoria University of Wellington. In 1991 she was made an Honorary President of PEN New Zealand. In 1994 she was awarded the German LiBeraturpreis for her book **Potiki**, which has been translated into German.*

I was born in Wellington in 1937, lived in Melrose and attended St Anne's Primary School in Newtown, later going on to St Mary's College in Thorndon and to Wellington Teachers' College in Kelburn.

I grew up with a brother a few years younger than me, and have a sister and brother eighteen and twenty years younger than I am. I left home when my sister was about two. My brother was born two months before my eldest son was born. I have come to know them more as adults than I knew them as children.

My maternal grandfather, whose mother emigrated from the Shetland Islands and married a French Canadian seaman who jumped ship in Nelson, lived with us for several years. My maternal grandmother, whose parents were both born in Ireland, lived in another part of Wellington. Also in Wellington were my mother's two sisters and their families – living in the early state houses in Miramar and Seatoun.

My father's parents, brothers, sisters, aunts, uncles and cousins – of Ngāti Toa, Ngāti Raukawa and Te Ātiawa – lived at Hongoeka Bay in Plimmerton. These were my grandmother's people. My grandfather was Pākehā, his family originally coming from England. He married our grandmother and became part of that community.

So I grew amid two families, having close, continuous and frequent contact with each. These were two different worlds – the contrasting worlds of my mother's and my father's families.

My maternal grandmother, my mother and her two sisters took it in turns to visit each other every Thursday. In each house, ours and my two aunties' houses, on a mantelpiece or windowsill among other glass and china ornaments, was a version of the three monkeys – See No Evil, Hear No Evil and Speak No Evil. In close proximity to the monkeys was a photo of the three angelic-looking sisters. We could choose whichever version of the sisters we liked (though I suppose if you see, hear and speak no evil that makes you an angel anyway). My aunts were, and still are, women full of fun, mischief and good humour.

On Fridays my grandmother, mother and aunts met in town and tried on hats – or that's my impression of what they did. They took us for ice-creams at Adams Bruce's and later went for afternoon tea at James Smith's Tearooms. Sometimes they called in for a few quick ones at the hotel where my grandmother lived and worked as a cook. (But Nanna had a stake upstairs too, being a friend and companion to the owner proprietress.)

The cousins on my mother's side of the family, the ones near my own age, were boys. We were quite streetwise, spending much of our time on old bikes, or playing war in backyards or up and down the pavements, climbing trees and jumping off sheds. We had an active life and our playing was adventurous.

Our own vertical section in Melrose was a challenge. We tapped our way round its paths and banks with our eyes shut, pretending to be blind. We went tearing down the paths on anything with wheels, went along ledges and up and down steps on stilts that our grandfather made for us. We could roam the hills, or if we wanted to play ball games, skipping, or kick square we went out onto the footpaths and roads.

There were 'games of the imagination' too, with cousins on both sides of the family. But my closest companion for these games was my brother. We became pirates, jungle dwellers, tank drivers, orphans and a range of characters from the comics that our grandfather brought home for us each week and were a regular part of our reading diet.

It was when I started school that I learned that I was 'different'. Yet in saying that I realise that I was already aware that I was 'like' my father, 'like' my aunties (my father's sisters), 'not like' my mother or her sisters and their children, apart from having their blue eyes. This was something that both my families were interested in and positive about. One of Mum's sisters had a Māori husband, too, whom she had married in Egypt while 'overseas' with the Women's Auxiliary Army Corps during the war. This uncle used to lay special claim to me by calling me 'black nigger', and I thought it great fun to hide and have him going through the house saying, 'Where's this black nigger?' Another uncle, one of the Plimmerton ones, used to challenge me to 'brownness' competitions. He'd call me to him, rolling up his sleeve so that I could match arms to see who had most colour. Others would enjoy this and join in.

So, being 'different' in this new way was a shock to me.

It meant that I was questioned, out of curiosity by some children, as to why I was brown. By others I was accused of brownness and being a Māori. I was told I had a 'brown stomach' when the neck button came off my blouse and there was a little vee of chest showing. I didn't know what to make of it. When I complained to my mother about this teasing (my father was away at the war during my early years at school), she did her best to reassure me that 'brown' was a good thing to be, that I was like my father (who was a hero) and like my beautiful aunties. Once, one of my mother's sisters was present when I came home with my complaints. She said, 'Tell those kids that if they don't leave you alone your aunty will come and pull their noses as long as their arms and let them fly back and hit them in their faces.' This amused me greatly and it really did help. Even though I never told anyone what my aunty would do to them if they didn't lay off, I did think of it. I knew I had people (not like me) on my side.

I found that being 'different' meant that you could be blamed – for a toy gun being stolen then thrown into a drain, for neighbourhood children swearing, for writing appearing on walls, for a grassy bank being set on fire.

Being 'different' also meant that there was a low expectation of me by some teachers, and that I was continuously having to prove what I could do. I remember feeling thankful, when on returning to my college and being introduced to a group of people as a sports champion, that one of the other teachers present interjected and said 'and scholar'.

However, I don't want to make too much of all this. Even though, as a young child, I was a little nervous at school, for the most part silent and often worried about mistakes that I might make and the punishments I could receive, I liked school, liked learning, liked the games that we played. I was successful at school and had some close friends. (But yes, I was the only one in my Standard Four class left off the invitation list to a birthday party. I remember feeling hurt about that.)

I had a few neighbourhood friends, too, mainly those who attended the same school as me. But it was in that mainly working class, but

Family outing.

upwardly mobile neighbourhood, that I came in for a rough time. What I disliked most was being told I was dirty and that I needed a good scrub. (I tried the scrubbing.) I had continuous reassurances from my mother that I was okay and that I was the cleanest kid around. But I soon stopped telling my mother about this verbal stuff because I realised it was upsetting for her.

I actually handled the physical attacks much better (except for on the 'Going for the Bread' occasion). The attacks usually came out of the blue, always from the girls. In the neighbourhood boys and girls didn't associate much at all, which was very different from my 'cousin' experience. At school, boys and girls were segregated at a young age. My brother and the only other Māori child at our school went to Newtown Marist when they reached Standard Two. Anyway, I was physically agile and fearless, probably because of the robust games we played at Hongoeka Bay, and even though I was completely unused to fighting it wasn't a problem for me to stand up to these attackers. I always ended up with a hiding, though, because my attackers were always older and larger, or there would be two of them against me. Sometimes the attack would be just a heavy thump in the middle of the back before the girl dashed off. At other times attacks were prolonged, only ending when there was blood (mine). My mother used to give me tips on how to deal with this. I suppose it was all she could do. Once when I came home with a bite on my arm she told me I should have kept one hand up in front of my face, and that if my attacker tried to bite my hand I should have pushed it down her throat. I tried it once and it worked. I have written about the worst of these attacks in a story called 'Going for the Bread', so I won't dwell on it here, except to say that the incident upon which the story is based is sharp in my memory and, in written form, has been understated.

I don't want to give a distorted picture of my childhood. Looking back, I know I was privileged in many ways. I had a full, vigorous childhood. I had freedom, security and safety in two family environments among people who listened to me, indulged me, encouraged me, believed in me, and trusted that whatever I wanted to do I would be able to do. From meagre resources nothing was spared us. The reason I have not spoken of 'the edge' before is not because it is difficult to talk about but just because I realise it could be given undue emphasis. It was small in the larger picture of my life as a child. I write about it now because of its relevance to the topic under discussion.

My parents both attended Wellington Technical College. That was during the Depression of the 1930s. They both left school at a young age to work at John Dickenson's Stationery Manufacturers where they got to know each other.

It was not easy for them to find accommodation in Wellington after they were married. They were shown only substandard places – some unlined or without kitchens, one with a cooking ring and an old basin up a flight of stairs out on a landing. They eventually moved in to one of the better of these substandard places, a basement flat in a house in Melrose. It was while we were living there, when I was two, that I was hospitalised with pneumonia.

My parents decided that the only way they were going to get out of such accommodation was to build their own house. They bought a section on the vertical side of a Melrose hill and my father picked, shovelled and barrowed a twelve- to fifteen-foot excavation from it. While he did this, during evenings and weekends, neighbourhood boys came and performed mock haka behind him. My father chased them off once and one of the kids got such a fright that he stood stock still and wet himself. My father liked telling that story.

I have no recollection of the basement flat we lived in, except for a vague image of the outside steps leading to it. My earliest memory of living in a house is of the new house in Melrose.

But I also have early memories of our bach and of my grandparents' house in Plimmerton where we spent many weekends while I was little, and where I spent most school holidays as I grew. This land in Hongoeka (where I now live) is part of the ancestral, tribal land of the Ngāti Toarangatira people and looks out towards Whitireia, the maunga tapu that marks one of the boundaries of Ngāti Toa. It looks out also to the island called Te Mana a Kupe ki Aotearoa, named to honour navigator and discoverer Kupe, where ancestor Rangihaeata once built his stronghold.

Before the Second World War, my father bought a car. It was a two-seater with a canvas hood. The boot opened out to two open-air seats at the back. In the weekends we'd start out for Plimmerton, sailing down the Melrose hill towards Newtown, with the motor turned off to save petrol. We'd go through town, then chug our way up Ngauranga Gorge (that Dad's father had worked on doing relief work during the

Depression). We'd eventually come on to the winding metal road through Johnsonville, Tawa Flat, Porirua and on to Plimmerton.

When World War Two began, my father gave the car to his brother and went away to Italy with Māori Battalion reinforcements. So for a few years we were without our father, but our weekends at Hongoeka didn't stop. We'd set out on a Saturday morning by bus to Courtenay Place. Perhaps we caught a tram from there, though I remember walking along Lambton Quay and stopping at Gates for tomato soup and toast. On the trains were Americans, based at Paekākāriki, who gave out chewing gum and oranges.

Once at Hongoeka my parents hardly saw me. I was away with my cousins and my father's young sister, who is just a few years older than me. She was my big sister. When it was time to go home on a Sunday my parents would have to come looking for me in the homes of my aunties and uncles, or down at the beach or in the bush or out on the paddocks where we played our games.

Life at Hongoeka was a very different life to the life I had in town, in the physical freedom that we had in the beach, creek and bush environment, and the freedom that we had to be part of every household. The road came as far as 'the gate', where the settlement began and people walked round the beach to their houses which were a mixture of loan-assisted houses as well as smaller, less substantial, home-built places.

We learned to fish, handle small boats, collect shellfish – paua and kina from the shore rocks, but kina could also be obtained by diving from dinghies to collect them from the kina beds if we wanted larger amounts. At certain times of the year we would go 'round the point' for crayfish. It was the men who did the crayfishing, using short spears on the end of long mānuka sticks. They'd walk out on to the rocks at low tide and spear the crayfish in the shallow pools under the low rock shelves. It was the men who did the conger eeling too, reaching in under the flat rocks at Pauatahanui and hooking them out with hand-held hooks. Smoke drums were set up for the smoking of fish, especially the eels, or eels could be hung from branches or lines and dried. Fish and shellfish would be distributed to the various house-holds. We children were resourceful in many ways and had ingenious ways of catching herrings (trapping them in pickle bottles, stunning them by throwing a sofa spring, jagging), and whitebait (nets made from a loop of wire with an old petticoat attached round it by the hem – tied in a knot at the top end).

During tangihanga was the time I remember hearing the karanga and seeing greenery being worn. Because there was no meeting house the funeral ceremonies were held in the homes. A marquee was set up as a dining area, and cooking was done outdoors on open fires using large iron pots, with kerosene tins for the heating of water. Mattresses would be put around the room where the casket lay and family would sleep there, along with family visiting from elsewhere. It has been done that way up until recent times when the building of our marae complex began. All the homes would be full at such times. Food gathering and preparation, wood collection, preparation of the grave site, ritual welcoming of groups of visitors and the care of visitors was done by those a little more removed from the death, while the close family went through the mourning process. This is the same today. It was usual for cooks to stay up all night working, snatching sleep the next day when, and if, opportunities arose.

Māori wasn't spoken on a day-to-day basis, though there were smatterings of Māori words used within English sentences. I really didn't realise then that the people of my grandmother's age, and some of my parents' age, were speakers of Māori – that is in spite of the fact that I remember my grandmother saying once that her father didn't want her to go to school because he didn't want her to learn English. There is more Māori spoken and being learned in our community now than there was then.

I expect that most of the bigger jobs to do with the upkeep of the urupā were done by adults, but we children were given the task of keeping the urupā tidy, especially during the summer months when we'd go there regularly, climbing the hill with an armload of flowers and a beer bottle of water each, to weed the graves, clean out the flower jars and arrange fresh flowers. We were quite competitive about this and had arguments about whose handiwork was best and who had an unfair advantage because they'd taken the best flowers. We'd come down the hill when we'd finished, wash ourselves in the creek, wash the bottles and store them away under the shed.

I don't know how it was for those of my cousins who lived in 'party houses'. My grandmother was a non-drinker who didn't allow drink in the house (except what came home in my grandfather). But weekend beer parties were common and we kids were round the edges of it all having our own fun. There'd be singing all night long, with ukulele, guitar, spoons, sometimes a piano, teaspoon in the neck of a bottle, different solo acts, duets, a song without words, big-time foot-stamping, one song following on from another, without a break, for hours on end.

It was one of our visiting uncles who used to sing the song without words. Actually, the songs did have words. The one I remember was "In the Shade of the Old Apple Tree'. This particular uncle has a wide mouth, and for everyone's amusement he used to mouth the words of songs, with or without accompaniment. One night when he was giving his rendition of 'Old Apple Tree' a moth flew into his mouth; he swallowed it and kept on 'singing'.

There was a huge repertoire of party songs – songs in Māori, songs in English, songs from the thirties and forties and onwards, romantic and ribald side by side. The hits of the day would be sung over and over until everyone knew them. Sometimes someone would have a new *Songster* with words of songs in it. And we kids had old exercise books full of words. We listened to the 'Hit Parade' each week and took the words down. Long after we'd gone home to bed the singing would go on and would usually continue into the next day and sometimes the next, or at least until the party ran dry. These 'social events' still happen, with kids round the edges having their own fun, and though they are not frequent and not as enduring as before, many of the songs have survived.

There were a number of war songs that Māori people throughout the country knew and sang. These were songs in Māori especially composed to farewell or honour those who went to war, or were about the war itself. There were also German and Italian songs brought back by the soldiers. Some of these were translated into Māori, and some of the tunes had Māori lyrics put to them. These were all included in party repertoire. I was reminded of one of the songs, 'Buona Notte Mia Amore', when I heard it sung during a television programme a couple of years ago by a Māori Battalion 'old soldier'.

In 1949 when Ruru Karaitiana's hit song 'Blue Smoke' came out we were taken to see him at Beggs music shop in Wellington during a promotion. He was in the shop playing the piano, wearing his soldier's uniform, looking much like one of our uncles. I'm not sure how long afterwards it was that we found out that 'Danny's' new song was scheduled to come over the radio at a certain time. People crowded into my grandparents' sitting room to listen to it. I'm not sure whether this was because other people didn't have radios, or because they wanted to be together for this big event. We listened to 'Windy City', a song about Wellington that I don't think ever became a hit. But I was impressed that there could be a song about Wellington.

Weekends were also times for card playing. Some of the older people played during the week as well, but it was during the weekends that the bigger 'schools' started up. There was a fund raising 'kitty' for the purchase of a marquee and crockery, which were bought and jointly owned with our relatives at Waikanae. These were for use when there was a tangihanga, wedding or other social occasion.

There was a constant exchange of visits with relatives living in Ōtaki, Waikanae and Porirua. We were always expected to be present to greet relatives when they arrived and to say goodbye when they left. Our grandmother, in particular, would take us to Ōtaki and Waikanae to visit the older people, her brothers and cousins, and much of the talk and stories were to do with relatives, their deeds and misdeeds. One summer we spent the holidays with relatives at Whakapuaka in Nelson, another in Waikawa Bay in Picton and another in Waikanae. When I say 'we' I'm talking about myself, my young aunt, and cousins of a similar age, as well as adults and younger children. That's how it was done. It meant four kids to a double bed sometimes, or space being created in inventive ways, whether for sleeping, eating or getting from A to B (on the back of an open truck, for example. The open-air truck that we travelled on in Nelson had a comfortable old sofa on the back where the older people could sit.)

It was at Waikawa Bay in Picton that I first learned waiata-ā-ringa. After not too many practices, my cousins and I found ourselves on stage with adults, dressed in piupiu and bodices, at a full concert performance. On another occasion we performed out on a launch alongside the *Tamahine* which was berthed at the Picton wharf. There was a Queen Carnival taking place over the summer and we were part of a fund-raising effort.

Besides talk and stories of relatives there were the stories (not from adults, though they must have come from adults in the first place) of the kaitiaki Kopa who took the form of an owl, and of taniwha, especially the one resident under and around the Paremata bridge. These were not so much stories as talk topics among kids, which we embellished in our own way, and which I have found out more about as an adult. There were many kēhua stories which we frightened ourselves with at night, and our urupā, which we entered without difficulty in the daytime, became a scary place at night. On coming home from the pictures, even though we had walked by the urupā without thinking about it on the way there, we would make a run for it, flying past it on our way home.

I have mentioned the contrasting worlds and perhaps in some way these notes give an outline of what I mean. In other ways these notes are insufficient because they are selective and not greatly expanded. But there was contrast in all aspects of the contrasting worlds – in the way people related to one another, in food and in the cooking of it, in clothing, in values, attitudes, organisation, money, self-perceptions, group perceptions, language – 'contrast' but not 'conflict' for me as a child.

Important for me while growing up was the strong, positive identity given to me within my father's family, and this identity was strongly supported by my mother and her family. On looking back I know that this was necessary for how I saw myself, and for healthy survival.

Us Kids

MARGIE HOHEPA

Margie Hohepa was born in Auckland in 1960 and is of Te Mahurehure, Ngā Puhi descent. She went to primary school in West Auckland, with a brief sojourn in Hawaii and Massachusetts, USA, where, she says, the contrasts in schooling have informed her later interest in considering models for the teaching of young Māori in Aotearoa. On her return to New Zealand she attended Rutherford High, Wellington East and Wainuiomata College. She began her university career in 1979 at Auckland University and is now a lecturer in Māori Education at the University. She is also living back in West Auckland, married with three children and helping to raise her niece. She's a 'Westie' and proud of it. 'I never really got out of Te Atatū,' she says.

Margie Hohepa is passionately committed to all Māori kaupapa. 'When do you ever stop being Māori and thinking about everything to do with Māori?' she laughs. 'Never!' Like most of us, Margie Hohepa learnt Māori as her second language. Currently, she is doing her PhD about Māori parents for whom Māori is the second language, and their parental relationship with their children.

Growing up in Auckland the only close relations we had nearby were on our dad's side, but that worked out as a lot of kids. All our families lived out west until one of my youngest uncles also moved up to Auckland. Like many Māori families new to Auckland at that time, they ended up out south. But that wasn't till I was a lot older, into adolescence. For a long time there were just our four families.

My own family moved in and out of the country twice during my preschool and primary years. Both times we came back to the same place. The years we were in Aotearoa we spent a lot of our weekends swapping homes with these Auckland cousins. For twelve years I was the only girl in our family, with two younger brothers. There were heaps of girls in the other families, and I loved staying with them.

And then for a while I had an older 'brother', our second cousin. My family had gone up north, I'd stayed behind with my aunty and uncle and two younger girl cousins. On the night they returned to Auckland they picked me up. I'd climbed into the back of the station wagon to be met with green-eyed stares of a kitten and my cousin; this was the first time I had met either of them. While he stayed with us my 'cousin brother' increased my popularity amongst the girls at school no end. Apparently he was a spunk. All I knew was he was like a dream come true. Someone older so that anything that went wrong, especially if it involved the younger kids, wasn't always my fault, or my problem any more. And I had someone to stick up for me rather than me having to stick up for all the littler ones, when we were fighting first the Māori kids (until their parents told them to stop because we were their relations) and then the Pākehā kids (because if we were related to those Māoris then we figured along with the Pākehā kids that we must be Māori too) who lived across the park.

We had our share of battles amongst ourselves too. The worst fight we ever had was on my birthday. My cousin had pretty much taken over my party (my friends wanting to go out the back and play softball with him and my two brothers, rather than do girl party things with me). We ended up having a scrap because I accused him (probably falsely I can now admit) of breaking one of my presents. But any angers us kids had against each other didn't last too long: some days later peace was made, my cousin asking me to teach him knucklebones so he could hold his own at school.

Even though he was older, he allowed me to help him in other ways too. I was pretty good at maths back then, he wasn't. I used to help him with his. One day he brought a mate home, who also happened to be the big brother of one of my best friends. I remember feeling really good when my cousin still involved me in his homework, even with his big mate (who he had known from when he lived in Ponsonby and who went on to be a heavyweight boxer ... he was big!) there. I felt older, like I was someone who could really be trusted.

After our cousin went back to live with his maternal grandparents, I went back to the responsibility of the oldest sister until another family came to stay with us. The oldest daughter, man she was tough.

She wasn't big for her age or anything but she wasn't slow at taking on anyone she thought was giving any of us a hard time. Once she chased a boy years older than her across the park, because he had tried to make her baby sister dance by throwing stones at her feet. When she'd told him to stop he had tried the same on her. Bad move.

She advanced on him, he kept throwing stones until it dawned on him she wasn't going to stop. He turned tail and ran homewards, her hot on his heels, him screaming his lungs out. We all followed in hot pursuit, not sure if we really wanted her to catch him: most of us knew firsthand what she was capable of doing if she did. He made it through his gate, still yelling his head off.

His father came sprinting out the gate demanding to know who was the big bully who was picking on his son. The word impotent takes on its meaning for me in what happened next. On the sight of my scrawny, furious cousin, nearly half his son's size, standing in front of us even littler kids, who incidentally were ready to defend her in any way we could, but trying mostly to do so with our mouths, all at the same time, he stopped short, in impotent anger. She stood there, hands clenched, fists at her sides, her rage out and potent as hell. To have a go at her would destroy what little remaining mana his son had. But not being able to sort out this 'little black bitch' as his son had called her, I think galled him.

I learned heaps about what was on and what was not from my older cousins. I learnt how to play and fight and work in ways that were so enjoyable and fun and so belonging. Now when I'm where lots of kids gather with their families, I feel sorry for the many kids and young adolescents who aren't playing together, fighting together, working together like us kids used to. I guess because our family came and went with such regularity, sometimes for over a year, my brothers and I had to renegotiate our membership into this larger family of kids whenever we returned. Maybe that's why these ways of growing up and belonging still seem so clear and strong to me.

I don't remember ever being physically disciplined by my father. From him we learned what was appropriate and not appropriate in ways that didn't involve beltings or even smackings. Of my mother I have a few memories of incidents such as raps on the knuckles with a spoon for dipping a finger once too often into the bowl and a slap on the backside when attempting a rapid retreat after realising I may have pushed my luck a bit too far. These are dim memories of childhood – my youngest brother and sister hadn't yet arrived on the scene so I couldn't have been older than nine or ten, probably younger.

It was the Pākehā kids I grew up with who brought stories of electric jug cords and wooden spoons to school. It was a Pākehā kid I knew who was thrown down the concrete front steps of her house for losing her glasses. Other Māori kids I grew up with had similar experiences, but we didn't talk much about them. Some Māori families got talked about, but it was usually about their being dirty, the parents lazy or poor or the family plain just too big.

When I became a parent I often drew on my memories of smacks and hidings, or rather the lack of them. For a long time (the eight years my two older children were going through kōhanga reo) I believed, was encouraged to believe, that my ambivalence about the use of physical discipline with our tamariki and indeed generally, was mainly the result of my so-called middle class upbringing. My father, Māori, was a 'professional'. My mother, a Pākehā. We'd had probably what could be considered a liberal, 'reason with your kids, don't hit them' sort of upbringing. If I had problems with 'the Māori way' of disciplining kids, then it was probably because I too was Pākehā. Well I bought this for years, whimping out at whānau meetings and would-be confrontations around the issue of physical discipline. Now I hear some of these same whānau members talking about physical discipline not being the Māori way of doing things. I'd laugh if I could only erase the images of our children being hit.

We must stop beating up on our kids. But we also must stop beating up on ourselves. There are people out there who do a much better job of it, as a letter written to a suburban Auckland newspaper shows:

Motherhood

Recently I witnessed, in Henderson, a young Māori woman swinging a toddler by the arm and kicking it to shut it up. When I intervened to stop the assault I was promptly abused, asked what right I had to interfere and told that she was the mother ...

In today's society, I have noticed that the darker races (in New Zealand anyway) inflict on their offspring, much abuse and suffering. Others of their race turn a blind eye and if a European intervenes, she/he is called a racist. Abuse is a perpetuating phenomenon.

(Western Leader, *April 16, 1993*)

In today's society Māori, as one of New Zealand's 'darker races' abuse and use physical punishment on our very young. I've heard it said that this is and was the Māori way of doing things. I'm not so sure how much of a general traditional practice disciplining children physically was among Māori. I am definitely sure that beating the shit out of kids wasn't. So why does it seem to be seen as common practice today?

Perhaps we just happen to be good learners. Maybe it's only taken us a century or so to take on physical punishment as a way of making children toe the line. In 1862, a 'European' commented about Māori disciplinary practices compared with the prevailing Pākehā practices of the time.

> *Corporal punishments and an over-rigid discipline have done much to drive away many children from the schools. A punishment, which to us would appear by no means harsh, would to a Native seem cruel and excessive.* **As Native parents never inflict chastisement upon an offending child,** *our summary mode of dealing with young delinquents must seem strange and tyrannical. It would not be unwise in future to pay some little deference to their feelings in this subject.*
>
> (Report of Inspectors on Native Schools, *1862, p35*)

This was by no means an isolated observation. The native school reports of the 1850s to 1870s contain many similar ones. It is a pity that those teachers from the 'lighter races' didn't heed the words of one of their own! I agree with the sentiments that abuse is a perpetuating phenomenon. Obviously over the last one hundred and forty-odd years we Māori have learned well, or rather badly, from the 'lighter races' about how children should be disciplined!

The young mother described in the above letter justified her actions by contending she was the mother and another had no right to interfere. Where did this view of having exclusive rights over your child come from? Obviously this letter got to me. And I talked to my dad about Māori disciplining our children harshly, physically. As usual, he didn't directly respond to what was eating at me. Instead he talked about how kids in the valley would take off over the ranges if they felt they'd been hard done by. And sometimes other whānau would come down and deal to whoever. What he told me said that children weren't seen as belonging only to those who directly made them, their parents. They belonged to the wider whānau. They belonged to the hapū, they belonged to iwi. And they could call on any of those to protect their rights and their safety, and to seek retribution if they were mistreated.

I am not condoning the actions described in the letter; they pained me as a mother and a Māori. But it also sickens me how often the 'lighter races' seem to have made an art out of dirtying other people's backyards around the world, and then complain about the smell!

How do we try and stop this perpetuating phenomenon, and do we want to? I believe on the whole we do. Waiata written by Māori women to sing in kōhanga tell us so.

Ko te mea nui ko te aroha.
Kaua e patu
taku mokopuna
Me awhiawhi koe i taku mokopuna korikori e.

The greatest thing is love.
Don't hit
my grandchild.
You must embrace and care for my mischievous grandchild.

But we can't just sing our waiata: we must live the guidelines they give us, we must relive them. We have to reclaim our own experiences, both the personal and the historical, of childrearing and childhood, of growing up as Māori children and bringing up Māori children.

Eldest Son

TOM SMILER JUNIOR

Tom Smiler Jnr is an elder of Te Aitanga ā Mahaki and Rongowhakaata. Born in 1915, he grew up in Gisborne and the Poverty Bay district, where he continues to maintain a busy life. At 83, he is a revered and loved community leader, trustee of the Wi Pere Estate and farmer. He is married to Julia Keelan, 75, who works at the Sandown Hotel as a cook and kitchenhand.

Both Tom and Julia Smiler have come from large families. They themselves have a large family of children, grandchildren and great-grandchildren.

I was born in the Waituhi valley in 1915. My original name is Te Hā o Rūhia, The Czar of All The Russias, and my brothers always called me Czar. Māori had a habit of naming their children after events or places or people, and the Russian Empire was just beginning to be known by them. I had uncles, brothers and cousins with names like Caesar, Mafeking, Tunisia, Tripoli and Egypt. My grandfather, Manu Tawhio-rangi, used to call me, 'E Hā'.

In those days Māori women who were pregnant didn't go to hospitals to have their babies. The other women would put up a shelter near the house, and the pregnant woman would go there for the delivery. In my mother's case, a canvas tent was put up for her and she was in there for a few days. When her contractions began the midwife helped her. I was the eldest of what was to become a family of sixteen children.

My mother's name was Teria and my father was Pera Punahamoa. After I was born, so I have been told, my paternal grandmother came to pick me up and take me away with her. Her name was Hine Te Ariki and she was about forty-five at the time; Manu Tawhiorangi was her second husband – they brought me up. I don't know if my mother objected. The custom in those days was that the first-born was adopted by the father's parents and the second-born by the mother's parents – my younger brother, Winiata, was taken by Moanaroa Pere and Riria Watene Pere, my mother's parents. The third one in our family, Michael, came to join me at Hine Te Ariki's. Puku, the fourth, stayed with Mum and Dad, as did Mary and the others. But at some point another sister, Josephine, when she was older, also came to stay with Hine Te Ariki. This was possibly to make it easier for Mum and Dad, who were going through hard times during the Depression.

I think one of the reasons why Hine Te Ariki took me was because, when I was born, I had an abscess in my head, somewhere near the fontanelle. The scar is still there. I was skinny, emaciated, my eyes sunken into the sockets and the abscess, constantly weeping, still hadn't healed after a year. In the end, I was bedridden and people were waiting for me to die. I was told by my uncle, Charlie Pere, that Hine Te Ariki came into the room with a plate of kūmara. Looking at me, she started to eat some. I saw her eating, pointed to the kūmara and started to beg like a dog, 'Mmmn, mmmn'. Hine Te Ariki put some more kūmara in her mouth, mashing it because it was too hot, and then put it from her mouth into mine.

I stayed with my grandparents until my grandmother died in 1931, but sometimes I used to visit my mother and brothers and sisters. Sometimes my mother would say, 'Stay the night'. But I always answered, 'No, I have to go home to my nanny. She'll miss me.'

Hine Te Ariki and Manu Tawhiorangi lived across the gully on a high terrace on the Waituhi 2E Block about a mile and a half from the Waipoua River. Their land was never flooded until the Poverty Bay Catchment Board started to change the river. It was completely under water during Cyclone Bola in 1988.

Hine Te Ariki was the daughter of Pera Punahamoa and Terina Parewhai from Whakatōhea. Her first husband was Ihimaera Te Hanene Ringarore, from Tūhoe, and their children were my dad and his sister, Te Raukura. Hine Te Ariki lived in Tūhoe until Ihimaera was killed while bush-felling. A branch flew in the air and hit him in the head. Devastated, the young widow returned to family land inWaituhi – but left my father in Tūhoe in the care of her sister-in-law, the oldest sister of her husband, Mihi Te Hanene, who married a Meihana from Nuhaka.

Now, about this family land in Waituhi. Although Hine Te Ariki was from Whakatōhea, she was connected to Whakarau, the youngest son of Mahaki, the great chief. It is through Whakarau that she claimed the land and her rank. In later years she met Manu Tawhiorangi and they had Mini, Sid (Iriopeta), Wereta, and two other children who died at birth. Mini, my auntie, whom I grew very close to, must have been ten when I was brought as a baby to the house.

The house was painted white and had three bedrooms, a dining room and a lounge. Hine Te Ariki and Manu slept in one bedroom. I shared with my Uncle Wereta and Sid. Manu had a team of the best horses in Poverty Bay. They were chaff fed, grain fed. Manu was a farmer on forty acres of his own land, cropping maize and oats, and he also had some lease-land. He also used to grow grass to sell as hay and seed.

In the 1920s the Okitu dairy factories started up at Makaraka, one near the railway station. Hine Te Ariki and Manu ran a herd of cows and the revenue they got from the cream was exchanged for flour, butter and other goods. I recall that no money was exchanged – only goods. Hine Te Ariki was a great milker. She'd climb a hill, see where her cows were – sometimes a mile and a half away – put two fingers in her mouth and whistle her dogs to bring the cows in.

Me, three years old, in 1917.

In those days everybody lived close-knit. We stayed in our own homes but we shared everything with each other. My grandmother used to save milk and take some to my uncle Tip (Tipene) and others after each milking. If anybody killed a beast they'd go around sharing the meat. Any meat left over was preserved in a big drum filled with fat from the pork. The fat preserved the meat and it lasted for months. If somebody didn't have kūmara, resources would be shared so that *everybody* could get through from one season to the next. It was not unusual for families to feed up to twenty people at dinner, including those who were passing by or staying temporarily.

Our day normally started at five in the morning. Manu used to start the Ringatū himene but sometimes he would call out to me, 'E Hā, māhau rā te himene, you start the waiata.' When I was very young I used to get frightened of the droning sound and would hide my head under the blankets.

We had prayers for up to an hour and then we were out of bed by six. Breakfast was cooked in the kāuta on an open fire and normally comprised a cup of tea and oven bread. We always blessed the food before eating – in fact, there was a prayer for just about everything. Then, Manu and Hine Te Ariki would go off to work. 'Right-o, haere tātou ki te mahi.'

One of the main occupations was tending the kūmara plantation. I remember how Manu would say a karakia before digging the kūmara out of the ground. In those days people were always so *careful* handling kūmara and other garden crops. I remember helping the old man put the kūmara one by one into a flax basket, *so* carefully, that they wouldn't get bruised. If they got bruised they could go rotten in the kūmara pit. Then I would help him carry the kit to the kūmara pit – all the time he'd be saying in Māori, 'Careful, *careful*, e Hā!'. The pākoro was a small raupō house in the pit, so low that you couldn't stand up in it, where the kūmara were stored. It was constructed so that when it rained the rain would fall away on the outside of the pit and not come inside. Manu would crawl inside and I would start handing him the kūmara, one by one. And always he would be cautioning me, because I was always in a hurry. 'A! A! Don't tip the kūmara ! Be careful! Kei maru! You might bruise the kūmara!'

I loved watching the way he put the kūmara into the pākoro. The first row on the solid ground. Then the next row on top of it, giving a slight careful *twist* so that each kūmara fitted in nicely. The big kūmara were always placed at the back of the house and the small kūmara to the front. Always so much *care*. The reason? Because Māori lived from season to season and those kūmara had to last a year, between one harvest time and the next, so that there was sufficient food to keep everyone alive.

I remember once I tried to go into the pākoro to help him, but he wouldn't let me, just in case I did a fart – because even that could make the kūmara go off.

Kūmara was the main diet, supplemented with pūhā, pumpkin, ironbark pumpkin, and Māori bread baked from flour, water and sometimes yeast. Not many potatoes were grown at the time.

Our main drink was water. Whenever it rained we had to catch water by any means – and put it into three twenty-gallon wooden casks. We didn't have a tank. Sometimes, however, we had to get our water supplies from the Waipaoa River.

I remember, one day, Manu said to me, 'Haere tama ki te tiki wai.' We took two of our casks on the sledge down to the river. It was in flood and the water was dirty – I wondered why we were getting this dirty water. We started to bucket the water into two of our casks.

'This water is too dirty,' I said. 'How can we drink it?'

'Don't ask too many questions,' Manu answered. 'Turi turi.'

After we had taken the water home, he proceeded to bucket the water from one of the casks into the third cask, which was empty on the kitchen bench. When it was filled he said to me, 'Go and get a mug.' He turned on the tap at the bottom of the cask – and the water came out clear! I was so astonished, until he told me his secret. At the bottom of the third cask was six inches of shingle which filtered the impurities out of the water. Much later in life, I used this same principle when digging a well. I shovelled some shingle into the well because the water was so yellow. After a while, it came out clear.

These are some of the ways by which the people showed their simple, natural wisdom. And at the end of every day's work, there'd be a prayer of thanksgiving before going home.

As I have said, Hine Te Ariki was of very high rank through her whakapapa. She was a Ringatū and had been in her teens when Te Kooti established the church. She embraced the church with such vigour that she became a leader among them. Her personality was so strong that very soon she became the boss of Waituhi. For instance, the house, Takitimu, never used to be on the hill – it used to be on the flat, where it was too wet. When the decision was made to put Takitimu further up the hill, it was Hine Te Ariki who organised the people to level the ground out and move the house there.

My grandmother also became the main speaker on all the marae embracing the Poverty Bay, Māhia, up the East Coast and over to the Bay of Plenty.

I was still only a baby when she started to take me with her to all the marae, including those at Mangatū, Te Karaka, Waioeka and Māhia. As I grew older I used to look around during the welcomes and wonder who would do the replies – and it was always Hine Te Ariki. You know, she was physically formidable – about six feet tall, broad-shouldered, with a bell skirt and hat.

Hine Te Ariki was *some* orator. She had a big strong face. She had a moko. She was a very forceful, strong and clear-speaking woman. When she finished her speech she'd sit down. I never saw anybody else speak after her. Throughout Mangatū, Pūhā, Te Karaka, Waihīrere, Manutuke, Muriwai, Māhia, Ōpōtiki, Ōmaramutu – no men, nobody else spoke after her. She had a huge influence. Even in Waituhi, Rongopai, Pakowhai and Takitimu, although there were other important families like the Pere and Halbert iwi, none of the men stood up – I never saw Te Moana speak and the only Pere to ever speak in later life was Turuki.

Most of the kōrero at meetings was to do with politics. Either church politics or land politics or cultural politics or politics to do with the Pākehā.

When Hine Te Ariki stood to speak I used to stand beside her.

'Haere ki te noho!' she would growl at me. 'E noho! Te hōhā o te tamaiti nei!'

And the people would laugh as, using her walking-stick, she tried to push me behind her skirts.

If you want an illustration of Hine Te Ariki's mana, one example is that when she died *everybody* wanted to be a speaker and to take over where she had left off. Naturally, my dad was one of the first ones to do this. All the others, cousins and relations, were fighting all the time.

I don't remember much about the flu epidemic except that there were a lot of people dying in those days – but somehow I survived.

I was eight when I started going to Patutahi School. One day, Hine Te Ariki said to me, 'Haere ki te kura ki te ako ngā mahi a te Pākehā.' This was in 1923 and my brother Winiata was going to school – he'd started when he was five.

So I joined my brother. We were lucky enough to go to school by horse. Other children had to walk three miles or more. I remember during the first week, on our way home, we came across a harvester, a haymaking machine. Our horse shied, we got thrown off, and the horse bolted. That was the first time I had ever seen a machine.

My dad registered me at school. He put my name down as Tom Smiler Jnr because he was afraid the other children would make fun of me if they knew my name was Czar – the royal family had been murdered during the First World War. My name today is Thomas Smiler Junior.

I learnt to speak English at school.

I was sixteen when Hine Te Ariki died in 1930 or 1931. Māori were very susceptible to all sorts of illnesses and she contracted the flu. There were no doctors for Māori – they used herbs, massage, poultices from other herbs and plants and, for breathing problems, they boiled bluegum leaves and inhaled the fumes.

On the morning Hine Te Ariki died I was out getting firewood on the sledge. I had cut some mānuka and I was on my way back along the hill ridge behind Rongopai. Then, from far off, I heard wailing coming from the direction of Takitimu. I had this terrible feeling of emptiness and knew straight away she had died.

My father came to pick me up at Takitimu meeting house to take me, Mike and Josephine home. At the time, Mini, Hine Te Ariki's own daughter, was looking after us. We had lived together all our lives and we loved each other. Mini said to me, 'Please don't leave me. Stay with me.' So I said, 'Okay.' I told Dad, 'I'm sorry, I have to stay with my auntie.' So, although Mike and Josephine left with him, I stayed with Mini until my 21st birthday.

My mother, Teria, wanted to give me a 21st birthday party but I didn't want one, so I went out camping in the bush. A year later, in 1937, my mother sprang a surprise party. All of Waituhi was there.

Eventually, I went back to my mum and dad. By then, shearing had begun in Poverty Bay and the East Coast, and Dad started up a shearing gang.

My father was physically strong, a hard worker, and he expected everybody – including the animals, like his horses and dogs – to work as hard as he did. He started shearing with blades when he was fourteen. When motor-driven machines first came in, they got so hot that they were often difficult to hold. Every shearer had a bucket of water near his stand. When the handpiece got too hot, the shearer would plunge it into the water to cool it down.

The important happenings of life all occurred around the pā. We had our own community. Sometimes we had dances – our band was a piano and mouth organ. Māori and Pākehā would come to enjoy each other's company.

I have to say that I have never wanted tribal leadership. When Win (Winiata) was alive, I told him to do it. He used to say, '*You're* the eldest.'

Today, I have realised that I have had to grow into this role of a kaumātua. I think that Hine Te Ariki and Manu Tawhiorangi would have been proud that I have tried to do my best according to their teachings.

It was they who taught me to care, to look after people, to be unselfish, to give more than you take. To look after the kūmara – the royal children who will take the Māori into the future – and to try to stop them from being bruised.

And always to have aroha.

He Whare Tangata: He Whare Kura?
What's Happening to Our Māori Girls?

NGAHUIA TE AWEKOTUKU

*Ngahuia Te Awekotuku was born in 1949 and raised in Ōhinemutu, Rotorua, by an extended family of weavers, entertainers and storytellers. She is the author of a number of books including **Tahuri and Other Stories** (1991) and **Mana Wahine Māori: Selected Writings on Māori Women's Art, Culture and Politics** (1991).*

Ngahuia Te Awekotuku maintains a busy national and international career in indigenous, women's and cultural issues. She is one of our highest qualified academics (she completed her PhD at Waikato University) and taught art history and women's studies at the University of Auckland for many years.

She now lives in Wellington where she is Professor of Māori Studies at Victoria University of Wellington.

Hoki hoki tonu mai
te wairua o te tau
Ki te awhi rei nā ki
tēnei kiri e

The shrill, excited squeak of a two-year-old's voice lifted in the close night air, bounced off the dark wooden headboard of the great big bed. Bundling a soft feather pillow around her neck, the little girl rolled into the warm, warm cushion of her kuia's side. Her feet were snug beneath her koro's arm. She was wrapped up in bed with her Kuia and her koro, and she was happy. They were teaching her a song – one of the songs they did at the concert; one of the songs she loved.

My earliest childhood – before I first caught the school bus – was the time of both my grandparents, my kuia and my koro, and living down at the pā. How desperately I wanted to stay down the pā, to be with them all the time! But the two people who adopted me had other ideas, and moved a few miles up the road, to a Māori Affairs home in a new 'pepper-potted' suburb. 'Pepper-potting' was a government policy of mixed-race housing. Integration. Having Māori and Pākehā live side by side, with goodwill and purpose, as they had so diligently fought side by side in the Second World War. My mother preferred the pā, and her people. Her husband, a well-colonised person from another tribal group, preferred to foster friendships with the Pakehas next door, and across the road. Especially those ones who were English and had a little girl who did elocution and dancing, and got very exciting presents from her relatives in 'the old country' and her daddy who was always in America. I was simply fascinated; she had a stereoscope with views of the ruins of Pompeii and the Changing of the Guard, and she had games with numbers and other bits. And shelves and shelves of books. Books! We never had them. My kuia and koro had the Māori Bibles and heaps of the *Weekly News* – but not real books, with thick backs and hard covers. This girl was truly from another world.

But slowly, I began to explore that world. One of my aunties had become a schoolteacher, and she was very interested in 'tiny tots'. At that stage, I was very much a 'tiny tot', and she was very interested in me. She visited us a lot, and she often looked after me. We played games together, and some months before my fifth birthday I had stumbled through my first lines of reading, and written my first sentences. Aunty Toria encouraged my mother to give me books; I will always be grateful for that. And I devoured them. I memorised them. I treasured them. Even when I was down the pā, my books were my friends. They didn't hit and pinch and laugh at me for my asthma and funny way of talking and hakihaki (eczema); I was happiest with books and with the old people, especially my kuia, who sat weaving in a pool of sunlight, around her a mass of sweetly fragrant green flax. I was seen either as a loner, or a little bit strange. And I was very excited about going to school.

That first day, that first week of school. Rotorua Primary. Cluttered together with lots of other tiny tots. Fear, excitement, panic; we clutched our little chair bags and rattled their contents – chalk, duster, handkerchief. We peered up at the dark, endlessly high, polished walls, where the narrow windows seemed so far away. We sneezed on the smell of chalk dust. I made a friend – actually, she was my cousin. We swapped chair bags straight away. Hers was bright yellow with brown grapes and mine was navy blue with pink daisies. We chattered and made a noise. We got smacked. We learned fast.

By Standard Two, I had hopped a few classes and settled in when suddenly the world changed. Family matters shifted us to Wellington, where we stayed with another aunt. I had also acquired two newly adopted siblings, who came and went: one was a brother four years older than me; the other a baby girl, a tiny little sister. But during most of the Wellington time, they were not with us. Instead I had three older male cousins to contend with, and a vastly different, almost foreign, social and cultural environment.

My aunt had married a very wealthy and prominent doctor. Their home was a spacious nineteenth-century villa, densely carpeted and richly panelled with dark glowing wood and bevelled glass, gleaming antiques, heavy maroon velvet drapes, and landscapes and horse pictures edged in gilded wood. Huge trees framed their view of the sea, and embraced the house itself. And they even had 'native bush' – an acre of forest trees, just behind the house. And only twelve minutes away from the uncle's Willis Street surgery. The family was devoutly Catholic, and thus I became a somewhat bewildered pupil at the exclusive hilltop convent of Mount Carmel.

It was not easy. Catechism and Christian Doctrine were totally beyond me, and Sister Mary Aden took me into her special care. I was there two terms; I spent what seems, at this point so far along in my life, hours just wandering alone around the school. I examined the vaults below the red brick building, and one day I found some brilliantly coloured banners leaning against a wall. Amazing. I explored the basements, and avoided the classrooms – there were only two. And I became aware that I was different – not just because I was a 'Non-Catholic', but because I was Māori. The only one in the school – my cousins were at boys' schools, and together. I was by myself. And everyone expected me to sing. That was hard, and rather humiliating, despite my early lessons from the old people. After all, I was asthmatic and it was bleak winter in Wellington. However, my clearest memory of that time was the school marching, beneath one of those banners, in the Corpus Christi Festival – with all the trumpeting and pageantry – rich song resonant on the chill grey air. Hundreds of proud, happy people being Catholic. I thought about turning into a Catholic. Seriously.

But again, changes. A transfer for a painful half-term in a Palmerston North convent school, St Mary's. Competitive marching teams at playtime, and the nuns calling me a nuisance. The only good thing – dawdling to school through the hospital grounds: huge, gentle oak trees, softly greening. And daffodils.

My conversion had to wait another year. Back I went to Rotorua Primary; Standard Three and a Māori teacher who taught us his tribe's version of 'Hey Diddle Diddle Te Pereti me te Whira', and whacked everyone on the back of the legs with a leather strap if we misbehaved, which was often, though I only lined up for one dose. Though I cannot remember why – and had come from a household where a 'damn good hiding' was always threatened and often carried out. Corporal punishment was something I was very used to.

The last three years of primary school crawled by at St Michael's Convent, where I sheltered with the nuns, Sisters of Mercy, with soft Irish accents and gentle pink faces. My home life was in acute crisis; that's all I'll say here. My koro died; my mother's husband refused to live permanently down the pā. My mother refused to leave our kuia. And my older adopted brother returned to his 'real' (birth) family, while my baby sister stayed, because she was my mother's mokopuna. At this time, I also thought a lot about my 'real' family – but my father had been dead a long time, and my mother had a chronic, crippling illness. Unlike most adopted Māori children, I had no contact with my birth family, though my father's home was Ōhinemutu, and my mother would often visit other relatives in the pā. I daydreamed a lot about what it would have been like – I wrote long, complicated stories and made up plays.

I trundled about confused, unhappy, but safely concealed behind a veneer of much celebrated 'cleverness', which perhaps in its own way protected me. Once school was done for the day, I would hang about for hours. I did not want to go 'home' – to the suburban house – where I was forced by fear to live, away from my kuia and my mother, for varying periods. The house, the man in it: both frightened me. So I diligently remained at school, applying myself. I did my best to be brainy and productive, and the nuns loved and rewarded me for it. What treasures they shared! Christian Doctrine revealed not only the deep bewilderment of Eucharist and purgatory and Immaculate Conception; it also planted the seeds of strong political consciousness.

Apart from the lives of the saints – the chaste Agnes and Philomena and Catherine, who chose death before dishonour – we were read the most extraordinary stories. Of Violet Szabo, courageous woman spy and anti-Nazi resistance fighter. Of Douglas Bader, the RAF ace pilot who lost both his legs, but kept his wings and shot down even more enemy planes. Of the wooden horse, which enabled prisoners of war to tunnel valiantly to freedom. The Second World War was not too far behind us, and Battler Britain and Spy Thirteen and Biggles were comic heroes avidly consumed, and brought to life in the playground. Other issues also surfaced in the classroom – the Irish Republican Army and its own heroic struggle; the true meaning of Guy Fawkes Night; and, very poignantly indeed, the plight of the Black Babies in South Africa. I clearly remember being told about apartheid; Verwoerd had just attained power, and we attended a special mass for the native people. As well as the politics, and 'the moral of the story', there was the music, the drama, the plainsong, Latin, English and Māori. How often we were told, by visiting 'Inspectors', and church dignitaries, that truly we 'sang like angels'.

Although we were a small convent school, the second in the district and very new, we presented a fascinating ethnic fruit salad. A lot of Māori children. And a few of the others – Italian, Canadian, Portuguese, Cook Island, Yugoslav, Polish, Irish and Dutch, with the balance Pākehā. We were shaped and prodded and readied for secondary school – though there was then no church institution in Rotorua. Academically, the 'clever ones' were cultivated, in the first row of the room. We were groomed on 'Proficiency Test' cards; we sat outside examinations, and we did well. I was awarded the Ngarimu Essay Prize; I was an avid writer, and contributed the serialised version of my second novel to a Bay of Plenty Catholic School monthly bulletin. It was about some kids sailing a raft (not a canoe!) called Te Arawa from Maketū to Mōtītī Island, in earnest search for adventure. My first extravagant literary effort was about two orphans who inherit a haunted Rhineland castle, complete with Lorelei, and punctuated heavily with lots of 'Achtungs!' and 'Raus! Raus!' and 'Gott in

Himmels!' And by this time, I had a set of real books, Arthur Mee's *Children's Encyclopaedia*, with epics of the glorious Empire on which the sun never set. They satisfied me for a while, but they frustrated me too – because the flowers and trees were foreign, and I never did find a razor shell or a periwinkle on the beach at Maketū.

She scratched, a little to the left, a little to the right. The sunburn was still annoying, flaky and sore. Itchy. She moved again. And suddenly, above the clamouring hymn, a voice shrilled out – 'Stop! Stop this instant! You, there! Get out! Get out of this hall! You were doing the twist! Doing the twist at my assembly! Get out! Go, girl, go!' A muffled wavelet of gasps and giggles rolled down the hall. Row after row. She looked up, saw those dark red swan wing glasses flashing fiercely down at her. At her. No one else had moved. 'Do you mean me, Miss Hogan?' She gestured meekly to herself. 'Yes! You! Go to my office. Now!'

Three away from the centre aisle, she lurched across the knees. And walked the endless walk, under the gaze of a thousand eyes, to the Head's office. It was the Tuesday of the first week of the first term of her first year at high school.

That year was unspeakably, unprintably ugly. I ran away from home, I got into fist fights with other girls, I wagged school, I sneaked out at night, I imagined I was Elvis Presley and Connie Francis all at once. I chased girls who were running after boys and it looked as if I chased boys too. Which was blatantly untrue and unfair. I passionately, passionately hated that school. Its teachers. Its pupils (except my cousins). And most of all its headmistress.

I was placed in the top third form, privileged to learn Latin and French with the yachting, skiing set. I wanted to study Māori; was told that was impossible, my test results were too high. They were convinced they were doing me a huge favour; they were wrong. I was, after all, from down the pā. No different from all those rough Māori widgies in 3 Vocational and 3 Commercial B and 3 Remove – my cousins, my mates. And in the classroom, I had two strange allies – a Canadian immigrant from a family of seventeen kids, and a voluptuous, silky-voiced sophisticate whom I persuaded to run away with me (during one of my 'Elvis' episodes).

Three memorable items from that school year: for our class

fundraising stall, I offered to bring rewana bread. The response: 'Eeek! Oooh! We don't want stuff like that on our stall!' I raged, 'Look here you Pakehas, I'll bring it and I bet it'll sell before any of your butterfly cakes and coconut ice does!' And of course it did. Second item: hearing the reigning Miss New Zealand, a Māori woman related to many of us, come and address the assembly about poise and pride and all that. Then a few days later, hearing the headmistress request that all Māori girls, Māori girls only, remain in the assembly hall. The Pakehas filed out, even the dark, quarter-caste-looking ones. We stayed, and we were told some of us 'had been seen shoplifting. In school uniform. And I know it was a group of Māori girls. I know it.' We knew there was a very active group of Pākehā girls playing that game too. We said nothing. What was the point? Third melting moment: being pushed out in front of the class by the maths teacher, a golfing, cantankerous, vegetarian bigot in tweeds, with the announcement that I was a black abomination, because I hadn't done my homework. Balanced later by the French teacher, a plump, bespectacled matron with heart-shaped lips, who counselled in her most soothing voice that I was special because I was a Māori and I was clever and had a responsibility to my race. Ho hum. I was expelled.

I survived. Most of the girls I had been following around left school at the end of the year. Got jobs, got pregnant. Boring. I had had enough of being a rebel; I had never stopped writing or thinking, despite all that had been going on. And I desperately wanted to go to a boarding school, to get away. But the problem was simple enough – my family could not afford any fees, did not know about Māori Education Grants, and although I was 'scholarship material' academically, for a Catholic school, I was unacceptable, possibly even corrupt. So that was that. I was bad news.

Luckily for me, the headmaster of the only other high school in the area acknowledged my academic potential (possibly after a chat with the nuns), and offered 'to come halfway to meet me, if I came halfway too'. It was the break I needed. I applied myself; there were other Māori teenagers in the top stream, and we were related. One, in fact, was the cousin with whom I'd swapped chair bags in the infants' room.

Those four years at that high school whipped me through a series of changes; I tried to bury the Elvis part of my personality in a flurry of affected femininity that never did quite fit. Māori culture, the drama club and amateur theatrics, hiking, classical records from the library, and reading Shakespeare aloud to myself were all part of it. Plus writing, copious amounts of writing, in journals long since and tragically lost (that's another story!). And hours in the whare rūnanga, the house Tamatekapua, with the orator/sage Tani Te Kowhai, who told me long, complicated stories. With so many of the other old people of Ngāti Whakaue, of Te Arawa Whānui. E kui mā, e koro mā; E kore koutou e warewaretia; moe mai. Most of my peers thought I was a bit peculiar.

Financially, life was far from easy. I never, ever had a full school uniform – I borrowed when necessary, and improvised with an uncle's reefer jacket, and mother's white blouses. My mother held down two jobs; her husband was seldom on the scene. I worked too. As a tourist and publicity model (those images are still for sale), as a takeaway bar and coffee shop attendant, as a tourist guide and hostess, as a dishwasher. To keep myself at school, I had to work weekends in my lower and upper sixth years. My mother could not comprehend why I refused to 'get a job in a bank' (high status choice for a Māori girl with School Cert.), or later 'go to training college' (even higher status choice for a Māori girl with U.E.). By doing this, I could bring money into the house, and also be independent. But these options were not for me – I was determined to go to university, and my determination was seen as rather selfish.

There was only one known model for a Māori woman academic: I followed the achievements of Ngapare Hopa proudly, and with great pleasure. Her success motivated me. She was an anthropologist, as was Te Rangi Hiroa – Sir Peter Buck. Anthropology – what wonders. A way of helping our people, by studying our culture. That was the career for me. I wrote an essay about this ambition, and won another national prize. I was very clear about things when I was fourteen years old!

Not so, two years later. Contact with a family of lawyers convinced me that Law School was the preferable direction – and I believed I had 'the making of a good lawyer'. Until I got there. Totally unprepared for university life, the pace of a big metropolitan city, and the horrors of an elitist hostel, where the only other Māori women were domestic and kitchen staff. How I loved them. Totally unprepared for the snobbery and cliquishness of the Pākehā students – each and every one of whom had attended private schools – I was neither in their club, nor their league.

So, with the other Māori girls new to the big city, I inevitably flopped into a life in the fast lane – searching the city's festering underbelly. I discovered Japanese ships and drag queens and nightclubs and hard (and soft) drugs. I experimented, I explored. And I fell – with a sharp push from the faculty fathers – out of Law School. Eventually, after a long series of misadventures, I became an anthropologist, a Doctor of Philosophy. But all that is another story, another chapter, in another book.

He mihi atu tēnei ki a koutou, e kui mā, e whaea mā
Kua wehe atu ki te pō
Kua ngaro atu i te aroaro o Papatūānuku,
Tēnā rā koutou.

The Rhythm of Life

TE KUI

Te Kui (Merimeri Penfold) was born in 1920 and is affiliated with Ngāti Kuri ki te Aupōuri. She was born at Te Hapua, Northland. She has been a lecturer in Māori Studies at the University of Auckland for some years, an inspiration and support for many students. She has held numerous public offices and was for many years a board member of New Zealand on Air. Apart from her academic work, Te Kui is a composer, editor and historian. She is completing a novel in Māori. She lives in Auckland.

Every now and again, when I look back to the time I was a child growing up in my home village, I experience a warm glow welling up within. My childhood was like one long summer's day in which I was very much at home within the environment of my family, local primary school and the greater community. Ours was a close-knit family dominated by a lean, tall, upstanding father. He was twenty years my mother's senior. She was quiet and retiring in demeanour. Their relationship was one of caring and support.

My background is Māori as is my mother tongue. My parents were Christian and adherents of the Anglican and Catholic churches which they later left to join the Ratana faith. Our home was a very orderly place. Each morning all the family members came together on the flax-mat-covered floor to join in prayer before breakfast. Likewise, evening prayers followed the last meal of the day. During these occasions we were encouraged to say individual prayers, blessing sick members of the family, our parents or people known to be ill within the community.

As the second eldest of the family, and first daughter named after my paternal grandmother, I received a great deal of attention from both my parents as a young child. My siblings, who numbered twelve, followed me in quick succession. Caring for such numbers was demanding for my mother, more so because each year brought a new addition to her flock.

Under such circumstances I grew up very quickly. I became my mother's daily chief help at a very early age. I fetched and carried, cradling or feeding the baby, watching or adding wood to the fire, removing and replacing flax floor-mats when tidying the house, and gathering the washing from the fence line. Yet life for me was exciting and indeed great fun and my bonding within the family grew from strength to strength. I adored my parents, particularly my mother. At night I often feared losing her.

Very early in my childhood I sensed a definite rhythm about our lives. The seasons of the year greatly influenced our lifestyle, year in and year out. Our lives seemed to revolve particularly around gum digging, mustering, planting and harvesting kūmara, and fishing and gathering seafood. And, of course, for us children, there was school. I recall clearly my first contact with school. I was four years old. It was my duty to deliver milk to the schoolhouse which was not far from home. Milk-can in hand, I walked along the path leading to school and up to the school house gate. With some trepidation I opened the gate and was struck first by the size of the house, the woodwork and panelling on the door with its shiny bronze knob. A profusion of honeysuckle and grapevine created a welcome and cool bower along the verandah. A curious gentle perfume permeated the whole scene. I felt I was in another world, new, different and it left me full of curiosity. Timidly I moved forward and thumped on the door. In a few moments the door opened and there, wide-eyed, I beheld a small, white-haired lady with sparkly blue eyes, pale skin, long, skinny fingers and a tiny, sharp nose. She may have greeted me but I cannot recall the words she used. She had a thin soft voice. I stood and handed the milk over to her. She took it and retired. I waited for her to return the milk container, a billy-can. Meantime, sweet, new and interesting delicious food smells emanated from within. The old lady returned, handing me the billy-can and a lovely golden apple. I smiled, 'Thank you,' turned, ran down the path and out the gate to admire the apple I held in my hands. It was perfect. My first Pākehā apple! Yes, that was the moment of my first contact with the Pākehā world, the inevitable new world that awaited me. The sensation and wonderment of that passing moment remains with me to this day. So, in delivering the milk to the schoolhouse daily I became familiar and at ease with the school environment which was to be part of my growing up for years to come.

The vision to be part of that world was born.

My father always had much in hand to attend to. At times it was mustering the cattle which roamed the hinterland, branding, culling and getting them ready for the annual cattle sales, where he would receive much-needed cash for the needs of his family. He rose early in the morning, had family prayers followed by a good meal. Then he saddled his horse and, with stock-whip in hand and dogs at heel, cantered his way out onto the open highway to join other musterers from the community. Mustering meant he was a whole week away from home. He often returned with comb honey from a large pūriri tree-knot which he had located some years back. The honey was delicious and a real family luxury. The end of my father's mustering endeavours was always celebrated by the butchering at home of chosen beef cattle. The meat was cut up and salted to store for future use. Parcels of meat were often served out to some families in the community.

Early in my childhood I was my mother's constant companion whenever she went fishing with fishing lines in her kit. I mastered the techniques early: baiting and casting a line, gathering shrimp for bait using a kit, scaling and gutting my catch. I learnt and grew sensitive to the care of the fishing grounds we visited and used. Pollution in any form was not permitted. I learnt fast and revelled in the challenge that came my way.

On occasions I accompanied my father and brother when they went netting for mullet and other fish. Our vast harbour surrounded about seventy-five percent of the village coastline – a veritable food-basket for people who never feared starvation. We netted when the tide was on the turn. A spot was selected to one side of a channel. There, one end of the net, attached to a solid ti-tree pole, was firmly planted into the seabed, a wading distance from the shore. My father then boarded the boat and with my brother rowing, proceeded to feed out the net, folded concertina-wise across the stern. Across the channel and up the opposite side towards the shore they went, and there the other end of the net was planted firmly in the seabed. By that time the first catch were leaping and struggling to free themselves. This was great excitement for us! My brothers and I would board the boat and move along the top edge of the net, marked by cork floaters, gathering in the fish we could reach. It was quite an art to seize the catch, free it from the net and load it on to the boat. Sometimes scaling and gutting took place by the bank away from the fishing grounds. On returning home we were greeted by all and sundry of the community, who shared the catch. This was a venture that was repeated often throughout the year with the whole family or with just father and boys.

The kūmara season played a significant part in our lives. The cycle began in August with my father visiting the traditional kūmara grounds, approximately ten miles distant from the village. The soil was alluvial, the site was sheltered and had a northerly aspect. Kūmara grow well in the hot sun. The land was ploughed and allowed to fallow. By the months of October and November, the serious matter of planting was upon the family. This often necessitated the whole household moving to the site for a whole week or more. Other whānau members would join the trek. The gardens were large and required the skilful use of horse-drawn equipment, with disking followed by harrowing and then ploughing up of the hillocks in readiness for planting kūmara shoots. This was intensive work, involving many hands, young and old.

On arrival at the gardens the makeshift camping site was made ready for habitation by whānau members and part of the planting team. My father and others would fish for the first evening meal, after which prayers followed, and then it was to bed.

Early next morning, very early, we were out on the plantation behind the adults as they moved along the long rows, forming and watering holes ready for planting the shoots. And so it went on until dark. Day after day, for a whole week, the planting went on. At the end my family boarded the ox-drawn wagon to return home and back to school.

The site was revisited a couple of months later by a smaller team to weed and mound the rows before the kūmara shoots sent out tendrils that wandered across rows and hillocks. The last visitation was in autumn when the harvesting of the crop took place. As before, the whole family was involved with uprooting the crop and sorting tubers for storage in pits: seedling tubers into kits for the following season and damaged and smaller tubers for immediate use. The whole crop was loaded onto the ox-drawn wagon and transported back home. The pits used for storage were specially constructed to be cool and well-drained. It was not uncommon for our family to be still drawing from the crop of the previous season while harvesting the new. During the year contributions of kūmara and potato would go down to the marae for community occasions.

Gum-digging was a dirty game, particularly in the winter period when my parents would work in wet conditions, often standing in gum holes with water up to their knees. In such conditions they would discard what footwear they possessed and work barefooted. Gum was a cash crop for them and enabled them to better provide for their family. This manifested itself when, having cleared the gum of gravel, wood chip and other debris, they haggled with the gumbuyers for the going price of the day. Such sojourns into the hinterland to collect gum denied the family access to food from the sea – that's when pig-hunting became the pastime that we indulged in. Together with salted beef from home, the family fared reasonably well. As ever, the family in the end looked forward to returning to home and school. For those of us of school age there was much catching up awaiting us as well as the fun of rejoining our schoolmates.

School was always a place of interesting happenings. All oral activities such as reciting numbers, times-tables, poems, sounding words, the alphabet – all were done in a singsong fashion. From the day I met the white-haired lady at the schoolhouse I had been struck by the shrillness of our teachers' voices. It was difficult to warm to them. Instead, my friends and I were great mimics and would spend endless hours imitating the different teachers we had in a ponderous manner. A great source of amusement for the watchers-on. Singing sessions were very popular for me. We apparently learnt new songs easily and with great enthusiasm. However, I often had no real appreciation for the meaning of the words, including those we rattled off as endless nursery rhymes. Such activities were fun as it enabled me to learn how the English language flowed. But *speaking* English for me was agonisingly soul-destroying and challenging. I met the challenge.

However, I always had a deep-seated longing to use my mother tongue. If only my teachers would speak to me in Māori! Of course I would have engaged and responded readily and my whole being would have come alive – unlike the way I sat vacant-eyed in class with English the only means of communication. But Māori was never spoken in the classroom. As a result, all of the class at break would walk out and move away in small groups, speaking Māori as much as possible without being caught. Those sessions were delicious moments for all of us. It was manna from heaven. However, we were always aware of the likelihood of being strapped once back in class.

The obverse side to this linguistic debate, for my siblings and me, was the response of our parents when we got home after school. My father, in particular, was not concerned with our being punished for speaking Māori at school but rather that we dared to attempt to speak *English* at home! He would say, 'Kaua koutou e kōrero i tērā reo i konei.' Every so often we would return home with precious new phrases like 'Excuse me' and 'Thank you', and have to run away and practise saying them to each other without Dad knowing. We learnt very quickly to do our practice beyond his hearing.

So, linguistically, life for me and the rest of us school children was like being between the devil and the deep blue sea. We were safest in that area between school and home where neither our teachers nor our parents heard us. We made good use of the opportunity of speaking both languages.

My parents were greatly involved with all community functions like church services, funerals, dances, land court sessions, elections, school concerts and Christmas festivities, all held at the local hall. The whole community would assemble and participate in each instance. The elders led the assembly in prayer. Speeches of welcome and greetings followed. Matters of local concern were raised and discussed and eventually resolved. Ours was a very organised community. Controversial issues involving relationships, families, unacceptable behaviour and violence between members of the community were duly dealt with by the community. I, personally, was not aware of much violence. There was none in my family. The only violence that I recall vividly was that performed by the headmaster who caned senior kids using a supplejack switch. I can still hear their yelps and screams of pain and agony. But, on the whole, growing up, for me, was a very long sunny day.

Three Women

DEIRDRE NEHUA

Deirdre Nehua is the Regional Manager for the Royal NZ Foundation for the Blind. Born in 1950, she has been closely involved in the Māori Nationalist Movement, Te Ahi Kaa, and is a practising traditional Māori healer.

In 1996 Deirdre Nehua responded to the deep commitment of being a Māori woman by taking the moko kauae. It is from this beginning point that she makes the first cut on her own life and takes us back to the women who were at the very beginning of her childhood.

1.

I take a deep breath, close my eyes and say a final karakia.

I feel rock solid. I am buoyed up by the wāhine toa, the strong women, who have come from the four corners of Ngā Puhi to support me, to tautoko this ceremony by which I will receive the moko kauae. So much thinking, praying, negotiation and contemplation has gone into this, for receiving a moko kauae is not something to be done lightly.

Although my father was from Taranaki, a descendant of the fighting chief Titokowaru, those who nurtured and cared for me were my mother's people from Ngāti Wai. In particular, two strong rivers shaped my life – my mother and my grandmother.

My mother married at nineteen and had four children – two boys and two girls. I was the third child. We were the first mokopuna, grandchildren, in my mother's family, and I always felt we were extremely lucky for this reason. Our grandparents were still young enough to enjoy us, and Mum's brothers and sisters all spoilt us in their own ways. I have many fond memories of my aunties and uncles growing up, going through their courtship years with boyfriends and girlfriends who were later to become our aunties and uncles as well.

Early photographs of my mother show an attractive woman. She had wavy hair, which she hated, strong white teeth which we all thankfully inherited, and she was always – always – impeccably dressed. She was, so they tell me, a stunner in her younger days, and the life and soul of the party. She married our father, she told us, not out of love but because she wanted to escape Whangarūrū. Then, in 1955, while she was still in her late twenties, she found herself widowed with four young children. I was barely five years old.

All I remember of my father was that he was very sick all the time. He had come home from the war, his body broken and riddled with tuberculosis, which he'd probably contracted in a prisoner of war camp. At first he was isolated in TB shelters. Later, a small isolation hut was built for him at the back of our two-bedroomed state house. I was told that although TB was infectious, the authorities allowed him to live at home because Mum was so scrupulously clean. I remember him sitting in his chair in the kitchen, the chair placed so that he could look directly out the back door. When we said our evening prayers we knelt every night at his feet, our hands clasped and foreheads on his knees.

Now I lay me down to sleep, I pray thee Lord my soul to keep
If I should die before I wake I pray thee Lord my soul to take.

Vivid memories of Dad's funeral come to mind. Granny and all her sisters came to the house. Everyone was dressed in black. Mum offended Auntie Tari by putting the flowers she had brought for the grave in the house. Everyone talked quietly. I heard someone ask, 'What will happen to the kids?' I also heard Mum say, after seeing Dad in the funeral parlour, 'I saw him in his coffin and he looked awful. They had his hair parted on the wrong side. I don't want the kids to go to his funeral. They can stay with Auntie Bub.'

So we never went to the funeral. Later, my sister was angry and resentful about this. Mum had told her that Dad had gone to sleep. My sister kept waiting for him to wake up and come home, but he never did. He used to call my sister 'Daddy's little girl', and now he wasn't there. Who would protect her, and us, from Mum's growlings? He always did, and now he wasn't there.

After Dad's funeral, tangi, Mum gave away all his clothes and carpentry tools and, although we often asked about him, she never spoke to us about him again. But my uncles used to say, 'What a lovely man he was,' and 'How lucky your mother was to have him.'

2.

I know in my heart and soul that it is right to have the moko kauae.

Following the long period of contemplation I have fasted for a week. I have undergone three days of training, of wānanga.

Now, Pou does the karakia.

Strong fingers stretch the skin on my chin. And then comes a sensation like someone pulling a red hot razor through my skin. The moko kauae is not the end of a period of learning. It's the beginning.

I feel the first cut.

For reasons I've never understood, my mother never liked being Māori. She had a beautiful Māori name but would tell everyone it was Spanish. I suppose, to Mum, that sounded more exotic than Māori.

I think Mum was probably pleased that my two brothers and sister were quite fair-skinned, but me – I was blue-black. I was not allowed in the sun in case I got blacker and, when Mum was around, I was not allowed to go swimming and had to stay under the pōhutukawa trees in summer. Before we went into town, Mum used to put powder on my face and neck. Many's the time I can recall being locked in the shed when Pākehā visitors came to the house. I think it was so they wouldn't see how black I was.

The other problem, for Mum, was that from a very early age I kept seeing things, especially at nights. Old people who had died, tūpuna, would come to see me. They would talk to me. I'd also see taniwha crawling up the walls. Mum didn't like my having this sight and it made her quite afraid. 'All that Māori bullshit!' she called it.

As for me, I thought it was normal. I thought everyone saw what I saw. I was not scared by it. Not only that, but I could mirimiri people who were sick and make them feel a lot better. Mum didn't like that either and didn't like to discuss it. I'd tell Granny instead.

My mother actively discouraged us from mixing with any other Māori kids who lived around us. The nearest I could get to winning grudging approval was to excel at school – so I did. I was referred to as 'the smart one' in the family, although that was not necessarily because of my academic skills. I received prizes for excellence as a Māori student, which I always thought a strange thing. It was as though excellence in a Māori was the exception rather than the rule. If anything went wrong at school it was always the Māori students who were singled out. If anything was stolen or broken we were always lined up for interrogation. The Pākehā kids in the school thought all Māori were thieves. This was reinforced by the attitudes of the teachers towards us. The irony was that it was never the Māori students who were guilty.

I'm not really clear about the date but, soon after Daddy died, my brother and I went to stay with Granny and Grandad. It was a huge relief for me.

My grandmother, as a young woman, was a foundation pupil of Queen Victoria School for Māori girls. She and her sisters were renowned for their beauty – many an old kaumātua bore testimony of this fact to me when I was older. Photographs of her as a young woman show long flowing hair, heavy lidded eyes and an extremely stubborn jawline.

On her father's side, Granny was a direct descendant of the chief Patuone, of Ngāti Hau. Granny was extremely proud that Patuone had been a signatory to the Treaty of Waitangi. On her mother's side, she was descended from the chief Taiawa, of Great Barrier Island. Granny absolutely adored her mother and always spoke of her in glowing and loving tones. Granny and Grandad lived at Motu Kōwhai, Whangarūrū, where they brought up nine children. I grew very close to Granny; those days that I spent with my mother were made tolerable only because I knew that Granny would be coming to get me and take me with her.

Whereas my mother constantly shouted, 'Being Māori is not a good thing to be,' my grandmother whispered, 'Being Māori is the best, indeed, the only way to be.'

Whenever I saw my tūpuna ancestors, Granny wouldn't go up the wall. Instead, she'd ask me what they looked like. When they spoke to me she would ask what they said.

'You have a gift,' she told me. 'It has been passed on through our bloodline for many generations. You are so lucky to have been chosen. Not everyone is. Only special people can carry this taonga.'

I never really knew what Granny meant.

But I did know that she made it okay.

3.

So what has brought me to this place in my life? Here, taking the moko kauae?

In a sense, this story is being written in my head while the moko is being done. When the pain gets too bad I find myself leaving this place.

Journeying homeward.

Back to Motu Kōwhai.

All of my most precious childhood memories revolve around life at Motu Kōwhai.

Every morning, my chores were to help with the milking of the house cows, collect kindling and bring in the wood for the woodbox. The first sound I heard those mornings was the poker in the grate as Grandad cleaned out the woodstove before setting the fire for the day. I helped Granny with breakfast – porridge with thick cream skimmed off the top of the boiled milk – and, after breakfast, Granny and I would do the dishes and scrub the floorboards with sandsoap.

The rest of the day, Granny and I would work in the vegetable garden or the flower garden. Sometimes I helped Grandad tend his vast orchard. He taught me how to graft the fruit trees, prune them, keep the insects at bay and create new strains. Every couple of days Grandad went fishing and I helped him clean the fish. Up to the time they got cleaned they were *his* fish. After they were cleaned, scaled, gutted and strung together by a flax through their mouths, they became *Granny's* fish.

On many days, Grandad took me for walks in the bush to bring the cows home. Every step along the way he had a story – and he would tell me a different one every day. Stories about the history of our people as we walked through battle trenches, hundreds of years old, on our land. He showed me how to lie in the trench, how to make yourself invisible in the bush so that you could leap out and ambush your enemy. Sometimes, when he was tired of telling stories he would sing to me as we walked. He had a beautiful singing voice. He often sang to Granny, usually when he was in trouble with her.

We lived in a small, galvanised-iron hut with floors sandsoaped white and walls lined with old newspapers. One of the

Here I am at three-and-a-half.

newspapers, I remember, told the story of an earthquake in Napier and had a photograph of the devastation. Another newspaper, in the bedroom, had photographs of some very glamorous women at the races. They wore close-fitting hats with a flower on one side, ankle-length lace dresses and shoes with a T-bar. I loved the styles and the clothes – this was a world which fitted my fantasies.

Our reading material was the pink-covered *Weekly News*. The centre pages were glossy black and white photographs of what was happening around the country. Later, we got the *New Zealand Woman's Weekly*. I loved the cartoon strip called 'Through the week with Mopsy'; Mopsy was very glam and had a wardrobe I coveted. Even at the tender age of seven or eight it severely bugged me that Granny would buy my clothes from Woolworths and not one of the flash shops – or worse, she'd make my clothes.

My auntie, who lived in America, sent us the *National Geographic* magazine and *Ebony*, which was a magazine published by Black Americans. Many of the people in *Ebony* were seriously glamorous. I was determined that when I grew up I would dress the way they did, and not continue to wear the cast-off clothes that Mum sometimes got from Pākehā who lived around her – the kids who used to own those clothes often teased me about being in their old clothes. Although I think we were poor, I never felt as if we were. We were never ever hungry, and the only thing I recall really wanting – apart from flash clothes – was one of those kewpie dolls on a stick that they sold at the winter show.

When I was older I began to get *Te Ao Hou*. I read it from cover to cover.

Granny worked incredibly hard. I don't ever recall seeing her resting or sitting doing nothing. She was always baking, fussing around the house, gardening, bottling, making jam, making butter, sewing, washing or doing some chore or other. Visitors always commented on how spotless her home was, even though it was a tiny shack. There, in the middle of nowhere, was this home with starched tablecloths and lace doileys, polished furniture, shining silver cutlery and spotless woodstove. The mats may have been sugarbags, but they were beaten and aired every day. Even the steps and boards outside the house got a daily scrub – usually by me.

All the Māori called Granny, 'E Ani'. Everyone Pākehā called her, 'Mrs Strongman'. Whereas Grandad was the storyteller, Granny was the poet. She collected poetry and glued it into an exercise book she had for that purpose. At nights, by the flickering light of a candle, she would read to me. Sometimes she would read from other books – her father's diaries – or tell me stories about our family, her mother, her father, our tupuna Patuone, or her namesake Ani Kaaro. The stories were all about the wonderful mana of our people, the land and the Treaty of Waitangi. They created a picture in my mind of a proud, strong and handsome race who I was proud to be associated with. They were stories in stark contrast to those that my mother told me.

Granny's stories helped me appreciate where I was from.

Grandad's stories helped me appreciate where I was.

Then, one year my mother came for me and sent me to health camp. I'm not sure why this happened, but I was told she was worried because I coughed a lot and my father had TB. Most of the kids there were Māori, and many were my relations, whanaunga.

I hated health camp with a vengeance because it was there that I got my first real inkling about how the rest of the world considered Māori. The staff constantly talked down to us and made derogatory comments about Māori. The regime was rigid and although I struggled to do my best at my schoolwork I was caned and told my lack of intelligence was because I was a 'dumb Māori'. I was beaten and punished in an attempt to make me conform. The one person I could run to, whenever things got difficult to bear, was the cook. She was Māori.

I couldn't understand why Granny didn't come to get me like she always did. I knew she didn't want me to be there because I heard her and Mum arguing about it.

It was about this time that I inherited Granny's stubborn jaw. I developed survival skills that were to help me, when I got out of the health camp, to deal with my mother.

4.

The tohunga tā moko is continuing his sacred work.

At each cut he makes I go further back to Motu Kōwhai.

My footprints are in the sand. I can never go back there, either in the body or the spirit, without seeing my darling grandmother, my grandfather, my aunties and uncles as vibrant young people with their lives ahead of them. As I take my voyage into the past, I see Granny's sisters, all dressed in black, perched on the island cracking oysters open with a rock and eating them.

All my memories are here, at Motu Kōwhai, and all the people who shaped me and made me who I am.

All have helped me endure some of the pains of growing up Māori.

They are helping me now, as I endure the pain of taking the moko kauae.

The very few photographs of me as a child show a little girl who looks like she's dying to break out and show who she really is.

Indeed, growing up Māori was a constant battle with my mother. Somehow I felt I was never able to measure up to her expectations – something I desperately wanted and tried to do. Whenever I was around her I learnt to suppress my emotions, my dreams and, indeed, myself. Nonetheless I loved, and love, her dearly.

Because of this I lived a kind of double life. The first life was under my mother's influence where I always behaved, anticipated her every move and mood and became invisible. The second life was at Motu Kōwhai, under my grandmother's influence, where I was never yelled at but I always listened. Granny encouraged me to go with my flights of fancy and to explore the world both around and inside me. She always spoke to me in Māori when we were alone. Travelling around with her exposed me at a very young age to the everyday kōrero of our people. This was often political – about the government, the Treaty of Waitangi, te reo Māori, land – all leavened by the odd bit of gossip. I have no doubt that hearing these kōrero planted the seeds of what would become my future political leanings. The things the old people discussed then were not really different from Māori political discussions today.

Mum's complete denial of her Māori-ness, and her subsequent attempts to pass her attitudes on to us, had the total opposite effect on me. Yes, I masked my Māori-ness when she was around but the core, deep inside me, always identified as Māori. Granny had established this well inside my very being and I was very clear about who I was and where I came from.

This core was my great resource when I later entered high school – after all, Granny could only help me part of the way but there had to come a time when, in the confidence of her love and pride, I could strike out on my own. At high school, Māori girls were, it seemed, automatically streamed into cooking and homecraft classes, geared for careers as waitresses, cooks and good wives. I didn't aspire to being any of those things. I went into the commercial class and did shorthand typing. There were only a couple of other Māori girls in the commercial class.

I loved school. I loved learning, loved writing and had great dreams of being a doctor. But it was made very clear to me that this was not a realistic or attainable goal for a Māori girl. It was suggested that I should look at being a waitress or perhaps an air hostess, as I was so well groomed. I took the nearest career to being a doctor. I went nursing.

I can only guess at how hard my mother's life must have been. Being widowed, at such a young age, with four children to bring up, she had to make her own choices. They may have been right for her but there is no doubt that it was her attitude that made me strong, arrogant, and stubborn – all good traits in the right quantities.

All I know is that Mum felt inferior about being Māori. She never spoke te reo Māori. She never went to the marae. She never went to a tangi. All this further alienated her from her roots. While I still love Motu Kōwhai – my home and hers – with a passion that has ruled my life, Mum hates it and seldom goes there. Perhaps Granny saw this gap in my mother's life and tried to compensate by pulling me into it.

Whangarūrū became my sanctuary and, there, I had a wonderful childhood.

My grandmother died in her ninety-fourth year.

While I am sure it was not her intention, my mother gave me a fierce determination to be Māori and, with it, the strength to endure the hard times that were to come. As for my grandmother, she gave me the compassion to understand. Her world was Māori and she lived it that way. She never considered herself above anyone else and I never once heard her make a derogatory comment about anyone.

These are the two rivers that have ruled my life.

In the end, they have joined in me to make a third river.

The river I have had to follow inside myself.

And now it is over, and I have the moko kauae.

And the moko, I now know, is a symbol not of an ending but a beginning.

The tohunga tā moko says, 'Kua mutu. It is done.'

I return from Motu Kōwhai.

My journey into a new world is about to begin.

My Beginnings

MIHI EDWARDS

*Mihi Edwards is the author of **Mihipeka: Early Years** (1990) and its sequel, **Mihipeka: Time of Turmoil**.*

Mihi Edwards was born in 1918 and has affiliations with Waikato, Te Arawa, Ngāti Raukawa and Ngāti Maniapoto. In the preface to her first book she writes, 'I wanted to write about how the Māori people lost the language, to let it be known how it really did happen. I made a vow in my heart that one day I would tell it from every point, every pinnacle, every roof-top, so that there would be no more misunderstanding. I would let people know how important it is to hold fast to your identity, because without your reo you are nothing.'

My mother died when I was three weeks old. She passed away of the flu epidemic. We had no doctors to bring us into the world. My father brought us all in the world. She was six foot, my mother – so they tell me – very much in command of herself and of how she felt. They say she looked you straight in the eye. She was as thin as a reed.

My father was very very good at helping with the births. He had to be because there was no money for doctors, and doctors weren't going to come miles and miles through the bush to come to a Māori woman.

There were hundreds of us living there at Maketū. People were dying like flies. That's what I have been told anyway. I am lucky to be alive.

The soldiers went away overseas, and they brought back dreadful viruses. We had no immunity, as I understand, to fight off these things, because our people were nature's children. We lived by nature, and our medicines were all in the bush.

There was a plant for everything – infections, infected sores, sterilising, stomach upsets, blood poisoning, poultices – everything. And fresh air was one of the most precious medicines that they had. But they had no medicine for this flu. They had never had it before. They didn't know what it was. They couldn't cope with it.

They were just dying like flies, not only in Rotorua but all over the country. And they couldn't stop it because one would give it to the other. They were living close together as whānau, sharing everything, sleeping side by side. It was easy to pass the sickness from one to the other. There was no isolation from each other.

They were just carting the dead away by the cartload to be buried. My poor father. He wasn't carting flax, he was taking the dead – it was quite terrible in those days.

We ate natural foods. We didn't have any sophisticated foods. I'm seventy-one and I've still got my own teeth. And I think that's the reason why – we didn't have any rubbish to eat – that's all I can put it down to. My father, I didn't know how he stood up to the flu, but he was out in the fresh air all the time and that could be why he survived. Whereas my mother, she was weakened. She had blood poisoning and got the flu on top of that. There was no medical attention.

My father was half-caste. He was born from a liaison of my Māori grandmother and my Pākehā grandfather.

As far as the Māori was concerned, grandmother and grandfather were legally married, but according to the Pākehā system they weren't, so my father wasn't very happy at all. He saw his Māori mother and her people being degraded. Father was very fair, he had grey eyes and light hair, but when he opened his mouth the most fluent Māori came from him. He was absolutely a Māori and had love and compassion for Māori people. He was Māori in his heart. He was respected in Maketū but was treated as something of an outsider in Manakau.

When I was born, my father journeyed with me to Rotorua and I was looked after by his friends there until I was old enough for my sisters to cope with. I think I was about three months old when they brought me back. My oldest sister was only twelve or thirteen years old at the time.

In later years, when we met, my sisters always said to me, 'Gosh, you used to howl all the time. We had to cart you round on our back everywhere. In the end you wouldn't go to sleep unless we carried you.' They used to give me puha water in a bottle to shut me up!

I lived in Maketū with my father, brothers and sisters until I was five years of age, there amongst the flax. I remember a lean-to place and the inside was loaded with flax. My father and his horses used to bring the flax. It was a sort of depot. We had no house, but there was a roof over these loads of flax, and Bobby, our dog (I can remember Dad's dog, he loved animals), slept on the floor. I distantly remember sleeping there amongst older people. They must have been my sisters. But of course that was no place to bring up a child. We had no house and I was born on the ground, on Papatūānuku.

There were a lot of us living there. We had no houses. We had our camps in the clearings, under trees. No tents. No one could afford tents. The old people were clever at making whāriki. The women made these flax mats and they tied them over four posts or to the tree branches to make shelters. They spread some of the whāriki on the ground. Put dry fern underneath to keep them off the damp earth, and it was good to sleep on. They made shelters for food too.

Flax was all around; it was a good resource. And the old people were so clever. They made ropes and hats and footwear, all out of flax. All types of kete – for every conceivable thing – for kūmara, for rīwai, for meat, for kānga wai. They had straps for tying their children to their backs while they worked, and different little pouches to carry a baby in the front. All sorts of dishes and bowls – all from flax.

They all lived that kind of existence in those days because they had to live where the work was. The men were cutting flax for eight shillings a week – that's the only money they got. They had plenty of land but they couldn't work it. The system had tied it up. There was no money to develop and they had to go and earn money. They didn't know how to farm in those days because that was only a concept that the Pākehā were trying to teach. Anyway, they had no money to build up a farm. But this flax milling was their livelihood at the time. I followed Dad around wherever he worked.

The Māori were a simple-living people. They lived by nature – from the bush and sea and land – and they grew their food. Mum and Dad did have a house of their own, but it was right back in Rotorua. There was no work in Rotorua. They had to go to Maketū in the backblocks, and later on sawmilling started. But at that time, all I can remember is the flax.

Then I was brought up (in Māori terms to travel from the north south towards Wellington, 'the head of the fish', is to travel up) from Maketū to Manakau by my oldest brother, who was already living that end of the North Island. I think Dad must have got in touch with him because he couldn't cope. Dad had lost his wife and he had six other children to look after besides me. My brother brought me to Manakau – I can just remember – to live with my kuia, Dad's mother, because I was too young for my father to take care of.

There were tears in her eyes when she saw me.

Well, I just looked at her. I looked at this kuia, this little person, supposed to be my father's mother. My father was such a big man and this little person was his mother. I was told she was only about five foot two. She was so very thin, but then of course all the Māori people were thin in those days, because they worked very hard. They had a very very plain diet, and often only one meal a day. They never ever got fat, they worked too hard.

She was crying. When my kuia, like any kuia, cried, she cried with big sounds. She was wailing as she was crying. As I understand it now, she was wailing not only for me, the child, but for the mother who was gone. She made such a terrible noise, it frightened the life out of me.

But not for long. When she took me in her arms then the warmth and the love flowed through from her to me, and then I felt I was safe.

My koro, her husband, was very very good to me. He just stood in the background. What I remember of him, he was a very kind person, very very good to me, very loving. I felt secure, very secure, all the time I was with them.

My kuia's house had no verandah. I can remember a footpath leading up to the front door. It was sort of L-shaped. Their house had no paint on it, but it had four rooms. She had a front room with big windows, no curtains on them. On the walls were pictures of Pākehā women – actresses. One of them was Gloria Swanson, and another was Marlene Dietrich. There were two others – I think they were Mary Pickford and Ethel Barrymore – famous women of those days. They were posters from picture theatres that someone from Porirua had given to my kuia.

I thought they were great. She did too. She wouldn't even let me touch them. There was no wallpaper so those became very nice coverings for the walls. And when I looked around, there was the *Auckland Weekly News* pages on one wall. It was in layers with all the best news on the front, and the walls were never boring because we'd go around and look at all the pictures.

There were two bedrooms and a kitchen with a big table in the middle – a rough-hewn table. There was an open fireplace with bars across for pots to stand on, and rods up higher where the pots hung. This is where we cooked. The open fire had a wide chimney for the smoke to go out. There was no wood chopped – no short pieces – so big logs were put into the fire. Two of those were put on and they would last all day. There was a lean-to porch outside. One side was open to the weather. It was an airy place where they hung dried foods and stored some types of vegetables. The air flowed through so the food wouldn't deteriorate. I suppose according to those days' standards it was quite a nice house.

My kui had a beautiful garden outside. She had very green fingers – flowers growing in profusion, fruit trees all over the place. No order, all higgledy-piggledy. My koro used to dig the garden, but that flower garden was really Kui's domain. I don't know where she got her cuttings from. She wouldn't let anyone touch her flowers. I remember huge roses, snapdragons, sweet-william, anemones, ranunculas, climbing roses, dahlias. There were lots of flowers I don't know the names of. There were big cream freesias growing under the window. Lilies grew wild. She had blue, purple and white violets. There was a snowball tree. There were gooseberry bushes and plums and nectarines, pears, apples, peaches, all growing in amongst flowers. They grew wild in those days. And further round the back there were great pine trees and then the bush. This is where the moreporks and the other birds were. The birds were my friends, I can remember. Lots and lots of birds. We were surrounded by birds, beautiful birds.

There was forest, dense native forest, from the Tararua Ranges right across to where we lived – until the Pākehā came and cut the trees down.

The only time my kui gave up working was when she couldn't walk any more. That I can remember. Her Pākehā friends used to come forward with beautiful delicacies for her to eat. Her Māori family was always there too of course. It was the family's responsibility. But there were some Pākehā who lived very happily with my kui's generation. They were pioneers. They shared everything. They had better houses of course, were well off compared to us, but they always kept an eye on my kui. I never went into a Pākehā house, not until I was much older, but I knew they had better houses than us. They were painted and had pretty things hanging at the windows.

I was five years of age then. I was happy living with my kuia and koro, very happy. They were very wairua people.

I couldn't understand it then, but nothing was done unless there was a karakia. It was just the whole way of life in those days, to pray. My kuia and all the other old people, they couldn't speak English. They accepted their spirituality from the beginning. I would go with my koro into the bush and he'd always karakia if he wanted to cut a tree down to use for making posts or things like that. Everything was precious to them, because those things came from the creation, the bush especially. Even when they were hunting for kererū, because kererū – the pigeon – was a very sacred bird to the Māori. But they had to kill them sometimes – every so often when they were numerous. They were so beautiful, these birds, I used to cry when I saw Koro killing them. They wouldn't run away, they wouldn't fly away or anything. They were so fat and heavy at certain times of the year. They used to sit there and get killed. Koro used to just hit them with a stick. They were so fat and full. They were so beautiful. I used to cry. I wouldn't eat them.

There were about twenty or more Māori families living there, all of us connected tribally.

There were three Pākehā neighbours. We were friends with these neighbours. They had a nice house and they had a square motorcar. It used to smoke along the road. They had traps and gigs. I don't know where they got their land. I think they were leasing it at first, then all of a sudden they seemed to own it. This is what I saw as a child.

It's all that Haka in
the Kūmara Patch

HONE KAA

Hone Kaa was born in 1941 in Rangitukia. He is of the great Kaa family of Ngāti Porou, Rongowhakaata and Kahungunu. If any family on the East Coast could be described as 'Shogun' the Kaa whānau would surely win this accolade.

Hone Kaa was educated at Rangitukia Primary School, St Stephen's and, in later life, attended the University of Auckland. He has had an extraordinary career, embracing, among other fields, the Māori Ministry, television and radio. Most Māori associate him with the heyday of Radio Aotearoa when he was Māori Director and Manager of the station, as well as one of Māoridom's most articulate and controversial spokesmen. He has also held many public offices, including Commissioner in the Programme to Combat Racism in the World Council of Churches. The issue that most interests him now is the role of leadership in the Māori world: is leadership solely the male preserve?

Hone Kaa is currently at St John's Theological College as a lecturer in Māori perspectives and cross-cultural studies. He is doing a Masters degree at Auckland University in Education with the intention of undertaking further doctoral studies in the United States.

Hone is the name my father gave me when I was born on 9 April 1941 at Whatamoa, Rangitukia. Whatamoa is the kāinga and is an old tipuna name, and it obviously has something to do with the storage of kai, but I'm not sure. It doesn't really matter I suppose but I do wish that I knew for certain.

I was named after my father's youngest brother who had just been posted overseas with 'C' Company of the Māori Battalion. I understand he left Aotearoa as a sergeant and was soon after sent to officer training school in Cairo from which he graduated as a sub-lieutenant. My birth coincided with that graduation, and I like to think I was responsible for his success! I met him after the war and was terrified at the thought that I might have to go and live with him if he ever decided to marry. Being a returned serviceman, an officer, and an accomplished saxophonist meant he was not short of willing partners.

It was not until I turned twelve that my father discovered that I had also been registered with the full name of Te Kauru O Te Rangi and that it was Uncle Poihipi Kohere who had given me the full name. My father never let on as to why he was delighted that I was so named. It was not until 1978 that I learned the name I bore belonged to one of the Waiapu Valley signatories to the Treaty of Waitangi.

Whatever the name or the circumstance, I'm here and I'm number eight in a family of twelve – eight boys and four girls. We didn't all grow up together. Rutene, one of my older brothers, was brought up by my mother's brother, Uncle Horace Whaanga. I always considered him lucky because he didn't have to milk cows and weed kūmara. But it was good being eighth because it meant that your older siblings had to look after you – even if some of their treatment left you wishing them something other than good health and God bless! My big sisters, though, were wonderful surrogate mothers as they made up for the bullying from my big brothers.

Dad was born and bred in Rangitukia and was fiercely Naati – or Ngāti – Porou. He seldom ever referred to himself as being such as he preferred to be known as Takimoana – but you knew he was Naati just by the way he carried himself. We knew not to pull the wool over his eyes, and many a bruised bum in the household attested to the wisdom of that fact. He was fluent in te reo Māori and his English was impeccable, written or spoken, and he wished us to be the same. Not for him sloppy diction or bad grammar. He loved the English language as much as he cherished his own. He would often quote excerpts from Shakespeare. If you were smart you picked up on the quote and either completed it or parried it with another of like power and depth. He was also a master of the art of Naati haka. I can remember many a night when Arnold Reedy and Peta Awatere would turn up, usually in the dead of night, and they would keep my father awake learning haka and mōteatea. In fact, they kicked Mum out of the bed and she had to sleep with us or in the sitting room. Mum didn't seem to mind, or at least she never complained.

I grew up milking cows and weeding seemingly endless acres of kūmara. I don't know which I detested more but, as a whare wānanga, it was great because it was here that our father instilled our passion for haka and our Ngāti Poroutanga. Milking and weeding were not only back-breaking, they were mind-numbing. Breaking into a haka was a wonderful way of overcoming the drudgery and the monotony. Our mother, of course, not being Naati, was not always appreciative of our need for such literary refinement. She saw it as time wasting, as it probably was, but what a way to remember things! Many of the locals would ride by on horseback and make rude comments about those loony Kaas, but it didn't deter us in the slightest. It probably explains why we are such an extroverted bunch of people – it's all that haka in the kūmara patch and the cow dung.

Education was another of Dad's passions and he made sure we did not miss a day at school. Living over the fence from the school was a distinct disadvantage as we had no real choice about being present. Like all other families in the village we went to school to learn to speak proper English. It was the time when Māori was discouraged from being used in the school grounds. I can't ever remember anyone being punished for speaking Māori, but that's not to say it didn't happen. The only books in our house were prayer books and they were all in te reo Māori. We certainly learned to read those pretty early, as Dad made sure we could. We each had to take turns leading prayers at night, often without prior warning. For us younger kids it was a great opportunity to show off in front of aunts and uncles who called in to join in the karakia that they knew would always be on at 7pm every night. Sunday night karakia was a longer affair with a couple of hymns and a reading from the bible. Locals would often stop and sit outside on the front lawn and participate in the karakia. As soon as karakia was over we went to bed while the adults talked the night away.

Our dad was so passionate about us being educated that he made sure most of us went to boarding school. He himself had been successful at school and had gone to Te Aute College in Hawke's Bay for his first three high school years. However, because they did not offer matriculation at Te Aute he made the decision to go to St Stephen's School in Parnell. It was a long way from home but he was determined to succeed and his father was willing to help him. He matriculated in 1919. Dad was also keen to follow in the footsteps of his older brother Pekama who, sadly, died on the battlefield in Belgium in 1917. Pekama rose to the rank of Captain and was, at the time of his death, leader of the Ngāti Porou contingent. Pekama was the first of that whānau to matriculate and was training as a solicitor with the Public Trust when he enlisted. He was, from all accounts, extremely gifted intellectually and one wonders what he might have become had he not gone to war. Dad didn't pursue an academic career, principally because his father had decided to develop their property and start dairy farming in the Waiapu Valley. The other reason was that Dad's younger brother, Te Hihi, had decided to offer himself as an Anglican ordinand and, as that meant study at university, the decision was made by the older brothers to assist him in achieving his ambition. Te Hihi went on to become the first person to major in Hebrew language in this country, his other major being Greek. He was ordained a priest in 1931 and he died in 1965. The one regret he had in his life was that he was not able to go to London University to further his study in Hebrew and possibly complete a doctorate. He was an amazing man because he seldom carried an English or Māori Bible and used to do direct translations from the Hebrew and Greek testaments. He found my lack of passion for these languages perplexing.

It was nerve-racking growing up in this whānau as every school report was examined with a very critical eye, especially Dad's. I had more fails than passes but I was forgiven because I did extremely well in English and Māori. I too went to St Stephen's School and spent seven years there. I guess I must have been a slow learner although my headmaster at the time reckoned I was lazy.

Perhaps the greatest influence in our lives was the fact that we lived across the river from the bungalow and home of the late Sir Apirana Ngata. We became devotees of this old man early in our lives, as Dad and his cohorts spoke in almost reverential tones about him. We sang songs about him, and songs that he had composed; in fact, we sang and spoke of him in a manner not unlike that of our parents. The intellectual heights he scaled became the measure of our ambitions and his prowess in the story of the nation became the benchmark. His name was indelibly impressed upon our minds.

There is one other person who cannot be left out and she is my mother Hohi Pine Whaanga. She was born in Iwitea in the Rakaipaaka rohe and she was extremely proud of her Rongomaiwahine and Kahungunu roots. It was not easy for her living in a place where she was clearly an outsider and on more than one occasion was reminded of that fact.

Hohi, or Sophie as she was more commonly known, was if nothing else an extremely determined and defiant woman. She brooked no nonsense from anyone, male or female, as her father-in-law discovered very quickly. Her tenacity in the face of the constant hostility she lived with made her a force to be reckoned with. I can't say she was a gentle mother but she was always busy ensuring that we never went without. She laboured long and hard for us and it is for that I remember her most fondly. Her father had left her a lot of land in Kahungunu and she used the dividends she received to keep us at school and to provide us with a house. Her cousin Turi Carroll made sure she got the help she needed especially when it came to the education of her children. Whenever we visited Uncle Turi, sister Keri and I were made to tell him what was in the daily paper and woe betide us should we omit anything at all.

Mum wore her fingers to the bone and kept us well clothed while she and Dad went without. She herself had not enjoyed a good education even though she went to Hukarere School in Napier. Ill health had meant that she had to leave there after only three months, but it did not abate her thirst for learning, which continued until she died at the age of eighty-nine. Her passion for debate after having read a particular novel or narrative was testimony to an able and agile mind that refused to know defeat. This, I believe, is the single most important characteristic we inherited from her.

I guess Mum was the one who taught us never to give up. I remember her having to sit an examination in order to become a playcentre supervisor at the ripe old age of sixty-five. She passed with flying colours despite the fact that she hadn't sat an examination at any other time in her life! She was a devoted member of the Māori Women's Welfare League and in her seventieth year entered an essay writing competition and won first prize.

Some time ago I was sitting at an outdoor café on the shores of Lake Geneva, reflecting on how far I had moved from that cowshed and that kūmara patch in Rangitukia. Although they were miles away in terms of distance they were there in my mind and in my heart. I also thought of the two people who had nurtured me, Mum and Dad, and their memory was sweet to recall. To them both I have an eternal debt of gratitude for the opportunities that life has offered.

Taura

WAERETE NORMAN

*Waerete Norman lectures in Māori Studies at the University of Auckland. She is affiliated with Muriwhenua, Ngāti Kuri, Ngāti Rehia and Te Aupōuri. She dropped out of high school when she was 14 but, as an adult student, graduated MA (Hons) in Māori from the University of Auckland. She is one of Māoridom's most influential thinkers and fully involved, when she has the time, in Waitangi claims work and other work to do with kaupapa Māori. Her piece for **Growing Up Māori** is an illuminating, luminous and lovingly detailed account of those years of transition between the worlds of Māori in the country and city.*

1.

For me growing up Māori and being Māori is to be involved in all facets of life, to be exposed to the rawness of life as well as the poignancy and heart-side of it. There were two sides to my growing up Māori, a country side and a city side. While I have fond memories of the former, most of my growing up was really done in the city, so I have no problems identifying with the current debate concerning what constitutes an 'iwi', and whether urban Māori are 'iwi,' per se, as I come and go between the two lifestyles and always have (as I write this, the decision from the High Court on what constitutes an 'iwi' is still pending). Pat Hohepa, my esteemed friend and mentor, once said that, 'Some of us are the original urban Māori,' and I fit easily into that notion, as do my own tamariki and our mokopuna who were born and bred in the cities.

Another term, coined by academics, and applied to Māori who

regard the city as home now, is that of a pan-Māori identity. However, I reject that label, as I do most labels, because, to my mind, it sounds like we have all been put into some huge tauiwi frying pan, mixed and stir-fried and come out as an alien people. It is probably more appropriate as a definition for multiculturalism, reminiscent of the American waiata, 'What you need is a great big melting pot, big enough to serve the world and all it's got.' In rejecting this I prefer to think of myself as a taurahere, a person still linked to our beloved homelands, the lands of our kāinga, whilst at the same time maintaining an urban Māori existence.

In some ways, life experiences could be said to be back to front. For example, one's formal education may be put on hold for a period of time by dropping out of school, despite the pleas from parents and teachers to return. After having children one may go back to kura to sit School Certificate, or even take up serious tertiary studies at polytech or university.

Running away from home was another matter; but if this was done within the confines of the kāinga, the homelands, or even to the home of a brother or sister or relative in another town, parents didn't worry, as it was considered that one was still within the whānau network. Running away to the homes of outsiders, however, people unknown to your mātua, like Pākehā, gave cause for real concern.

Going to strange homes and running away from home began within the city environment when new experiences began to shape life, with outsiders, who became insiders, your friends. Before that people of your own generation, close kin, met the needs of friendship, and became your most trusted pals, with whom you shared and exchanged your inner-most secrets. Even today recognition of that close bond still exists for me, even though I may not have seen my tribal brothers and sisters for some time. When we meet, greet, and gossip, it is as if it were only yesterday, and parting is made lightheartedly, jokingly, to mask our aroha, how we really feel.

Growing up Māori is also having dreams and aspirations, being involved and participating in some kaupapa Māori, an aspiration, some worthy cause. Being dedicated to the kaupapa at the outset, be it the Muriwhenua fishing and land claims, as in my case, or working and fighting in a collective effort at the coal-face, adding your contribution, 'Ko tāu rourou ko tāku rourou ka ora te iwi', and working together in an attempt to change the face of poverty and oppression. It is also loving and caring for your tamariki and mokopuna and setting trails and pathways that they can seek for their own future.

Growing up Māori means many things for many people. It is driven by te reo and tikanga, which create a distinctive identity which we have strived consciously, or perhaps even unconsciously, to maintain and preserve. That maintenance extends to our keeping alight our cultural fires with our whanaunga in the homelands, those who live and maintain the ahi kā, warming the marae in the safe zone of the kāinga, the lands of our tūpuna. It means keeping alive the dream to return, to re-light those fires, even though some of the whanaunga may not be so keen for that to happen, because of the lack of resources or no mahi.

2.

When I think about growing up Māori, the earliest memories I have are when we lived between three or four communities. I was born in Kaitaia, the eldest of the second marriages of my parents. My brother followed two years later. Our mother, who was a widow, had seven children from her first marriage, and there was a gap of some ten years between her youngest child, our brother, and myself. My father too was a widower but had no children, except for a love-child, I was told, a son, someone that I knew from a distance, who physically looked like our father. I longed to meet him, but this was not to be as the opportunity did not present itself and he died early.

I lived in Te Kao and began kura there. I often went to Te Hāpua, where both my parents were from, and then there was the settlement of Ngātaki, where I attended Ngātaki Native School.

The best part of schooling was being with your whanaunga, but the negative side was having to line up and spread out your hands to show the teacher that your fingernails were clean, and the most hated part of all was having to open your mouth to take a daily dose of cod-liver oil, poured down your throat in the same line-up. As school monitors, we were also given milk powder to mix with water for our daily calcium needs. We preferred to eat the powder in its dry form, and this we did, by the mouthful. Needless to say, when attending the Pākehā schools in Auckland, cod-liver oil was not part of the school curriculum and, instead, all pupils were given a half-pint of milk to drink daily, sometimes accompanied by an apple.

Some of the most exciting times of all, growing up in the kāinga, were the school holidays: the fun days camping at the East and West Beaches (the East being Te Rarawa Beach and the West being Ninety Mile Beach), swimming all day and coming back, or being called back, to the camp to the smell, drifting on the wind, of parāoa parai, fresh fried snapper or ngākoikoi, rock cod, kina, toheroa, pāua and all manner of kaimoana. For our whānau these were some of the happiest moments shared, some of the best days of our lives, and we looked forward eagerly and excitedly to all the school holidays to go camping. We never had flash caravans, just basic tents. We did, however, have a cot, an old army stretcher, which was shared with other children. It was something that one of our brothers came home with when he finished his army service.

Holidays were also spent in Te Neke and Te Tauroa in Ahipara, and both as a child and as a young mother with two children of my own we returned from Auckland with other family members to re-visit these places. When going to Te Tauroa we journeyed along the sea-coast for about an hour on my brother-in-law's tractor, towing a trailer-load of kids, with enough provisions to last for a week or more, staying in their bach alongside other neighbouring baches situated along the sea-coast. The sounds of nature reconnected us to the land; the cries of the seabirds, falling asleep and waking up to the sound of the waves, and breathing in the sweet smell of fresh salt sea air. For us every day was a new day, relaxing in sun, sea, and air, to the heartbeat of nature, with never a care.

These days permits are required from DOC to enable one to camp in some areas and there is also competition with the flash camping gear that city slickers bring back. Our family, our city children, were introduced to the old style of camping that I experienced – a modest tent, a kerosene lamp, sleeping on low stretchers, in the tent, at the Ninety Mile Beach. They still talk about it, even though it was twenty years ago.

Then there were always the meetings, the gatherings on the hui circuit, such as weddings, birthdays, hui whenua, hui mate, hura kōwhatu, family and school reunions, among many other hui. When these events occurred it was often a case of breakfasting at Te Hāpua Marae, having lunch at Te Kao Marae, and dinner at Ngātaki Marae. This gives an indication of the many miles travelled by both whānau living in these communities and visitors, who had come from Auckland and even further afield – it is still like that today.

My parents came from fairly substantial families in Te Hāpua, which had a reasonable standard of living because of the gum-digging economy in the early decades of this century. As they grew up, they were accustomed to having such things as pianos and tēpū piriota (billiard tables), good china and silverware and to having their older brothers and sisters being educated at established mihinare (missionary) schools, such as Tīpene (St Stephen's) and Wikitōria (Queen Victoria) and, as a consequence, the tradition of trained teachers became established in our whānau.

Mother and Father, however, being younger members of a large whānau, missed out on formal education, as it was not too long after these boom years that they experienced years of 'bust' or economic depression. They both had upbringings away from their immediate families. Our mother was, as a baby, brought up by her kaumātua on her mother's side, out of Te Hāpua in a community called Taka-paukura and father with his mother's people in Matangirau and Whangaroa, in the Bay of Islands. Some of these communities are no more because of the effects of the Depression. They were old kāinga and were always occupied in some form. They are now old camping grounds.

Along with everyone else in these communities, they got caught up in the Depression of the 1920s and 1930s when the gum went out of the land. From the nice comfortable homes that they had lived in with their whānau, they were gradually relegated into poverty and the corrugated tin shacks provided as 'housing' to meet the needs of such outpost rural communities as Ngātaki. I remember a poem that I wrote once which went: 'Tin shack tin shack, billowing smoke from your chimney, relatives you all are billowing smoke from your chimneys'. Ngātaki, Te Kao and Te Hāpua survived, but many of these small communities died as people had to leave them for the cities in order to survive.

The alternative to living in tin shacks, of course, was to have a nice neat little 'matchbox' farmhouse, if you were eligible for a farm loan for dairy farming under the Māori Affairs schemes of the day. This was not the case for my father. When I go home now and travel over the Mangamuka Gorge or travel along the Mangōnui coast or even up and down the Motu, the North Island, one can still see these tiny sad little two bed-roomed matchbox homes, with little or no adornment, some left to weather the storms of nature. They are stark reminders of abandoned whare left by whānau who, no doubt, once kept them warm and alive, but now, like our own whānau, are domiciled somewhere in some city suburb such as South Auckland, Ōtara, Otāhuhu, Māngere East, G.I. (Glen Innes), Panmure or as a 'Westie' in New Lynn, Te Atatū or Henderson, in what is called overall, the 'Big Stack' or 'Big Smoke' of Auckland. The great poet and philosopher James K Baxter more aptly called it 'Auckland you great big arsehole you' and in the same off-handedness referred to its 'blue black hemorrhoids'. But 'blue black hemorrhoids' and all, and with the statue of the rangatira in front of what was once the Chief Post Office in Queen Elizabeth Square, saying (as put by another great poet, Hone Tuwhare), 'Me all hollow inside, longing for the cliffs at Kohimaramara', and asking in his nostalgia, 'Now why didn't they put me next to Micky Savage [at Bastion Point], now then he was a good bloke,' Auckland had become our home. Returning to Auckland from a northern visit, the sight of the sea stretched out in all its magnificence, waves breaking in perfect harmony above Ōrewa, held its own mana and attraction.

In the Ngātaki landscape three of my uncles had farms allocated under the Ngata Development Scheme, farms that they too would leave later for the cities. We often visited our brothers and sisters, our 'cussy bros', or, to use Pākehā terminology, our first cousins, during long weekends or for some social events. When I went home to holiday in Ngātaki and Te Kao in the fifties an aunty and uncle ran the taxi service then and I was picked up by one of my tribal brothers in the taxi from other relatives' homes within the community. They would dispatch a car especially for me alone, and in triumph I would be conveyed back to stay with them. This gave me a feeling of importance. I felt like a princess.

When we lived in Ngātaki, a highlight for us in the mornings was to hitch a ride to school on one of my uncle's pānuku, sledges, which was drawn by two draft horses, carrying the cream to catch the cream truck on the main road near our kura. The pānuku never actually stopped, but slowed imperceptibly to give us just enough time to jump up on board, given just that extra boost by catching the outstretched hands of one of our cousins. We got quite good at jumping on to the pānuku. If for some reason we were late, because my uncle never stopped the pānuku, as the cream must go through, then we took the short cut which was at the back of our tin shacks. If the kōnēnē berry was ready to eat then we would eat this delicious berry on the way to school. The kōnēnē grew in a khaki-coloured tangled mass on the kānuka trees and the berries that we picked were not unlike sultanas or raisins in taste and size. We grew up eating this wild berry and when I look back we did a lot of eating wild things. Mushrooms, which grew to almost the size of dinner plates, were a favourite when they were in season, and we resorted even to sucking the ends of particular grass stalks – we were healthier for it. At lunchtimes we always came home to eat.

I think of my mātua, my aunties and uncles, now mostly gone to the mysterious homelands of Hawaiki and realise now that only one aunty on my father's side remains. Now in her eighty-ninth year, she is from one of the larger whānau of that time and still displays her aroha and gentleness towards her kōtiro and her tamaiti. I remember how they were always welcoming, warm and loving people, who often slipped us a bob or two. Harry Dansey, who was the first Race Relations Conciliator in the 1960s and 1970s and a prolific writer, in his poem *Pamupurupi* (Bumblebee), reminisces fondly of his 'Aunty Lil who gave him a kiss and a ten dollar bill'. It was like that: everyone had an Aunty Lil or an Uncle Bill, for that matter. Again, when I think of my mātua, for me this included not only my mother and father but also mother's and father's brothers and sisters and also the whaea and mātua of their generation, they being the hapū brothers and sisters of our parents. They too played very important roles in our lives and in our case we were regarded no more nor less, as, in my case, their kōtiro, and my brothers as their tamaiti, their sons.

All my mātua were involved in growing communal gardens at that time, and you name it, we had it; our kāri were always full of produce such as kūmara, merengi (melons), kānga (corn), raka (rockmelon), kamokamo, kūkama (cucumbers) of both the apple and long green variety, and what my mātua called African Zulus. African Zulus were a kind of cucumber, though very different in taste with large sharp spikes on the outer skin. They were sliced lengthwise and we ate them sprinkled with sugar. For us, he tino kai tēnei, a delicious food indeed. It has been many, many years since I have eaten, let alone seen, an African Zulu. Sadly, no one grows them any more. The kamokamo were also of a particular variety which had a pale yellowish colour when cut. Kamokamo were picked when they were very young and tender and were sometimes mashed like kūmara with fish water and sometimes with butter, especially for young babies. The kamokamo tips were eaten, as were most marrow tips. They were a delicious green vegetable to eat as an accompaniment to ham or boiled bacon. To keep the kūmara dry we stored them in a rua especially dug out for this purpose and lined with rahurahu (bracken fern), which grew wild everywhere. There was also pūha and wātakirihi (watercress), in season and in abundance. For fruit in season, one of the brothers, in company with other young male relatives, went on horseback with their pēke pīkau (saddle-bags), to an old abandoned homestead called 'Ēpeha', returning with their pēke pīkau overflowing with āporo (apples), pea (pears), pītiti (peaches), pāramū (plums), rīpeka (passionfruit), piki (figs), and kuini (quince). There was also kūpere (Cape gooseberries). Fig and quince jam were particular favourites, especially the former, and our aunties set about making hāmi piki (fig jam), and hāmi kuini (quince jam), and preserving peaches and pears.

Our idea of a bit of fun was teasing some of our sisters, our cousins, to the point of distraction about their English pronunciation. For example, when Mum asked our cousin Keiti, a six year-old, 'Kei hea tō Māmā me tō Pāpā?' (where is your mother and father?), Keiti replied with: 'Kei te darden', meaning, 'in the garden'. Like horrible children we would repeat this 'kei te darden' incessantly, much to the irritation and annoyance of our cousin.

Most of us called each other by nicknames as well. I was given the title of 'Sharp Nose', 'Ihu Koi' because they said my nose was koikoi, sharp, like that of a Pākehā nose. I was also considered to be too sharp and smart for them. Another person would be called Pita Kamokamo, Blinking Peter, merely because he blinked a lot. My brother was called 'The Slowman' because he was often perceived to be slow in his movements and it also rhymed: Norman the Slowman. My father was a large man in stature and he was fondly referred to as 'The Big Man'.

His nephew, to whom Dad taught haka, was called Wī Tētē. He acquired his rather comical nickname thus: each time he practised the haka, slapping his hands vigorously on his thighs or chest, it was noted that these movements made fart-like sounds. Whether in fact he really farted or not didn't matter. He still earned the nickname of Wī Tētē (Wī the Farter). Then there was Peg-leg, who had a wooden leg and his wife Pērē, (Bucket). I never knew why she was called 'Bucket'. This nicknaming, however, was nothing new in a close community of this nature. When I asked my mother to identify a handsome character in a photograph from her generation she just said his name was Hone Whenguwhengu (John the Sniffer), simply because he sniffed a lot.

We played simple games such as hopscotch, whai (cat's cradle), marbles, tag, hide and seek, and skipping. The game of whai enabled us to make all manner of shapes out of string, beginning with the one of diamonds, to the ten of diamonds, and more diamonds. Moeti, a girl with pigtails, is a string game taught me by my mother, which I have now taught to my eldest mokopuna.

A favourite pastime involved playing and spinning the kaihōtaka, the spinning top. My father and one of the brothers were good at whittling and shaping the kaihōtaka out of the mingimingi tree. A flax whip was also plaited and wound tightly around the kaihōtaka, from the base to the top end of the top, to enable it to spin upon its quick and sudden release at the subtle twist of the wrist – then it was whipped along the ground to keep up the spinning motion. The top was then whipped, spinning, high into the air, spinning still as it landed on the ground. Another favourite pastime, aside from foraging for food, was to fish for cockabullies in the drains. We also collected kauri gum nuggets, which could bring in a little bit of money.

The idea of large mahinga, communal gardens, remained with us and was transplanted by my mātua into the city to the extent that, initially, our corner section, pepper-potted as it was amongst Pākehā ones in Mt Roskill, was like a large garden with all manner of vegetables growing therein, and whose produce my mātua often shared with our Pākehā neighbours. In Auckland it took a while for our mātua to adjust to buying less things for our family, like one or two cabbages instead of a sack and of course to growing a smaller garden. Both mother and father had green fingers and loved to till and feel the soil. I grew up similarly and when we collectively planted a mahinga of kūmara on part of their section our mother ensured that the proper tikanga associated with the planting of kūmara was adhered to, where the tupu (tuber), was folded with the roots facing east. I sat down between each mounded kūmara row sliding along on my posterior in this sitting position, much to Mum's amusement and her commenting on the fact that she had never, in all her life, seen people sitting down to plant kūmara in the way I did. Despite my unorthodox planting habits, we did succeed in having a decent crop of kūmara, but this I put down to mother's whakamoemiti, her blessing of the kūmara crop.

In fact, when I think of growing up Māori, I think of sharing. The kai we shared as a whānau with the entire community in the kāinga. This āhua, way of life, of sharing, extended even to our Pākehā neighbours in Auckland. Even today when I go home to Te Hāpua to some hui or other (I served twenty years on the Committee of Management of Te Hāpua 42 Incorporation, now Muriwhenua Incorporation) up to about 1995, Te Hāpua is the only place that I know of where someone ranges up on horseback and yells out, 'Mea nei tō parakuihi!' (here's your breakfast), being a freshly caught fish from the Pārengarenga Harbour which may be kanae (mullet), tāmure (snapper), or parore (gumboot), delivered on the front lawn. The sharing, reciprocity and exchange still continue even today when particular whānau members bring fresh and smoked fish and oysters to distribute among some of our Auckland families, who in turn provide accommodation and other goods and services.

Kaimoana was, for our family, kaiwairua, spiritual or soul food. In our Auckland life we always had to have some form of it at least weekly, otherwise you would hear the parents say, 'Hiakai mātaitai', in that they longed for, hungered for, the pure and unadulterated taste of the salt of the sea. For them kaimoana also contained some healing and curative elements. I am the same, as I grew up eating most kaimoana in its raw and pure state such as pāua, toheroa, tio (oysters), mainly of the native and Bluff variety, kūtai (mussels), and raw fish, particularly tāmure, and arara (trevalli). There are times when I too yearn for the taste of mātaitai. It has taken me some time to get used to the Pākehā cooking methods of disguising pure taste with the likes of white wine and garlic, such as in garlic mussels. My father had a horse called Lucky Lindy and the horse was used by him mainly to go to the beach for kaimoana. If no fish were caught because the sea was too rough he never returned empty-handed. The kai would be pūpū (periwinkles) – a pot of cooked pūpū were indeed very sweet to eat, as was kōtore moana, the sea anenome. Dried shark was another favourite kai of ours along with tuna (eel). Our mother, however, disliked both these foods intensely because of the strong odours they emitted. Kānga kopuwai (rotten corn), with an equally strong smell, in my view worse than shark and tuna, was, however, a favourite kai of mother's. My brothers and I spurned this healthy Māori porridge and neither of us ever acquired a taste for it.

Thus living back there in Ngātaki, Te Kao, and Te Hāpua there were no strangers in the community. We were all whanaunga, very closely related kin. One could say you had very little privacy but that's a Pākehā way of looking at life. We had all we wanted and needed, no lack of aroha, warmth and security from certain adults in our lives as we grew up. Without sounding too idealistic and nostalgic about our Māori communities we learnt from our own experiences of different adults who were our teachers and mentors and moreover we learnt who we could trust and who we couldn't. As a consequence we grew up without the terrible trauma of violence and horrific molestation suffered silently by some of today's children. Sometimes knowing what was going on with others of the whānau had its own peculiar advantages and nothing was really hidden from us.

In Ngātaki, for example, my father's brother lived on one side of us and my mother's brother on the other side. The strangers were the Pākehā schoolmaster, his wife and family, plus the supervisor of the block, another Pākehā, Billy Teed by name. The youngest member of my family, my brother, was terrified of the block supervisor and knowing this we used to scare the living daylights out of him just for the fun of seeing him react, or rather over-react, which contradicted his nickname of Slowman. He was only about four years old and we achieved this by saying: 'E haere mai nei a Willy Weed!' (Here comes Billy Teed). No matter what he was doing his reaction was to scream and run instantly to hide behind our mother's skirts or to our father. It happened all the time, even though we were threatened by mother or father that we may get a hiding.

Our father always referred to him as Koro or even Korokoro in soft, gentle, loving tones. However, most of us who didn't use his nickname called him Son. Even as we grew older I never did find out exactly why it was he was so terrified of the block supervisor. I can only surmise it was because Billy Teed was so white and therefore alien to our community.

Needless to say it was not always like that. When we were living in Auckland my brother and I grew up to be quite close in our teen years and there was no real competition between us. He, being younger than me by two years, and still at kura, was delighted when I took him along with me to some of the kanikani sessions at the Māori Community Centre. I was working then as a toll operator at the telephone exchange (my first job) and if I stayed later at the centre or at a mate's place I always paid his taxi fare home. As he grew older he became very nimble on his feet, becoming an excellent dancer, just like our father. We were told that when Dad was a young man, growing up in his Whangaroa life, he was referred to as 'The King' and sought out by many women to partner them because of his dancing skills. My brother distinguished himself by winning the talent quest competition in one year at the Rātana twenty-fifth celebrations, through dancing 'the twist', a new type of dance technique that became the rage at the time.

He was also a very nifty and natty dresser with the latest gear. People were in awe of him when he bought and wore one of the first pair of 'winkle-pickers', shiny black patent leather with very sharply pointed toes and a huge gold square buckle, not unlike shoes that were worn and described in Dickens' novels. Accompanying his gear were also black stove-pipe trousers. Our parents bought him three bikes, as he was sickly at one stage, but it never bothered me because he always shared. Our relationship distanced only after I left home and married. He had very good taste and always chose and bought lovely presents for my birthday.

In our Ngātaki life the butcher was a Tararā, a Dalmatian chap, who came weekly to deliver the meat. Our mother almost always bought us shin meat, which was the cheapest of all cuts and made the best stew. The taste of stew and parāoa made in an umu on an open fire is unforgettable, particularly in the winter months. Shin stew was considered the mightiest stew of all stews. Although we stayed initially in the Ngātaki tin shacks our parents always ensured that we slept in proper beds, ate off crockery, and sat at the table on chairs. Furniture then was obtained through terms (now called hire purchase) and ordered from the Farmers Trading Company in Auckland.

We almost always attended church every Sunday. My parents were from Te Hāhi Rātana and were very devout in their whakapono, so going to church for us was a regular family event either in Ngātaki, Te Kao or Te Hāpua. The latter communities had temepara (temples), our places of worship. This habit of going to church continued even in Auckland with services held initially when we first came to Auckland in 1950 at the Manchester Unity Hall in Albert St in the inner city or in a home later bought for this purpose at Herne Bay. Services were also held at the Māori Community Centre or other community halls in Ponsonby.

My mother is an āwhina (deaconess) of the church, as are two of my sisters, and my father was a kaipatu pere (bell ringer) and served also as a wātene, a warden. Usually two lots of bells were rung by the kaipatu pere, who could be either male or female. The bell ringer ensured that all those present were aware that the service was about to commence. They were also responsible for counting the number of church attendees. The count was announced at the conclusion of the service. First the adults were counted, followed by the children, then ngā pou o te hāhi (the presiding āpōtoro (apostles) and āwhina), at the conclusion of which the whole was grouped together. The first bell was to call the flock together and to announce that the service was about to commence, as well as to give time for the āpōtoro and āwhina to don their kākahu (vestments). The second bell was the final bell. This came about ten minutes after the first one, prior to the commencement of the service, at which time it was expected that all the congregation would be inside the church.

Nowadays, when a service is held in a private home, and where there is no bell, the back of a saucepan may be used by tapping the back of it with some implement, or knocking on the wall for morning service in the marae, or even on the table when the food is being blessed before the meal is eaten. The mātua often spoke of a Pākehā kaumātua who married into our whānau and became a bell ringer before my dad took on the role of kaipatu pere. Our mātua, our uncles and aunties, often imitated his reo Māori, or made mirth of his pronunciation at the conclusion of the ringing, when it was reported that he used to say: 'Kua muchu che changi o choo chachou pere, ki ngā āpōchōro che chaima inaiānei.' Properly said: 'Kua mutu te tangi o tō tātou pere, ki ngā āpōtoro te tāima inaiānei (The bell has stopped ringing, it is now time for the Apostles to commence the service)'.

I don't recall ever being bored while attending church. We all gathered together as whānau, attended iriiri (christenings), and knew as children when and how to behave. The church colours and symbols were, for us, very vivid. Purple smocks were worn by our kuia and gold smocks by our younger female novices, or 'rōpū raupō', some of whom were only about thirteen years old and were learning to become fully fledged Āwhina. The whetū marama (moon and star symbol), the white smocks and vestments of the āpōtoro rēhita, adorned with the colour red, signified their rank as an ordained or registered āpōtoro or the ākonga. Those learning to become fully fledged āpōtoro wore a gold caul. In between ākonga and āpōtoro rēhita were the āpōtoro wairua, whose garments were blue. The founder referred to them as 'He pūāwai nō taku kāri (Flowers from my garden)', for every colour held a spiritual meaning.

Then there were the trips to the pā, where almost every year at the end of January we joined other whānau groups who travelled to Ratana Pā in Wanganui. The distinctive sound of the Rātana brass bands, and in particular, the charismatic Piri Wiri Tua (a philosophical fighter for Māori rights and the tumuaki (president) of the church) in her coloured veil, added to the aura of mystery and magic for us. The march to the temepara was led by the brass bands. The crowds behind them were followed by local politicians who 'strutted their stuff' to ensure the maintenance of the Rātana vote.

The journey to the pā was a pilgrimage, always begun two or three days earlier, leaving around 21 January. In that time we caught the train, the special train, which was called the Rātana Express. The train was originally arranged by one of the four Māori MPs, the then Tāpihana Paikea, the member for Northern Māori. Today everyone who goes to the pā travels either by private car or on special vans or buses hired from within their own communities.

Another feature of our visits to Rātana Pā was that, as young people, we roamed everywhere quite freely, stayed up all night, sometimes assisted the cooks with the breakfast kai and waited on the tables in the wharekai, Kī Kōpū. When we finally crashed out to sleep in the wharemoe, sometimes our male cussy bros slept near us – we slept with little or no fear of being molested in any way. Most people slept at one of the seven sleeping houses at the Manuao, the headquarters of the movement. Something I still do even today is go to the Rātana 25th celebrations with my whānau. Te waru o ngā rā o Nōema (the eighth of November) was another significant day of celebration for us and indeed for all of the Mōrehu Movement of Rātana adherents. Sadly, the days of the Rātana Express are no more.

3.

My mother and father were both classical speakers of te reo Māori and we were not prohibited from or inhibited by speaking te reo in any way, although our upbringing was fairly strict. The shift to Auckland, however, resulted in the loss of reo for my two young brothers who understood clearly what was said but couldn't speak te reo fluently except for some rude and swear words. One of my father's brothers upheld the then kaupapa of speaking only in English – it was a conscious decision he made so that his children would be educated and competent in the ways of the Pākehā. The same uncle, however, was an avid debater in kaupapa and tikanga Māori and knew his Bible from beginning to end. Although he was a devout Rātana, he could and did outsmart his Church of England relatives in many Bible debates held on our home marae.

Our mother, now in her ninety-eighth year, was also a kind of matakite (visionary). She also had a very powerful personality, and it was she who made the decision to leave the Ngātaki settlement for Auckland City. At first our father refused but she was adamant that we were going and she stuck with her decision despite enormous pressures from other whānau members not to leave. Close whanaunga who had opted not to leave said to her:

> I te haere koutou ki te tāone, ko pēnei koutou i nga kīrehe nei, haere kotiti noa ture kore. Ka mutu i te hokinga mai o nga kīrehe na, hahaha, he brindle kē te kara o ētahi. (When you go to town, you will become like mongrel dogs roaming all over, lawless. And

when these mongrel dogs return home, good heavens, their colouring has become shades of brindle.)

Being a matakite, mother had already seen and interpreted the nature signs:

I a mātou hoki e noho ana ki te kāinga i tētahi wā ka kitea e ahau ngā tūtae kēhua i runga i tā mao mahinga ko Pāpa. Ka mea atu au ki a ia, 'He kāinga mahuea tēnei, i kitea anō i Ngātaki.' (When we were living at home, one time I saw these mushrooms which we call ghost droppings. They were growing on the garden that Pāpa and I had tilled together. I said to him, 'This is an abandoned place, I saw them again at Ngātaki.')

So our mother was the driving force behind our leaving the kāinga. Ironically, for our father, after initially stubbornly refusing to go, and our mother giving him an ultimatum, he began to enjoy what the new city life had to offer, more so than our mother. His first job was a steady job painting the blue boats at the Downtown Wharf, which he thoroughly enjoyed. Father being a hardworking man, a labourer, never missed mahi (work) just for the sake of an MDO (a Māori Day Off). As a consequence he didn't go back home for some years, until he was forced to at the time their lands in Te Hāpua became incorporated in the 1960s and he and our mother became shareholders.

Although fundamental attitudes had been set in early life in the kāinga, growing up Māori for us was really mostly done in the city. Yet in this move it was always thought that the land base, the whenua tūpuna, would always be there to return to, and thus our links to tribe, tūpuna and land were never really severed. My mātua were old and wise and our uncles and aunties visited us constantly in the apartment or boarding house where we lived on Grafton Rd. This continued even when we finally moved to our own Māori Affairs-built home in Mt Roskill and Mother and Father always called me in to listen to the kōrero, the talk of my mātua, which I found at the time a bit of a hōhā (boring). In later years I began to understand why my parents had tried to educate me for it was those very mātua who selected me to sit in on such committees as Te Hāpua 42 Incorporation and to get involved in land issues.

Other relatives were also instrumental in encouraging us to move to the city. My father's sister and her family were renting houses in Freemans Bay, while others were in Ponsonby and Grey Lynn. By then two of my mother's brothers had left their Māori Affairs farms, one to live in Whāngārei with his family, the other moving with his family to Auckland. Mum and Dad were, thus, pioneers in the urban drift, and were instrumental in encouraging others of their whānau to move to the city, rather than ekeing out an existence on poor rural farming lands. Father's youngest brother eventually sold his farm and also moved to Auckland with his family. Of father's immediate whānau, only a brother and three sisters remained. They lived on in these communities, a sister and brother and their large families in Ngātaki, and two sisters and their families in Te Hāpua. Another of mother's brothers went with his family to the Huntly coal mines and I enjoyed many a holiday in Huntly and Glen Afton. One of mother's brothers lived in Pukepoto (Ahipara) and another in Te Hāpua. A sister and her family lived in Te Kao and Pukenui, while other sisters – having married farmers and fishermen – lived out of these communities, in Whāngāpē and Whangaroa. Yet another sister of our mother's moved to Auckland and for a period lived with us in our Mt Roskill home. All these mātua had large families, which gives an indication of the extent of whānau, the spread of whānau and how they alone constituted an iwi.

Fortunately for us – mother, father, my two brothers and me – one of our sisters and her husband were already established in an old two-storied villa which had been converted into a boarding apartment house with single and double rooms to let, in Grafton Road, Auckland. They had become the landlady and landlord and when rooms became available our family was ready to move in. Initially, cooking and bathing facilities were shared with other Māori and 'Islanders', as they were called then, who were, mainly, Rarotongan and Samoan families. You had to have plenty of shillings to feed the gas stoves, and pennies to operate the copper califont, so you could have hot water for a bath. In Auckland, trips to the beach for kaimoana still continued but they were more in the way of picnics, travelling to beaches like Torbay, Browns Bay, Muriwai and Ōrere Point, this latter moana having the most succulent kūtai.

Of course, growing up Māori in Auckland was very different to living in the kāinga. Our mātua were devout followers of the Labour Party because of the Four Māori Seats forged by the founder of the Rātana Movement, Tahupōtiki Wiremu Rātana. Our eldest sister and brother-in-law were key people within the Mōrehu Movement. Aside from yearly visits to Rātana Pā, life for us and all our whānau also involved fundraising for the Mōrehu Movement, attached as it was to the Labour Party.

Fundraising also involved play-ing cards, gambling, raffles and Queen Carnivals. Our father was a 'gun gambler' at cards – poker, five hundred and euchre – and even backing racehorses. Father could call your bluff on a pair of twos in his hand in a game of poker. In fact, he won twenty-five pounds this way in the 1950s – twenty-five pounds would be about the equivalent of one hun-dred and fifty dollars in today's currency and was considered to be quite a lot of money at that time. As I grew older I kind of inherited his skill for playing cards. On our trips to Rātana, in the marquee

A school portrait, eleven years old.

tents used for the overflow of manuwhiri (guests) for sleeping purposes, I was always chosen to partner someone in a game of rima rau (five hundred), or euchre. Father's favourite way of saying 'Away' during the game if you could not call a set, say of seven hearts, would be, 'Gone to Hong Kong'. Given the same situation when I play cards, remembering my beloved father, I always say the same phrase, 'Gone to Hong Kong'.

At the age of fifteen I acted as a courier for the Hon Matiu Rata. After a fundraising event I was given a small suitcase by my sister, a taxi was rung and paid for, and told to take me to the Māori Community Centre. At that time our sister and brother-in-law had given up the jobs of landlady and landlord of the boarding house in

Grafton Road, shifting into a long-awaited state house in Mt Albert. The huge garage in their backyard was used for many social occasions, including fundraising. In acting as a courier my instructions were that, upon my arrival at the Māori Community Centre, I was to give the case to no one else but Matiu, instructions which I followed to the letter, for my sister too was a woman to be respected and obeyed. Later, when Matiu opened up the suitcase he found it was crammed full of money.

The Māori Community Centre was a significant gathering and meeting place for all Māori who came to Auckland from about the 1940s until the 1970s. It was a kind of pouhere tāngata, a place where Māori people forged common bonds and made long-lasting relationships with other Māori, no matter where they were from. As whānau and with friends we attended the church services, talent quests and dances held there. The Gandhi Hall in Victoria Street East, and the Jive Centre, the Trades Hall in Hobson Street, were also places we flocked to for dancing and meeting up with relatives and mates. There were few Pākehā who went to these places and as budding city-ites we walked everywhere, although, sensibly, we moved in groups of two or more. Rape and violence towards our aged and young was unheard of in the 1950s. In the 1980s the Māori Community Centre was still used by Māori, although somewhat differently. Rātana Church services were still held there regularly on Sundays even up to the 1990s and then the centre was occupied by relatives who assisted with the rehabilitation of prison inmates.

Sporting events were also important when we grew up, particularly rugby and the All Blacks, to the extent that the Lions and Springbok matches were always played and re-played in our house *ad nauseam*. These were very important games and relatives came from the north and stayed with us in our little matchbox three-bedroom home in Mt Roskill. Toilets in these homes were built outside on the back porch of the house, and as I recall, our house was built with cheap Māori Affairs apprentice labour. As a consequence, when the toilet was built and the wooden toilet seat attached, the door could neither be opened nor closed. The only way around it was to saw off the side of the toilet seat on the door side of the seat.

My mātua were humble people and didn't complain. They were a generation that always paid their nama, their debts, on time and never owed anybody anything. I became very fluent in reo Pākehā, which helped them considerably, although when we journeyed home on the then rough metal roads of the Mangamuka Gorge and the sandstone roads to Ngātaki and Te Kao, my mother always begged me to speak only in reo Māori, which was good for me because growing up Māori meant being eloquent in reo rua (two languages). Although she was proud of me and my facility with reo Pākehā she was also kind of whakamā, a little concerned, and didn't want our relations to think that I had become too Pākehā-fied.

My experiences of the Pākehā world were mainly at kura, for in most instances, maybe out of a class of twenty or twenty-five, only two of us would be noticeably Māori. I was never fazed by this for I always felt equal to Pākehā and when I look back some of those school friends probably had Māori descent but could never declare it, whereas it wasn't a problem or an issue for me. I didn't like some of the teachers at school, particularly at intermediate level, and as a consequence I started 'wagging' school. I don't know how this began but I was unhappy, despite the fact that I could beat others in the class intellectually. In my school reports, I always appeared in the top tier of the class. I got very good at forging my mother's signature on the sick notes. The only thing, of course, was that I lacked the maturity of hiding the evidences of the practised notes which I had not removed from my desk. As much as I wanted to I was never made a prefect, not even a bus prefect.

When I look back on it, it was probably some sophisticated form of discriminatory practice. Thus, a reality of growing up Māori was also to experience the hurt of such practices of distinguishing between different skin types and colours, to learn the implications of this as one grew older and, moreover, not to accept it but to learn to live with it.

Despite it all, however, Pākehā people fascinated me: their social ways; their homes, which held smaller families but were so large; sporting space that was lacking in our Māori Affairs 'matchbox' homes, especially when our whanaunga came to stay, and often remained to become 'star-boarders' – those who stayed on and on in the household, virtually outstaying their welcome. I was invited to my Pākehā mates' birthday parties, to tea and to dinner. This posed somewhat of a dilemma for me because I could not invite them back to my place, simply because our kai was different: brisket boil-ups, pork bones and watercress, fish heads, which could only be eaten with your hands. Then there was parāoa parai, sweet breads, oxtails, pigheads, pig trotters, black pudding, sheep and ox tongues, liver and brains. There were also terotero (pig colons) accompanied by fat hens, which was a type of wild green. A brother living with his family in Christchurch sent us tītī, the muttonbird, and smoked silver-belly eels, which were a delicacy. Father, my brothers and many of our whānau members worked at the Westfield, Southdown and Hellaby's Freezing Works – which explains why we ate the types of meat we did. Mum never cooked cakes or made ginger beer like the mates' mothers. For sweets or dessert we had burnt sugar pudding with cream or custard. Another food indulgence we enjoyed was to toutou, to dip white bread into the cream.

The responsibilities of home life were such that growing up Māori sometimes meant growing up to soon. Because I knew the Pākehā reo so well other whānau members relied on me, as the need arose, to interact on their behalf; for instance, at the tender age of fourteen, when I had to accompany my sister-in-law to the National Women's Hospital to have her seventh baby. Growing up Māori was also to experience some cross-cultural misunderstandings. I recall my father being totally incensed with a neighbour who remonstrated with him about his pigheadedness, and Father saying to Mother: 'Tērā wahine kino ka mea ia he upoko pero poaka ahau' (That terrible woman to refer to my head as that of a pig head). All things, however, reverted to a semblance of normality after a period of avoidance between our neighbours and our household.

Our little Mt Roskill whare housed many people, big families, until they moved on to greener pastures. These families who were our close relatives learnt the foreign ways of the city from us. Some learnt how to behave, how to dress, how to live on a quarter-acre section. One thing that held true and strong was our intense loyalty to whānau no matter what the circumstance. A common solidarity about mātua and whānau existed as never before. Little though it was, I was proud of our Mt Roskill home, with its new wall-to-wall carpet and a brand new lounge suite bought on terms from Smith and Brown, a department store in Symonds Street. My parents allowed me to choose my own wallpaper for my bedroom. A treat for us was to go shopping with our parents, sometimes for second-hand clothing, but there were new clothes and shoes as well. By then our mother worked a week of day-shift, 7am to 3pm, alternating with a week of night-shift, 3pm to 10pm, at the Auckland Hospital Laundry in Newmarket. At that time, in the late 1950s, there was also a large Islander population with whom we got along really well, working alongside each other at the same laundry.

The new dresses we bought were made out of jersey silk, organza, bubble nylon, everglaze, polished and pure cotton, and shantung – beautiful materials to smell and touch. My eldest sister was once again a pivotal person in the city. Having secured a job from another relative, she made sure that she got jobs, not only for our mother, but for other family members as well. She was a very stylish dresser and had beautiful clothes and high-fashion shoes to match. I remember most clearly a pair of emerald green suede high-heeled shoes which had straps with gold buckles, that buckled around the back of your heels. Although they were too large for me, like any younger sister I tried them on and strutted around. My sister taught us how to dress for the city scene so that we were not whakamā (ashamed), and often we were the envy of others in the whānau for the style and flair we displayed. Gloves, stockings and hats were also the correct apparel of that period and as much as I disliked donning gloves and wearing hats and making sure the seams on my stockings were straight, my sister made sure we dressed accordingly. Our sister also encouraged us to go to the pictures, and introduced us to the fantasy of the Civic Theatre in its heyday – its wonderful ceiling of twinkling stars, green-eyed lions and the Wurlitzer, the pipe organ which appeared like magic from beneath the floor. The Civic Theatre was one of our favourite picture theatres and meeting places, along with the Regent, the Roxy (where most of the cowboy features, popular with Māori, were shown), the Century and other places on Queen Street which no longer exist.

Growing up Māori also shaped my politics. Te Tiriti o Waitangi was a household theme in our home, and as we were close within the ranks of the Rātana Labour Alliance, our mother always kept alive for us burning issues about the Treaty. The mātua never ever missed placing their votes during the general elections. My mātua always voted Labour until Matiu Rata resigned from the Labour Government, forming the Mana Motuhake Party of which I was a foundation member.

Growing up Māori meant that we never lacked anything in the way of kai and the nurturing, sharing and caring of our mātua. We were never left alone at night, even as teenagers. The simple forms of entertainment we had, even the parties we attended, were within the Māori communities of the city.

For me, though, the most significant thing about growing up Māori were the whakamoemiti, the prayers. Nothing was done in our home without whakamoemiti. Pathways were always cleared for us no matter where we travelled, north or south-east or west, or even overseas. Mother was a miracle-maker, and in our Mt Roskill house, in unity with our father, her prayers always bore fruit. Sometimes the prayers were for little things, like finding the handbag she left in the public toilets in Māngere. At other times they were whakamoemiti that ensured that when we went far away the protective force-field, the kahu whakamoemiti, remained always with us. I think of these, our mother's prayers, as vital to growing up Māori.

We continue them today as our own tamariki and mokopuna face the challenges of growing up Māori in the city.

Dad, Mum and Ruatāhuna

SIR HOWARD MORRISON

Entertainer Sir Howard Morrison was born in Rotorua in 1935 and is of Te Arawa descent. He comes from the great Morrison family of entertainers and has had great success as a singer, both nationally and internationally. He has been the star of many television and stage specials about his life and remains one of Māoridom's most loved personalities.

I remember the trip to Ruatāhuna; me, aged ten, with Dad and the driver in a truck loaded with everything including the kitchen sink. And in another truck were two Jersey cows: Betty, and Daisy, who was in calf.

Taking those cows was an example of Dad's initiative. He had made a couple of advance trips and discovered that milk wasn't available in the district. He reckoned that growing kids needed fresh milk. Butter, too, was still rationed so the cows would be a handy source of home-made butter.

Well, one house cow would have been sufficient for our needs. But Dad could see that there would be wider demand. And that led to me going into business at the tender age of ten, supplying milk to the postmaster, storekeeper, ranger, Sister Annie (a Presbyterian missionary who was famous in the Urewera country) and the school principal.

So why were we leaving the comparatively bright lights of Rotorua, travelling over narrow, dusty, twisty metalled roads, for the remote bush settlement of Ruatāhuna?

My father worked for the Māori Affairs Department. He started off taking contracts for scrub cutting, living in a tent with Mum when they were bringing up my brother Laurie, Mum washing the clothes beside a cold creek. He moved up with Māori Affairs during the war and he was a field officer when the war ended and the Department started rehabilitation programmes for Māori farm units, trying to bring them back to the land.

They decided to send Dad to Ruatāhuna where they were in a bit of cactus fungi; the land had gone back and a lot of farmers were in debt. I guess they thought Dad couldn't do any worse than what had been happening. The bottom line is, he got them debt-free in five years.

And I guess this is a good time to tell you something about my father.

Dad was a very good athlete and a very good rugby player. He made the Māori All Blacks and he was also selected for a team that was to tour Australia. But the way I remember hearing it, the tour was called off because of a strike on the *Wanganella*.

He was the second youngest of five brothers and told me that he was originally the slowest. But he worked at improving his speed – his eldest brother was a good trainer – and Dad eventually became a very fast runner.

Part of our family lore is that Dad and his youngest brother competed against some English professional runners who came out before the war. There was prize money of two hundred pounds, a lot of money, and my eldest uncle had worked out a way to beat the Poms with a bit of team running. Dad was to be the rabbit and set a hot pace for the English runners, while his youngest brother would swoop on them in the last fifty yards. But it didn't work that way; they couldn't catch my old man!

Dad took a pretty technical approach to his rugby, too: to his training, to improving his ball skills, learning how to step off both feet. He was a very good five-eighth; he played through all the district rep teams and when he made the New Zealand Māori team his five-eighths partner was John Rowles's father, Eddie Hohapeta Rowles, who was also a very good player. And, as Mum says, they were both a pair of blow bags!

Dad was a bit of a Sheik Ben Hassan, according to Mum. She couldn't stand him at first, because he was a bit of a teaser and a show-off. I wonder where I inherited that from!

Anyway, I said to Mum – how come you got married?

Just one of those things, she said. A love-hate relationship, and the love got stronger than the hate.

Mum has been very frank. Dad was told by the elder brothers that he had to do the decent thing and marry Mum, and they just made it, to quote Mum. They got married and one month later my elder brother was born!

But those were the days when chivalry was alive and well. Those were the days of innocence, when sex education was non-existent. It had an avantage where the purity of the person was concerned; it had a disadvantage, in that innocence was being exploited. But then, if a pregnancy was the result of taking advantage of a girl's innocence, then the young chap usually 'acted the man' and accepted his responsibilities.

So there was Dad, a great athlete but a bit of a go-getter in other ways, too. He created a lot of initiatives, made use of his natural talents and skills. OK, he was inclined to blow a bit ... all the Morrisons are known as blow bags. But when the blowing was over, Dad had put his money where his mouth was. He was an achiever as well as a talker.

Of the five brothers, all of them as physically talented as Dad and some more, he was the one who made the New Zealand Māori team. And he was a success in his work as well, as his achievements in Ruatāhuna showed.

I guess you can feel the threads of my admiration for my father showing through and why there has been a huge gap for me in my adult life ... in what I've achieved, I've missed his acceptance, the pride I think he would have taken. It drew me closer to my uncles, two in particular. But there have been so many times in my life, like at the investiture, where I wished so much that Dad could have shared those moments.

Anyway, that was all a long way in the future as that little Māori boy and his dad arrived on the truck at Ruatāhuna – to a culture shock!

For me, it was to discover that I wasn't a Māori – well, as far as the Ruatāhuna kids were concerned I wasn't. You see, they all spoke Māori as their mother tongue; remember at that time the culture and language were alive and well, and the rural to urban drift had not yet occurred. I was the new breed of Māori, with English as the first language. I couldn't speak Māori at all.

So here was this new kid arriving at Huiarau Native School at Ruatāhuna with his cap and tie and socks and shoes, as if he was still going to Rotorua Primary (Mum took pride, of course, in sending us off to school neat and tidy and 'dressed right'). The kids, of course, thought I looked a cissy. And they couldn't figure out how I could say I was a Māori when I could only speak Pākehā – and looked like one!

I soon fixed the first part. There was a big rata tree on the way to school, with a hole in it. I'd stop off, take off my cap and tie, shoes and socks, stuff them in the hole and get a bit of dirt under my fingernails.

But the second part was tougher. I'd try to get the other kids to teach me Māori, in the playground. I was desperately trying to learn the language, just to a conversation level. I didn't realise how important it was, in a cultural sense; I just didn't want to stay on the outer.

But those were the days when you weren't allowed to speak Māori in the school grounds – the teachers would come down on you. It was all right for the other kids; they knew the language from their mother's knee. But I was trying to learn the language, and I guarantee I got the strap more than anyone for speaking Māori in the school grounds. I don't know how many times I had to write on the blackboard: 'I will not speak Māori in the grounds again.'

One evening Dad found me having a bit of a cry behind the woodshed, because I couldn't resolve the dilemma. The kids were giving me a hard time because I couldn't speak Māori; the teachers were giving me a hard time because I was trying to learn.

So Dad marched up to the school the next day and bailed them all up, teachers and pupils. He said to the kids, 'I realise there are going to be misunderstandings and a few fists flying but I don't want to hear of you kids giving my son a hard time for trying to learn what you have got by privilege, by your right, and he hasn't got it. If he's a showoff or whatever, you can give him a hiding if you like. But not for that.'

And he said to the teachers that they had to make an exception for me. And he got his way, too!

By the time I left primary school, I wouldn't say I spoke Māori because the chances to use it were too few. We didn't speak it at home; it was restricted at school. But I got the tone, the feel, the flavour. Forty years later I'm still weak on vocab. But it doesn't take long to come back when I'm among Māori people. Especially when I'm back here, at Ruatāhuna.

Ruatāhuna ... Mum hated it. She'd had her fill of loneliness and isolation as a child. She'd become a 'city girl'. There was only generator power, which you could use only at certain times. It would be lights out, then you'd use candles. It could be hard there in the winters; it was a hostile environment. All the household tasks, with none of today's conveniences, would have made it hard for Mum.

But for me, once my assimilation problems were over, Ruatāhuna was a boy's paradise – the open spaces, the bush, the adventure of living there.

Dad loved it. It was a challenge. He was a stranger, going into a different tribal area. But quite early in the piece he was accepted by the big chief, a man named Paketu; he gave Dad a horse, so he was mobile, and that was the sign that he was accepted into the area.

Dad negotiated the cutting rights for Fletchers in the bush there. It had an upside in bringing money into the area but the downside, as local elder Mac Temara saw it, was different – the cash ran away like water and the farms were allowed to degenerate again.

I suppose some of the things about Ruatāhuna that made it seem a hard place for Mum were what made it seem an adventure for me. We had our daily chores but again Dad had that way of making them seem a challenge, almost a privilege.

Mind you, Dad was fanatical about doing things properly, of finishing what you started. Everything had to be right before you could relax. He could be a hard taskmaster that way, give you a clip over the ears or a boot up the bum if the kindling and firewood wasn't chopped for the next day; if the stable where I milked my cows wasn't properly cleaned up; if the billies we delivered the milk in weren't scoured clean. Nothing must be done 'half-pie'.

But the important thing is that we knew as kids why the chores were important and had to be done correctly. If you didn't cut the firewood, you didn't have a fire and you froze. And if you didn't milk the cows, apart from the distress to the cows, you didn't have a business! Those cows were my introduction to the commercial world; Dad taught me how to milk them and from then on I used to sell the milk to the Mission House – Sister Annie – to the head teacher and the ranger, to the postmaster and the Indian shopkeepers.

You wouldn't expect that the way of life in a remote bush settlement would produce influences which set anyone on the path towards a career as a performer. But I can think of two aspects, in particular, of those childhood days ... three, actually, when you consider the positive influences handed on by Dad's example. Things like, 'If something's worth doing, it's worth doing well; no shortcuts.'

Because we had only limited use of electricity, our radio was battery operated, used sparingly, and Wednesday nights were something to look forward to: the *Lifebuoy Hit Parade* with Selwyn Toogood. Because we were starved of entertainment, that communication from outside stimulated me to listen more intensely to what people were singing on the air.

I used to get so into it that I would mimic whoever was singing, male or female. I knew all the hit parade songs by heart.

More than that, it gave me a sort of subconscious knowledge of what people wanted to listen to. And what the majority of people want to listen to is middle-of-the-road popular; specialist areas like jazz and classical were never part of my childhood influences.

The other aspect, or attribute, of those childhood days in Ruatāhuna that came back to me years later in my professional career was an ability to imitate accents, specifically the accent of the Indian family who ran the store.

I mentioned before I used to deliver milk to them. Charlie Kalan and his father and family were from the Punjab and we became very close to them. Often we would share Sunday dinner. Mum would prepare the traditional roast with steamed pudding and the Kalans would supply the Indian food. So at the age of ten and eleven, I was not only getting exposure to cosmopolitan cuisine – in little outback Ruatāhuna! – but I was surrounded by their dialect, their intonation.

Twice a week, on the way back from school, I would call in to chop wood for Sister Annie and co because they were, well, spinster ladies.

Saturday was Town Day, when everybody would come in to shop from out of the hills, the maraes, from all over the valley, into Ruatāhuna. Funniest sight you've ever seen, some of them. The big chief sitting on the horse, the wife walking behind holding the horse's tail, and all the kids walking behind her. Talk about male chauvinism... Then all the women would sit outside the shop on one side, all the men on the other side.

Going back a bit, I remember that on the first Saturday we were there, Mum went into the store to buy groceries. Because Mum was fair the locals were amazed, when she got a greeting, that she responded in

Māori and carried on the conversation in Māori. They said, in Māori, that it was quite outstanding that this Pākehā could speak fluent Māori.

Ruatāhuna may have been a one-horse town – well, it wasn't; there were lots of horses – it may have been small but it was still an occasion going into the store once a week – on Town Day.

Once a month came Big Town Day, when we'd go into Rotorua on a Friday afternoon. We had a Buick Straight Eight. There were two Buicks in the town, Sister Annie's and ours, the red one.

It was my job to clean the Straight Eight, and once again Dad's psychology came into play. I could start the car and move it fifteen yards to where the hose was. And then I'd clean it. Clean it? I'd wash it, wax it and polish it until you could eat off the bonnet. Just for the privilege of moving the car those fifteen yards.

When we left on those once-a-month trips to Rotorua, our car would be shining like a new pin. But you're talking about metalled roads from Ruatāhuna, and the car would soon be covered in dust again. At Waiotapu we'd come off the dust road onto the tarseal for the last eighteen miles into Rotorua. We'd stop at the little lake there and us kids would get out with the buckets, the cloths, the shammy and clean the car again, all over. And then drive proudly into Rotorua.

That was Dad; he taught us to be meticulous about looking after things and keeping them clean. The car, yes, but little things, too. The rifle, the rods, the shovel and other tools; the things that we throw into the corner these days or replace with disposables. Those were the days of necessity. You had to make sure that what you had was looked after; it had to last.

It was a good life, a real good life, out there. Quiet people; very reserved people; hard-to-get-to-know people. But when Dad finished his tenure there they paid him the ultimate of all compliments. They gave him a huge farewell and presented him with a cloak made from the feathers of native wood pigeons – which, incidentally, were protected then as they are today. But that was overlooked for certain special occasions – like when the ranger wasn't looking! I still wear that cloak now, with great pride, on really important occasions. I wore it to the investiture; I wore it when I sang at the Commonwealth Games.

When I was getting to the age of not so much fearing my father as looking at him as an example – knowing more often what to do to please him – I was whisked away to boarding school.

For three years, from ages ten to thirteen, I'd been learning by example from Dad about farming: when to dag, when to dip, when to crutch, how to milk; about the importance of breeding to improve the quality of stock. Dad improved the level of breeding by bringing in pedigree stock: Aberdeen Angus bulls and a better class of rams.

At that time, it was my expectation that I would become a farmer. But not just a farmer; I'd be a farmer in charge of other farmers. Because when you're growing up you don't see things changing; you want to be like your father. So I'd inherit his job; I didn't know how, but I would.

Of course, things do change. And your life has turnings that you sometimes don't recognise until afterwards.

My life's next turning was when I was rising thirteen, in Standard Six, and had to sit a scholarship exam to go on to secondary school. We had to nominate the college we wanted to go to; it was a privilege then, not like these days when they're throwing the net out to get kids to go. Well, we all chose Te Aute College because of the mana.

And – great stuff! The two of us from Ruatāhuna who wanted to go to Te Aute College both passed the exam, Reti Apirana and myself. From little Ruatāhuna I was off to the big boarding school – and another culture shock.

First Things First

DONNA AWATERE HUATA

*Parliamentarian Donna Awatere Huata was born in 1949. She is affiliated with Ngāti Porou, Whānau-ā-Hinetapora and Te Arawa, Ngāti Whakaue. She has always been in the frontline of Māori politics. Her book, **Māori Sovereignty** (1984) is one of the great political statements of our time. She is an educational psychologist. She lives in Hastings.*

I was brought up by my sister whom I called Mum. My father never took to me as a baby; he didn't like me when I was little. But there were forty-six other people in my immediate family, and I could eat at any house I liked – or sleep there if I wanted to.

We had a little house by the riverbank with willow trees round it. Next door, Uncle Bobby had eleven children and Uncle Geoff had three. Over the road Aunty Gladys had four. Down the road Uncle Gosset had five and Aunty Homa had her four. Over the river lived all my nannies. As a child, I only ever met people who were related to me. Ōhinemutu Pā was a great place to grow up.

My father was very dark and very masculine. He was dark in the way that Ngāti Porou no longer are. At that stage they hadn't intermarried – partly because they had kept their land. They had stayed in the same place, married among themselves and their own people.

Perhaps for this reason his tribe valued fair skin. My mother was very fair: she had red hair and blue veins visible at her temple and in her throat. She was called Elsie, a delicate, almost fragile-looking woman. When you saw her with my father they looked like Beauty and the Beast. Even when the war was over, people more often commented on my mother's beauty than on my father's valour.

It says something for her beauty: after he died, ten thousand people came to my father's tangi. This was not an easy journey – he was buried on a small hill on a remote part of the East Coast, down dirt roads, across a river without a bridge. Ten thousand people came to farewell him: the Māori Battalion, his tribe, people from all over the country.

He came courting before the war. My mother's parents didn't want him, despite the fact that he was favoured by Apirana Ngata who was of our tribe. My grandparents said he was arrogant. He was a man of many talents, a great sense of learning, and very high standards. And with his bearing and his very dark skin he looked the epitome of evil.

They sent him to Wellington for a year hoping that their feelings might change, but when he came back they wanted each other just the same. They had a grand passion.

When the Second World War was declared, Apirana wanted Māori to join up. He argued that we had to show that we were as much a part of the country as Pākehā. He later set out his ideas in a pamphlet called *The Price of Citizenship*.

When you consider the reputation of the Battalion and their appetite for war it is surprising to learn that Māori did not want to go to the Second World War – and the reason was because they remembered what had happened to them in the first one. My own two tribes – Ngāti Porou and Arawa – formed the backbone of the Pioneer Battalion. They suffered great losses, like the Pākehā. But there was a difference when they came home. Māori came back and found they weren't eligible for a war pension. And even though their tribes had gifted large tracts of land to the government for rehab blocks, none of those blocks went to Māori.

So our two tribes were mocked for losing so many men for so little reward, and this mockery was a large factor in my father's generation's reluctance to go again. You may expect to die in battle, but not to be laughed at for doing so.

But Apirana had enormous mana, and he also had a protégé in my father, and so my father was one of the first to enlist, to set the example. He went away to war. All I know about what he did comes from other people; he never spoke about it himself. I came to understand that he was a hero; even among his comrades, he was a legend. At home, people would speak of his genius for war – he'd get more and more uncomfortable until eventually he would leave the room.

His batman – Canon Wi Huata – told me my father knew he would not die in the war, but he knew when others would die. He had matakite (second sight). This may have helped him in his exploits – and he did become famous for them. The taking of Hill 209 was a fierce battle. When they ran out of grenades they threw stones. My father led his men into the fire advancing backwards, deploying his troops with a whistle and handsignals. He was badly wounded in the leg but continued to direct his men. He only agreed to be carried off the hill when he could no longer crawl.

Another time the Battalion counter-attacked with bayonets. The Pākehā officers were staggered in the morning to discover over five hundred dead Germans and only five dead Māori. Our traditional combat style with the taiaha makes us especially adept at close-quarter fighting with the bayonet.

They used to admire German guns. They especially liked their lugers. So occasionally they'd go through the lines at night to kill Germans and get their guns. Although my father had been in reconnaissance he was a man who ignored what he was taught about stealth. Once, for instance, they went through the lines in a jeep.

His reputation grew so rapidly that he was recommended to be leader of the Māori Battalion. At his age he would have been the youngest-ever Battalion leader; but his appointment was blocked by Apirana – and for an interesting reason.

My father had been well trained in the martial arts, but his mana in combat came from another source as well. Every five or six generations the bloodlines of the hapū converged in one child and this child would have concentrated in them all the mana of their ancestors, and they would be a paramount chief. We had a great chief in the 1860s and another before him in 1913. This was my ancestor, Whetu Kamo Kamo, and he relates to my father in World War Two like this.

The people in the north had muskets. Hongi Hika had gone to England and been given a suit of decorative armour by King George the something-or-other. Perhaps at that court they thought such a gift would be of practical use to Māori combat styles. However, we have always been quick to embrace technology and in Sydney Hongi Hika traded in that medieval curiosity for some guns.

On arriving home he used these guns to avenge the wrongs he felt had been done to his people. One of the tribes that had crossed them generations before was Ngāti Porou. So they came south and Ngāti Porou collected their forces and came out. Whetu Kamo Kamo, their leader, had been advised not to fight but to take his people into the bush and disappear (a practical and almost honourable tactic). A disaster had been foretold at the Awatere River. But Whetu Kamo Kamo came from a great warrior tradition, and he led his people out. The invaders were routed, but Whetu Kamo Kamo was killed. Whetu's son – but not his daughters – was given the name Awatere.

When Apirana was asked whether my father should be made leader of the Māori Battalion he disagreed. He remembered my father's ancestor had been headstrong and had ignored good advice. So my father had to wait.

I believe one reason he was outstanding in battle was because he had a classical education. At Te Aute he did Latin: he was spellbound, even as an adult, by the great Roman generals. He studied Hannibal and Caesar's battle strategies and played them out with model hills and toy soldiers. All Māori officers had done this, all had had this academic military training.

People think the Māori Battalion were great warriors because they were brave and because they did not flinch from battle or from slaughter. This is true, but it should not obscure the fact that they were great strategists, great campaigners, intellectual warriors as well.

My father spoke Latin fluently. It was his joy to be asked to recite poetry in Latin – he could oblige at astonishing length. He translated the *Iliad* into Māori. An important scholar had translated it once already but my father found the work unsympathetic. He also composed epic choral works in eight-part harmonies, all in Māori, extolling the exploits of the 28th:

Arise! Arise! We have had this defeat but now we must rise up. We achieved greatness in battle, we must rise up again.

The words are laments for his comrades. He had us perform them with great feeling and for a very long time; I must say that we were drained after performing them. Later in life he formed a choir and they performed them too.

I find, by a trick of age, that his songs mean more to me now than they did then. When I think of his music I think of the war, his many dead comrades and his exhortation to our young – to adapt to the ways of the Pākehā but never to forget the ways of our ancestors. That's what his music was about.

When my father came back from overseas his war lasted two years longer than everyone else's.

When a Māori dies you have to take the tūpāpaku, the body, back to their marae, to their people. There were over five hundred of the Battalion who had died overseas. He had to take the spirit of each dead man back to their people. For two years he visited every marae to take their spirits home.

So it wasn't until 1948 that he came back to my mother, who was bringing up four daughters and working as a cleaner in a hospital. He remembered that it had been foretold he would have only daughters, so he and my mother began to try and defy prophecy.

He wanted to farm our twelve hundred acres out at Tuparoa. He tried to raise capital but was denied a government rehab loan and was turned down by every bank. He started a business selling mussels and crayfish with a cousin but it did not prosper. It must have been a difficult homecoming.

My mother was getting pretty tense and persuaded him into Māori Affairs. When Apirana got him the job, my mother fell pregnant again. He was ecstatic. He thought he was having a son. He assumed at a very deep level he was having a son. He composed a long waiata sending a canoe back into the past to ask the god of war, Tūmatauenga, to fill the canoe with the gifts of knowledge and skills of war for his son.

When I arrived he went into shock. I say he went into shock; all I learned later was that he went walkabout for another two years and my mother was bereft.

When I was born my eldest sister was twenty-one so she took me. She brought me up. She had eleven children after me (and adopted two others). I stayed with her until I was five and went to school. At that time I went back home to live with my parents. I was a very loved child by my sisters and mother – but not, as I say, by my father. But if you are sixteen years younger than your sisters you get a lot of attention. I was a living treasure for my mother. I was the darling of my sisters – but my father ... he brought me up as though I was a boy.

Usually there is a sharp difference in the way Māori boys and girls are brought up. In our case this wasn't so marked. Among our tribal leaders, my grandmother was a matriarch. One of her ancestors was an English lord, and she had been raised in a strict British fashion. She believed herself to be a cut above the local Māori, and she ruled with a heavy hand. I had her example – and though I'm not sure whether the example was always the right one, her independence of mind has been part of my character and part of my career.

The women's role in Ngāti Porou is dominated by the female line. One of my ancestors was a woman called Hinetapora. She was a very stubborn woman. My father always used to liken me to my nanny Hine when I wouldn't give in to him in an argument. I was apparently becoming more and more like my Nanny Hine. When I finally saw Nanny Hine at Tokomaru Bay I discovered she was a meeting house. I had thought she was alive but after all these years I discovered she was a building. She had died nine generations ago when one of her enemies came to kill her and as many of her people as he could. Knowing this, she sent her people into the hills because she believed that he would accept her mana and spare her people. And she was correct. They cut off her head and let the others live.

My mother's people, the Ngāti Whakaue, are a very elegant people. We'd had a lot of contact with the traders from early on and there had been children as a result. That was how a strong Anglican disciplinarian streak came into our people. Actually, there was an equally strong Catholic streak too. Both churches had been competing to increase their share of the congregation and we didn't want to offend either side. So when the time came to choose, we were gathered into the whare and were told by one of our kaumātua: 'All you on the left will be Catholics and all you on the right will be Protestants.' That's why, incidentally, David Bennett is a Catholic priest and Manu Bennett from the same family is an Anglican bishop. It worked well for me because my family was standing on the left side of the whare and, as I discovered, Catholics had the better schools.

I thought we were exceptionally wealthy. We had a piano, for instance, and an inside toilet. We had a bicycle. And we were surrounded by food. It was only when I went to Auckland that I realised we weren't rich. I am probably not the only one to have experienced that feeling.

Our house was always a centre of people coming to stay. But my father led a very disciplined life – and therefore we did too. He felt that sleeping was cheating. He only slept three hours a night, and that on the floor. Between the hours of 2am and 7am he wrote poetry, music, discussed whakapapa and worked on his translation of the *Iliad*.

Before dawn, he always swam in the river: he believed you should enter the water before it was light. Therefore, we did too, every morning, in all seasons. I recently swam in that river and couldn't believe how cold it was.

That aside, I had a marvellous childhood. Life in those days revolved a lot around the collection of food, and this was often a family affair. We'd drive up the coast for mussels, crayfish, pāua, pipis, scallops, kina and whitebait. My cousins and I dived for kōura in the river and steamed them on my nanny's mineral geyser. We caught eels and trout and smoked them ourselves. We'd go pig-hunting on horseback with our blue merle pig dogs running ahead. We'd climb Mt Ngongotahā to collect pikopiko (the bud of the fern). We'd collect puha and wade in rivers to get watercress. We planted potatoes, lettuce, tomatoes and other vegetables.

This is what we did as a family. My father took us over to Ngāti Porou and showed us the particular rocks on the particular beach where our hapu had taken oysters, pāua, kina and mussels for generations. As his father had taught him we learned where to fish, as his grandfather had taught his father and as Whetu Kamo Kamo had taught my father's grandfather. This was how we grew to know our lands, in the same way as we learned about our family.

Then we would spend days pickling and bottling. There was a lot of water in my childhood and it was marvellous until I got rheumatic fever and was hospitalised when I was eight. For the next four years I left school and was either in hospital or convalescing. And that's why I missed out on my primary school education.

I believe that was a good thing. Unlike my sisters I never learned that I couldn't do things. And I learned that I was beautiful. (A lesson my mother taught me. I don't know how. It lasted until experience and observation taught me otherwise – when I was twenty-five.)

My parents bought me Arthur Mee's *Children's Encyclopaedia*. My cousin over the river also had a set of the series which she read like I did. She was the first Arawa woman to get a PhD. There were only two copies of Arthur Mee in the pā and the only two people who read them went on to be academics. I don't think this was coincidental. I read ten volumes in four years and learnt Aesop's Fables, a bit of French, German, Latin and Greek, how electricity works, why steam engines go, how blood circulates through the body and other things that ten-year-olds need to know.

During this period, they thought because I was weak that I must be by the sea, so they sent me to Tokomaru Bay to convalesce. It is a magnificent sweep between the sea and the hills. There I came under the influence of my Aunty Ngoi Ngoi. She wrote extraordinary songs about the Māori Battalion, and about the Treaty of Waitangi. This is where I first learnt about our view of the Treaty and the importance of our land and how it was being taken through legislation. She wrote the only waiata ever to get into the Top Ten.

I learned also about whakapapa. This is the great web of heredity that contains all Māori. It's the living net of relationships between all of us – whether we are dead or alive. It is the account of our bloodlines: it is the history of our families, a celebration of our ancestry and a record of how we all connect.

Burke's Peerage in Britain is the book of the aristocracy. All the lords and ladies and their children get their names in the book. Whakapapa does that for all Māori of whatever standing or status. Any street child, any lost, urbanised Māori can take the name of his grandparents to their marae and the whakapapa man will tell him the whole forty generations of his ancestors. Whakapapa is oral and is carried in the heads of about two thousand Māori (all men) who can whakapapa their way from one end of the country, and one end of our history to the other.

And here too the values of my father were passed on to me. Ngāti Porou are a very feeling people – our culture and our whakapapa give us very deep connection with each other. We were helped in this because the tribe was isolated, they never lost their land, they had never been trampled on or dispersed.

You don't realise the impact of these things until you start thinking about who you are. Later in life, these memories pierce you.

My mother and I formed a tight partnership. I was surrounded by her love and wellbeing. All my other sisters had gone on to be married and I think my mother transferred all her hopes in life from my father to me. She never lifted her hand to me – and I tried her sorely sometimes.

I remember I got my first communion dress early so I could wear it as a bridesmaid for my sister's wedding. My mother gets me dressed and I go outside to get into the barrel at the top of the hill to roll down. Unfortunately there is a fresh cowpat in the barrel and as I keep rolling the cowpat keeps falling on me.

The dress was spoilt, for that day at least, but she never hit me. My father was different. He had an extremely violent temper. I almost never attracted it but he often dropped thunderbolts on my mother. It sent us as a family into the black cave. Now we know these things are common but in those days we were the only family in the world who suffered these things.

I remember him clawing the clothes off her back, he knocks her down and as he is booting her she tells me to run. I remember her voice breaking as his boot goes in: 'Run, Donna, get out of it. I'll be all right. I'm all right.' Once he started hitting me and I remember her curling herself around me to take the blows.

My sisters were severely abused – broken noses, broken arms. My father didn't drink or gamble, he was a war hero, an intellectual, a visionary and a lousy parent. He was so intent on saving Maoridom he didn't pay attention to saving his kids.

My sisters are all exceptionally talented people. They failed my father only by not being boys. They are great sportswomen with so much casual ability that they all got to the top of their fields without any real effort. Three of them became international referees in sports that they only took up because of their kids.

But the violence they experienced as children had a shattering effect on their lives. Two became alcoholics. My second-eldest sister was a deeply spiritual woman – she was the cleverest of us all, brilliant and witty and when she spoke it was like poetry. But she went into an abusive relationship with a man who beat her as my father beat her. She went into a spiral of playing cards and drinking. Her eldest son, a gentle giant of a man, loved by all the family, killed himself and killed his children too.

That caused my sister to pull her life back together. Her sons broke the pattern and are loving and supportive husbands. Her grand-children are at university. Three of my other sister's four children graduated – lawyer, accountant and teacher. My eldest sister named after Hinetapora absorbed most of my father's anger, yet she raised her thirteen children in the gentlest and most loving way.

I've seen violence travelling through the family from one generation to the next from my father's line. It has stopped now. I escaped the worst of it by being so much the younger. My nephews and nieces have escaped it too. The cycle has been broken. Things can get better, and I know from experience that education is the key to it.

When my father stopped hitting my mother I was thirteen. We had come to Auckland and we had a telephone. He was hitting her one night in the bedroom and I had determined to call the police the next time it happened. I heard it start in the familiar way. I yelled out to him to stop. He didn't. I picked up the phone and yelled at him to stop. He didn't, and I dialled the number I had memorised.

He stopped hitting her after that. He kept hitting me, however. He'd wait until my mother wasn't around and from time to time he'd pummel the hell out of me. I was lucky to have a resilient nature so these incidents never spoiled a childhood as happy as childhoods should be in New Zealand.

He assumed we were close, and that we had a bond because we spent so much time together. We travelled to so many marae together – I was still travelling with him when I was at university. I think he did come to love me. I used to get the better of him but he enjoyed my company when I wasn't being argumentative.

My father was a man with a commanding intellect and an extra-ordinary range of abilities. Sometimes when I think of him I see him hunched over the piano, absorbed in his hidden life, writing music out in the tonic sol-fah scales. I remember him also speaking Russian (he'd met a Russian soldier once, apparently). He also spoke German and several Italian dialects.

He urged me to take up Japanese as the language of the future. I took his advice but it was an unrewarding experience. My professor couldn't actually speak English – he was ill-equipped to teach basic Japanese, particularly to me (I'm a plodder). So my father, who was at the time in prison serving a life sentence, offers to learn it alongside me. He takes my books and looks at them for a week. When I visit him next Saturday, he greets me in Japanese and talks to me in Japanese and already knows more Japanese than I do. In a couple of months I took my professor to meet him again and they held an hour-long conversation with each other in that language which is still impenetrable to me.

When people say I'm clever I remember that I was surrounded by genius. Not just the ability of my father to speak languages and play instruments shortly after picking them up – but in other Māori as I grew older. Contrary to what is generally thought, there was an intellectual genius in the old Māori society. Our society is not famous for intellectual achievements but there was a far higher mental capacity in those minds from those years than is given credit for today.

The culture was all oral, and that way of living develops the mind in a different way from the modern world, but the ordinary conversation of those men and women was beautiful to listen to – not just in the sense of poetry but the range of material that furnished their minds. In the intellectual feats of memory and agility that underlay the poetry.

My father had a very Māori view about the uniqueness of people – he never looked at someone's socio-economic background, he looked at them as individuals, the product of forty generations of families whose bloodlines he probably knew as well as the people themselves.

He also taught me his belief that the traditional Māori was very disciplined. They slept lightly, always on guard, and not too much. They were also disciplined in the creative arts. They could, as he could, stand up and improvise a waiata with the full reference of history and whakapapa, and bring history to the present. If you can sing a forty-five minute waiata about an ancestor and all the marae they affected – that is a feat of memory and imagination that is true knowledge. And it only comes from discipline.

They were disciplined in war but they had a powerful spirit that could make them unpredictable. A biography of my husband's uncle has a story of my father after the war had ended.

My father and his staff walk into Hitler's secret mountain hideout. He was Commander of the Māori Battalion, he was in the company of generals of the Allied forces and they were all surrounded by their staff. He was in Hitler's opulent secret headquarters at Ravenscrag, and he has unbuttoned himself and, for want of a better word, is making water on Hitler's carpet.

The generals and their staff are startled. My father's comrades rush to him and grab him but he pushes them off:

'I'm not finished yet,' he said.

'You can't do that here!' they cried.

'Watch me,' he said.

When he had finished he reminded them that the most absolute form of revenge on any enemy was to eat his head. In the absence of Hitler's head, this was the next best way of expressing the sentiments of the Māori Battalion.

My father the poet and warrior, my mother and family so full of love for me, both my tribes so proud of their lands, so determined to be educated. These were my people. And this was where my journey started.

My Mother Fashioned Me

SIR PAUL REEVES

Sir Paul Reeves was born in 1932 and has affiliations with Te Āti Awa and Taranaki tribes. He has had one of the most illustrious careers in Māoridom. Among his many offices he has been Anglican Archbishop of Aotearoa, Governor-General of New Zealand, Representative at the United Nations in New York and Ahorangi of St John's Theological College, Auckland. He is currently Asia 2000 Foundation Visiting Professor at the University of Auckland.

Sir Paul's contribution to this volume came with a note which read, 'It's really about my mother rather than me, but what happened to her happened to me.' In a subsequent conversation, during the High Court hearing on the definition of 'iwi', Sir Paul noted that perhaps what was happening in the court was only symptomatic of what had been happening all these years – the constant defining and redefining of ourselves not only tribally but also personally. 'There are as many ways of growing up Māori,' Sir Paul said, 'as there are Māori themselves.'

Here is Sir Paul on what happened to his mother.

And, therefore, what happened to him.

Somewhere there is a photograph of my parents sitting astride a motorbike on the foreshore, Picton. My father, D'arcy, has a big grin on his face. His cap is turned back to front. My mother, Hilda – her Māori name was Pirihira – is grasping him firmly around the shoulders.

Before they met, romanced and married, Mum and Dad both lived in Waikawa – but in very different circumstances.

153

Dad's parents had come to Waikawa from the Sounds and Koromiko. In Waikawa they developed an orchard. Years later an old Māori told me that as children they called my grandfather 'Cocky'. This had something to do with his goatee beard and the car he drove. At the time Dad met Mum he was a returned soldier from the First World War. The war experience accentuated the asthma and respiratory difficulties he had for the rest of his life.

My mother was one of five children who was raised in the pā at Waikawa. Her mother, Roka, was left destitute when her husband, a farmworker, accidentally drank a poisonous weedkiller. My mother was bright but she had limited job opportunities. She had spent time as a pupil teacher and then an employee of the Post and Telegraph Office in Wellington. Back in Waikawa she met Dad.

I cannot imagine what my parents' wedding was like. Both families had little in common. After the marriage things didn't improve much. For instance, I was told of an occasion when my paternal grandmother, Gertrude, gave my maternal grandmother, Roka, some fish which proved to be bad. The story was told in glee but also with a great deal of rancour.

Anyway, perhaps the difficult relationship between the two families must have been a major incentive for my parents to move to Wellington. The little house in Newtown, where they lived, is still standing.

My father got a job as a conductor and, later, a motor man on the trams. Then the Depression years came along. My brother and I were born during a period where life was a grim matter of economic survival and, for my father, persistent bad health.

I don't know if my mother realised that the move to Wellington would isolate her, distance her, so far from Māori friends and relatives. Even if Waikawa was not far away, her whānau did not visit often – except for my favourite aunt, Minnie Cocker, who lived in Island Bay. I have to say that my father did not make it easy for Mum as far as this side of her life was concerned. As far as I could tell, he did little to acknowledge or encourage my mother's Māori heritage. I doubt whether, in marrying Mum, he accepted in his heart that he was marrying a Māori. I cannot remember Mum and Dad ever going to any Māori events together.

In 1946, my mother got a job at the Peerless factory, Vivian Street, making handkerchiefs. My father was very upset by this, but we needed the money. He was only fifty-one when he died, in 1950. At his funeral, members of the Tramways Union marched in front of the hearse for what seemed to be an interminable time before we drove on to the crematorium.

My mother grieved deeply when Dad died. For some time I would hear her, at nights, crying. But life carries on – and Mum began to reach out and socialise. As part of this process she renewed associations with Ngāti Pōneke and the Māori Womens' Welfare League. The Māori section of the Anglican church also absorbed her time.

Even today, people still come up to me and talk to me about my mother's talent and energy.

She combined a serenity with a sense of purpose.

With my mother, at my brother's wedding, shortly after our father's death. I was about seventeen when this was taken.

At the time, however, I was confused about my identity. When I was a teenager the two things I worried about were my being left-handed, which made me feel embarrassed – and my dark complexion, which differentiated me from my friends. I was at Wellington College which, at that time, was not an easy place for Māori. When you feel so unsure, the easiest thing to do is to deny that you are Māori.

So I did not grow up as a Māori. I did not have access to relatives, language and culture. Those are things I have had to work for – but love and acceptance are there, not simply for me but for my wife, Beverly, and family. Beverly and I have two grandchildren. One is called Roimata and the other, Ben, has Pehimana as his middle name. What identity and growing up as a Māori will mean to them only time will tell.

What happened to me has happened to many people. If you commit yourself to learning from life – making choices, making decisions, making mistakes – then all will be well.

I was fortunate enough that my choices, although I didn't know it at the time, were influenced by the fact that my mother was Māori.

Ultimately, this has helped to fashion who I am.

To Find a Place Nearer the Sun

RIPEKA EVANS

Born in 1956 and of Ngā Puhi descent, Ripeka Evans maintains her career as one of Māoridom's most influential women. As a student she reorganised Ngā Tamatoa. Later, she became involved in radical Māori protest, culminating in her arrest and conviction during the Springbok Tour for activities leading to the enforced cancellation of the Springbok rugby match at Hamilton.

In later years, Ripeka Evans reinvented herself as one of our top bureaucrats. She undertook consultancies for the Māori Economic Development Commission and the Department of Māori Affairs. Then, in 1990, she moved into the communications field by obtaining a key position in Television New Zealand. Subsequently she became the focal point for transformational work within Māori radio and television, and was appointed Chief Executive of Te Māngai Pāho, the Māori board set up to develop Māori radio and television media.

Ripeka Evans now maintains her own consultancy. She lives in Whakatāne.

I grew up in the foothills of Ngā Puhi, beneath an interior pā of one of our greatest fighting chiefs, Hongi Hika. Although he had no issue, his strategist and elder sister, Turikatuku, did, and I am descended from her through my mother, Ann Dalton, and her father, George Graham Dalton.

My grandfather was a firebrand. He was dark, wiry and handsome, in a Clint Eastwood kind of fashion. If he squinted one of those deep-set green eyes and chewed the corner of his mouth at the same time, you knew that you had ignited the Irish flame and the sooner you figured out the odds as to who might win or lose, the better. I can honestly say that I never tested the odds, perhaps because I always asked why not, and because my mother always told me that 'his bark is bigger than his bite'. However, there were a few of the forty first-cousins who did and we would huddle in the corn crib and listen to their stories about how incisive the whips from Grandad's peach branch could be.

We grew up in a simple three-bedroomed house along Taheke Road, about three miles outside of Kaikohe going towards Hokianga. My grandfather had carved an acre out of the Puketaurua papakāinga for my parents, who had returned from Auckland as newly-weds with my eldest brother, David, on the way. After David, my eldest sister was born but died at birth. Then came the rest of us, just like the Partridge family, all in a row, some a year apart, some a little more. Naera, Freda, myself, Russell, Lorraine, Yvonne and Norman. The three boys squeezed into one room, sleeping on a set of bunks and one single bed, the five girls squeezed into one another, three on a double bed, two on a set of bunks, Mum and Dad in the third room, and visitors in the lounge.

There were cows, ducks, pigs, horses, hens and turkeys, plantations of every conceivable vegetable, waterfalls, the bush, big old trees, and thousands of little creatures. There were always sounds. I remember the soft blips against the window as I sat studying at the kitchen table late at night or early in the morning.

My uncle Winky, Mum's eldest brother, lived over the road with my aunty Kath, and their nine children, and my grandparents lived down the paddock. My sister Freda and myself went off down the paddock for a while to stay with our grandparents.

My maternal grandmother, Pahemata Clarke, then started carting me around to various places with her. I remember her taking me to stay with Parani Maihi Rankin for a little while after her husband, Hone Heke Rankin, who was my grandfather's cousin, had died. I guess she wanted a mōkai, to console her for a while. She spoilt me and humbled me when she bought me a pair of black patent leather shoes and a beautiful pink linen suit. She was on a widow's pension and could barely afford to fill up her big bright green old Plymouth, let alone buy outfits for me. The only time she spoke English was when we had to prepare her for a review of her driver's licence. She was partially blind in one eye and somehow or other managed to get a favourable recommendation from the optician in order to be certified as fit to drive, despite the impaired eye being noticeably larger than the other eye.

There were two places my grandmother cherished, Ngāwhā, and the East Coast. Both places were her papawhenua. Her grandfather, William Clarke, had come to New Zealand as a surveyor-cum-property speculator from Scotland in the early nineteenth century and married Te Owai Tauehe. They had two children, Hana, who had no issue, and my great-grandfather, Wiremu Clarke, who married my great-grandmother, Mere Kohau Huriwai, from Rangitukia. My grandmother pined for her mother all her life. I remember lying in our bed opposite her as she lay beneath her mother's picture and told us about the week-long trek back to Rangitukia to bury her mother.

Living with her after Grandad died, and even before, always centred me. Night-time was storytime. Sometimes we would walk over to Uncle Winky's old home and hear about how my aunties and uncles had grown up in the Depression years on a dairy farm. My grandfather was an economist when it came to story-telling, always cutting to the chase and putting a sting in the tail. My grandmother was more methodic and deliberate. Grandad's stories always had a strong focus, about land, land wars, politics and ghosts. When he told ghost stories we would watch my cousin Billy – William Taiapo Dalton was his full name. He would sit opposite someone and try to act out the story, as if he had some sort of mystical power because of his ghostly name. It would only take a few minutes for cousin Tiny, his older brother, to knock an ounce of sense into him and Billy was transformed into Casper the friendly ghost.

The telephone was Nanny's real forum. She would spend hours on the phone speaking in Māori to Aunty Kath and the relations in Ngāwhā. It was funny, because Nanny didn't speak Māori to her children to the same extent. She would chatter to me in both languages as she kneaded and tossed bread dough from one hand to the other. Her bread rolls always turned out a perfect golden brown. My cousins could smell our bread rolls as we approached the creamstand which was our bus-stop. Freda was always the weak one so I had to make sure we got a supplement or a good trade.

Both Mum and Dad's families had been encouraged to get a good education and I guess that is where the focus in our family ended up.

With my sisters, Naera and Freda (who are on the right), circa 1958.

Dad's family were from a long line of schoolteachers. Dad's mother was Ripeka Taua Evans, my namesake. Her father was Wiremu Taua, who was the first Māori principal of Rangiawhia School. We never really had all that much to do with Dad's side until later in life. But we did have a lot to do with his immediate family. My aunty Ava, Dad's eldest sister, was like an opposite of Uncle Winky in Mum's family. She was the glue and always encouraged us to achieve.

At primary school I excelled from being nurtured and stimulated by teachers who taught me the classics and coached me to lead. From an early age I could even run classes. Once, when Maurice Taimana was away and there was no relieving teacher, I took charge of the class. When Maurice returned he just smiled at the headmaster, Alan Wotherspoon, and told him that he knew that I could do it. Netta Brown and Miha Matthews were both fresh-faced young Māori teachers who were a great inspiration. My only disappointment was that I could not meet all of Miha's expectations. He was great on and off the field but I was not built for all-round performance. For a start I was too short and inclined to be built for comfort and not speed. It was always great fun being in a team and what I lacked in ability I made up for in effort.

Because my father believed that the boys should have first choice to go to boarding school, I missed out on the opportunity. It was a disappointment, because I knew that I wanted to go to university after I was the top Māori student at our primary school. Going away to school could have lessened the barriers and I had a hunger to learn, intensified by the emptiness I felt when my grandfather, and then later on my grandmother, died.

Northland College was an experience that I wished to get over very quickly. It was a mixture of being happy and distraught, most unlike the happy and encouraging environment of my primary school. You would never think that it was a predominantly Māori high school when I was there; it was like being Māori started becoming 'in the closet'. I remember kapahaka practice was in the film room with the windows blacked out. Bill Hohepa would make us learn all the waiata off by heart before he gave us the song-sheets. Then he would scream at us saying, 'Come on you lot, parts, melody, harmony.' He was a hard taskmaster, a perfectionist,

Of the events that characterised my experiences at Northland College, none was more poignant than the third form English exam. In those days final exams were the basis for determining the award of annual prizes, and term results were not counted, or so we were told. I had performed well throughout the year and topping the final exam was icing on the cake. I was stunned with disbelief when the teacher told me that she had decided to award the prize to the second-placed student. I pressed the teacher for an explanation but to no avail.

When John F Kennedy was assassinated the world uttered disbelief that one of the motives for killing him was his stance on discrimination. I remember crying because someone so rich and powerful had risked so much for his beliefs. He was a powerful flip side to Martin Luther King and I kind of felt undeterred when I thought about them.

My parents' generation grew up believing that education was the key to integration. It took me a while to stop being mad with the racist third form English teacher; then I decided somewhere along the line that evening up the odds was not going to be enough.

I left Northland College in 1974 and shifted to Auckland to go to university – and with a mission to find a place nearer the sun. I'm still searching.

When Pākehā were Māori

WHAKAHUIHUI VERCOE

The Right Reverend Te Whakahuihui Vercoe is the Bishop of Aotearoa. He achieved national headlines with his address, made in the presence of Queen Elizabeth II, at the Waitangi commemoration in 1990. 'Since the signing of that treaty 150 years ago I want to remind our partners that you have marginalised us,' he said. 'You have not honoured the treaty. We have not honoured each other in the promises we made each other on this sacred ground.'

I was born in 1928 and grew up in Tōrere, a small coastal kāinga near Ōpōtiki. As a child I thought my extended family was normal. I grew up with a myriad of relationships with old people, middle-aged people, and my peers, which established for me that human relationships are more important than anything else. The sense of belonging sustained me, not only in material things but in spirituality. The church environment was an important part of the community.

My old people were concerned with maintaining family relationships so that everyone understood their place. They told the history of who you were and where you came from. They sang their songs. They gave the genealogical aspects of one's relationships, not only within the extended family but across inter-tribal boundaries, which was important, because you became part of a wider and bigger society. They spent time looking after and nurturing children, the married couples and the family. I was never brought up just by my mother and father. I was brought up by my aunts and cousins and grandparents too. These were the parameters within which Māori society was upheld. Old kuia and koroua had a special place.

Today we talk about respecting our elders, but it's difficult to do that now. A technological world has made our children more knowledgeable. In those days, children were taught why certain things happened within the environment. We were taught the proper time to plant, to harvest, to fish, to hunt. You couldn't have the same kind of upbringing in the city because there you were under the rules of an urban society. Besides, there was almost a demarcation – the Pākehā lived there and the Māori lived down the road.

The only Māori and Pākehā mix that occurred was either at school or in the labour market, where a lot of Māori worked for Pākehā. It never occurred to Māori that *they* could become the employer. Yet Māori were indeed the employers in the earlier settler period when their whole economic base was firmly secured. From the Bay of Plenty right down to the Coast Māori supplied the food resources for Auckland. Māori had their ships, they grew and marketed food products; but this commercial infrastructure was destroyed during the Land Wars and afterwards with the confiscation of land. In the confiscation the economic base of Māori was also destroyed.

It was at Feilding Agricultural boarding school that I began to understand the process of democracy. Mine was one of the first schools in this country having a students' council with a voice amongst the elders in the institution. One day Canon Paora Temuera, the then pastor of Rangiātea, spoke at our church service about the Māori mission. As he spoke I felt my old people back home saying something to me.

I decided to study for the ministry.

One of the problems today is that people are not given the time and space to work out who they are, where they fit in society or what society's doing to them. So they are not making any contribution. Instead people are used like puppets to fit into what government is doing to us. We do not go to school to enrich or enlarge our lives or our understanding of life. We are pressured into understanding – by having an education, we are told, we will receive the commercial rewards of this world. We lose sight of the humanness of people.

We talk about being poor today, but I grew up in a poor society with no money and no work. Everybody was unemployed. But people worked to sustain themselves, to grow their own food and to buy only the bare necessities of life. People were careful with each other and cared for one another. The old people never talked about costs. They talked about hospitality and put their effort into making sure their visitors were cared for. The cost was shared across the whole community, the whole hapū. Our society planted for the whole of society, not just for individual families. A percentage of your vegetables, your beef and sheep, were designated for the common good of the hapū.

Nowadays we don't do that. Today at marae meetings people talk about costs and pay for everything. It's not that we can't share nowadays but that we're pressured by the circumstances we live in to be self-sufficient individuals rather than to think about the self-sufficiency of the total society.

As a country we're more concerned with our national debt and everything we do is geared towards paying off or minimising that debt. We have to maintain this ever-increasing concern, and, consequently, people suffer in the process and are not held in high esteem. We're destroying our society when we should be caring for one another. Human life is the cheapest commodity and now we haven't the wherewithal to sustain caring. We're driven to be individuals.

I believe that the human spirit will overcome these things and that there are enough honest and sincere people – even politicians – who realise that we have to work together. We're also realising, slowly and painfully, that there was a contract made at Waitangi between two peoples that we would live in harmony, accept each other as equal members of a society and strive for the betterment of this country.

It's unfair to blame politicians all the time. The people who control our lives are the financial pundits who control the economy and the whole international global money movements. We cannot live in isolation in New Zealand. We are influenced by international money markets and its financiers who call all the shots.

In Māoridom the acquisition of material wealth was never held to be important. When the old people acquired things they gave them away. The old people said, 'You never retain treasures to yourself, you always give it away because if you keep it you'll lose it.'

I grew up in my grandfather's arms. He took me everywhere. I listened to him talking. He told me why he did certain things. When he made handles for his implements, like an axe handle, he'd sit there and tell me why you made it that way, how you should wait a while before you used it and how the axe head fitted into it. Explaining was really a therapy for him, giving him time to be completely himself.

After the Second World War the middle portion of Māori society moved physically into large cities where they made a lot of money. The acquisition of money influenced the changing of Māori society, forcing us to become competitive. You had to have things you thought were necessary – like a car and, nowadays, a boat and a bach or the latest video and sound system. Māori are getting more and more involved with the acquisition of material things and, again, the human relationships are not fostered, not nurtured.

When my generation grew up we dreamed of winning a scholarship and being educated as highly as possible. The old people pressured us and said, 'You must have education, you must acquire all the Pākehā skills in order that you can live a decent life and not be poor any more.'

One of the problems was, however, that, although the first language of Māori communities was Māori, this changed when people began moving away after the war, into factories and then into large cities. The language changed to English because that was the financial language. Everybody spoke English and our children grew up hearing English rather than Māori – although they understood they were Māori. So they lost their language skills – and now they're rediscovering them again. We have a rescue operation on at the moment, especially with regard to the language.

I knew very little about Pākehā New Zealand. The only part I understood was the town of Ōpōtiki. I was quite contented not to go there. That was the Pākehā world. But as a youngster I went to visit 'the big smoke' at Christmas. I walked on concrete pavements, saw all the shops and the goodies that were displayed. I couldn't buy any, I didn't have any money. I liked the lollies and ice-cream and the loaf bread. The old people went to town and came back with these things and we children ate them, but there was no wanting to have them. We were happy to see and experience them and then go back home.

I knew where Auckland was, and Wellington, but I grew up knowing more about England because that's what I was taught at school. There was very little taught about New Zealand.

We had frequent visits from Sir Apirana Ngata, but I never placed him within a Pākehā environment like Parliament. I knew he was an important man but I regarded him first of all as Ngāti Porou. He wasn't a politician. He was this wise Māori, talking knowledgeably, and he used to talk and sing and quote poetry both in English and Māori. He and Bishop Bennett were visitors but I never placed them in a Pākehā society.

I never said I'd like to be like Bishop Bennett or Sir Apirana Ngata. They were beyond our ken. If I had any jealous desires it was to do with public works. I'd love to have driven a truck or a bulldozer.

We regarded the Pākehā people who lived among us as Māori because they were absorbed into the community. They spoke Māori and they visited our home. They would have Māori bread and they were accepted. We knew they were Pākehā but they were Māori in their behaviour and their participation within the society in which we lived. My grandfather on my maternal side was an Englishman. I never regarded him as an Englishman. He was a surveyor. He talked about land values and boundaries and about his understanding of life in England. I never associated that as being Pākehā. I still thought it was part of being Māori.

My paternal grandfather was a half-caste and didn't look Māori. He was very European. But I never thought of him – of them – as Pākehā. Much later I understood my background and realised that the Pākehā grandparents had been very much English in their lives. They had absorbed Māori values, but they still retained a Pākehā behavioural pattern of what was right, what was wrong, and what was correct.

Māori were all mixed in with and part of the settlers. Our people married the soldiers, settlers and farmers. We grew up as Māori with English names. Almost the whole tribe had Pākehā names because they had Pākehā grandfathers or great-grandfathers. Yet we never questioned why we were called Vercoe or whatever the name was.

Wanting the Stars to Play with

JC STURM

*JC Sturm is one of New Zealand's most important short-story writers and poets. Her first collection of short stories, **The House of the Talking Cat**, was completed in manuscript in the early 1960s and, although not published until 1983, historically comes before the short story collections of Witi Ihimaera, Patricia Grace, Keri Hulme, Apirana Taylor and Bruce Stewart. Her first volume of poetry, **Dedications**, appeared in 1997.*

JC Sturm has Taranaki and Whakatōhea ancestry. In 'Wanting the Stars to Play With', she deals with the years between 1933 and 1944 when she moved from school to school, eight in all, throughout New Zealand – and the expectations she faced during these years.

JC Sturm lives at Paekākāriki.

I don't know when I realised my foster father was different. I think I always sensed it: he was much darker than anybody else, including my foster mother and me, and when he got really excited about something, he would pūkana with his tongue hanging out. I didn't like it much. I'd hide my face or run away and Mrs Sturm would say, 'Oh Bert,' and he'd stop suddenly and go back to what he was doing before.

It was about this time that I realised I was different too. I started school when I was six at a big primary school in New Plymouth. It's unlikely that I was the only Māori there but I don't remember any others. One day the headmaster took me outside the main entrance where I was shown how to curtsy with a smile while a man took photos of me. They weren't unpleasant in any way but I'd never curtsied before and felt silly and awkward. And different. Apparently the man was an overseas journalist collecting material for a travel book on New Zealand. The Sturms must have known about it because they were given one of the photos. I don't know the title of the book or even if it was ever published, let alone how the caption described me. No one said I was chosen for the photo because I was a little Māori girl but I suspect that was the reason. I can't think of another.

Soon after, we moved to Auckland and I was sent to another, bigger city school. I learned nothing there except the meaning of the word 'nigger' and how it feels to be afraid. The teacher was a grim-faced middle-aged woman who used to whack my knuckles with a stick if my pencil was blunt or my nails not clean enough or I couldn't produce a hanky. She must have done more than that but that's all I can remember. On the way home from school some of the big kids would call me 'nigger' and bad names and beat me up if they caught me. I don't know how long the nightmare lasted – it seemed forever – but when the Sturms found out what was going on they removed me from that school and I didn't go to another simply because I wouldn't. Mrs Sturm tried to explain the meaning of the word 'nigger' but I had a block about it and I didn't want to know. As far as I was concerned it meant being something that plunged you into a nightmare of fear and pain. Some would say I was right. My memories of that time are dark and confused and probably not to be trusted, but a song Mrs Sturm used to sing to comfort me still haunts me. A friend found the words for me on a Paul Robeson record:

> *So lulla lulla lulla lulla bye bye*
> *Do you want the stars to play with*
> *Or the moon to run away with?*
> *They'll come if you don't cry.*
> *So lulla lulla lulla lulla bye bye*
> *In your mother's arms be creepin'*
> *And soon you'll be a'sleepin'*
> *Lulla lulla lulla lulla bye.*

She had a lovely singing voice. So did the singers on a couple of records I was allowed to play occasionally. I couldn't understand a word but I loved the singing. Years later I found out that they were early Parlophone recordings of Ana Hato and Deane Waretini.

Next thing I remember we were living with relatives in Hastings and the Sturms still couldn't persuade me to go to school. I made friends with some kids living in our street who were about the same colour as me, maybe darker. They used to play some amazing games. One day when I arrived at their place they were making headbands out of willow branches. We put them on and the girls and I stood outside the front gate waving bits of willow and sort of singing while the boys walked up and down waving sticks and talking loudly. I had no idea what it was all about but I felt something was going to happen and I was right. Suddenly, grown-ups came rushing out of the house, grabbed our branches and headbands and hustled the other kids up the path after telling me to go home. I think the other kids got hidings and Mrs Sturm questioned me very closely about what we'd been up to, which wasn't like her. I'm not sure who wasn't allowed to play with whom but I never played with those kids again. Soon after we moved to Palmerston North and I was enrolled at the nearest school.

I was six when this photo was taken at Central School, New Plymouth.

The headmaster was probably the best teacher I ever had. After Mrs Sturm had finished telling him that I didn't want to go to school and why, he showed me round the playground and when I stopped at the parallel bars he said I could play on them every playtime and lunchtime if I wanted to and that's what I did. I don't remember any other teachers or the rooms or learning anything except that school wasn't always a place of fear and misery. And I became a real whizz on the parallel bars. Then we moved again to the other side of town.

The new school was the biggest in Palmerston North. I must have been in Standard Two or Three when I discovered I could read more than textbooks and school journals. I found a book in the classroom library called *Tales of the Māori*. It was a bit advanced for me and a lot of words I'd never seen before so I went to the teacher for help. 'You must know what that means,' she said, when I pointed to the Māori, 'that's what you are.' I can't say I was thrilled. I thought the people in the pictures looked very fierce with painted faces and funny clothes. I didn't think I looked like that at all and I didn't want to either.

I'd been at the school for some time when Mrs Sturm took me to see the Māori Battalion leave the Palmerston North showgrounds to go and fight in the war. It was a very quiet parade, no clapping or cheering, just the sound of marching feet and a sort of rustling in the air like long grass moving in the wind. Mrs Sturm told me my uncle would probably go too and she looked upset.

And then we moved again, this time south, and I went to a one-room two-teacher school near a small rocky bay. I loved it. I got on well with the teachers, so my work improved and I made friends with a Māori girl who lived down at the beach. She showed me where to find pāua and other shellfish and how to eat kina without getting a face full of spines. I liked them so much I ate seven one after the other and was sick all that night. I don't think Mrs Sturm ever knew why. I spent a lot of time with a Samoan family who lived at the other end of the beach. We used to catch crabs and the mother would bake them for us over an open fire in their backyard. She did all the cooking over that fire because they didn't have a stove. And sometimes she would dance Samoan dances for us and then we'd all dance together. I think that was the happiest time of my childhood but then I got sick and couldn't go to school for quite a long time and soon after that we moved back to Palmerston North and suddenly I was in Standard Six with secondary school looming ahead.

By then I had taken on board the expectations of the Sturms, their friends and my teachers. I was expected to, simply because I was Māori, sing in harmony naturally, play any musical instrument by ear, have a perfect sense of rhythm, excel at all sports, especially team sports, be good at arts and crafts and anything that required manual dexterity, and I was, of course, a 'born' orator. I was also expected to be easygoing, happy-go-lucky, friendly, generous, have an unfailing sense of humour, and underneath all that, a certain dignity, even nobility. (Remember the Noble Savage?) If that lot makes you cringe, imagine if you can what my life would have been like if I'd been saddled with a matching set of negative expectations, as so many Māori children were then and still are. I was one of the lucky ones. And so, armed with the positive expectations of family and friends, plus a good scholastic record and a moderate bursary, I left home at seventeen and went south to be trained to work for the Māori people. But that's another, very different story.

Murihiku is in my Blood

REINA WHAITIRI

Reina Whaitiri lectures in Māori and Polynesian literature in the English Department at the University of Auckland, where she is respected and loved as a mentor to Māori and Polynesian students. She is also convenor of the Wellesley Programme, designed to prepare students without entrance qualifications to be able to enrol in undergraduate studies the following year.

Born in 1943, Reina Whaitiri is of Kāi Tahu descent. The second part of her piece for **Growing Up Māori** *conveys with aroha and sensitivity just why we must treasure our elders and learn from them while we have them.*

1.

I AM the only child of a Māori father and a Pākehā mother. My mother, Ida May Martin, was the eldest of nine and the only one to marry a Māori. My father, Robert Agrippa Moengaroa Whaitiri, won the popularity stakes with her family, as he was well-educated, good-looking, widely travelled, and a great hit with his mother-in-law, my Nanna – the two of them used to run away to the races together. And so, my earliest memories are of being treated as the favourite by my Pakeha aunts and uncles. We lived on Te Ika ā Māui then so I knew little of my Ngāi Tahu whanauka in Murihiku.

My father was the guide at Waimangu, just south of Rotorua, where, together with my mother, he established himself as a beautifully presented and knowledgeable man. My mother was the finest cook for miles around. The Waimangu visitors' books from that time pay tribute to both of them. My mother's scones became legendary. Hoards of her family came to our house, which was way out in the country, and

Two of a kind.

were entertained by my father's stories of the area – he was extremely learned in the local fauna and flora. Dad often took the more adventuresome aunts and uncles out pig-hunting with him. My mother would dish up enormous, delicious meals, put together on an old coal range. We had no electricity, no reticulated water and no sewerage, but people flocked to our house because my parents were such wonderful and generous hosts.

I was never really conscious of being Māori when very young. Not until I was taken south, to meet my paternal grandmother, was I made aware that I was Māori and somehow different. She called me her little Māori girl, at which point, apparently, I burst into loud, offended tears.

As the favourite grandchild of my mother's family, and the only child of an only surviving child – my father – I cruised through my pre-school years without a care for who or what I was.

This changed radically when I was sent away to boarding school. It was a very English boarding school with a very English philosophy. Here, I was very soon made aware that I was Māori. I was favoured by the teachers but mocked and humiliated by my peers. For example, I was chosen to read the lesson in church and I was singled out to meet Bishop Panapa, when he came to visit the school. (Much later, I learned that I was sent to St Mary's Collegiate School on Bishop Panapa's recommendation.) But, I was also called Hone Heke by my classmates (this being the only Māori they knew), and I remember not feeling very good about that. At our first elocution lesson, the teacher picked on me to speak, as, being Māori, she expected me to have perfect vowel pronunciation. I'm afraid she was disappointed as I spoke just like everyone else in the class. I was a Kiwi kid after all. None of this perceived favouritism went down very well with my classmates.

My next memory of being made to feel Māori and different was when they decided to name our dormitories after the various waka. They came to me asking what my waka was. I had no idea and I remember thinking, What are they talking about?

It was about this time I decided that if I were Māori then I should learn the language. I must have been ten or eleven. Somehow, and from somewhere, I found a book on teaching yourself Māori. I used to read this book every night and managed to learn about *tēnā, tēnei, tērā*, and that was it. With no one to teach me and no one to encourage and support my efforts, I soon gave it away. We were all taught French at this very English boarding school.

My parents moved back down to the Bluff when my paternal grandmother died. It was at this point in my life that being Māori and belonging to a large extended family became normal and positive. I discovered I had hundreds of cousins, aunts and uncles. There was a stage when I believed everyone in the Bluff, in Southland, in Te Waipounamu, was related to me. Of course we are, but I had a different idea of what 'related' meant then than I do now. I had a very Pākehā model in my mind, so was a little confused about having all these whanauka. I was also trained to call anyone older than me aunt or uncle.

My father became involved in re-establishing te reo and cultural activities in the Bluff. Every Thursday we would all gather in a converted house (the very house where my beloved father lay in state at his tangihanga 45 years later) to learn te reo, waiata, kanikani, waiata ringaringa, haka. We travelled to Invercargill and gave concerts. We were introduced to the Von Trapp family when they visited the city and put on a combined concert with them. We farewelled Queen Elizabeth II on her first visit to New Zealand. We grew strong in our culture, we knew lots of stuff which we were positive about – but we didn't really understand what it was we were doing. We didn't learn our history or hear about the terrible experiences of our old people. We weren't politicised in any way. But being Māori was a positive thing. We felt quite superior to those few in the Bluff who were not related to us.

For us kids, those nights learning our culture, singing and dancing, was really an excuse to meet members of the opposite sex. Not only were there the local boys, but all the beautiful young Māori men from the North Island. These young men were recruited for the freezing works and, to our limited experience, were exciting and exotic. They were different. The local boys were okay, but the North Island boys, as they were known, were the ones who held the greatest attraction. Many of us met our future husbands at the Māori House.

Many links with North Island people were formed, through marriage and subsequently through the children. The Māori women of the deep south and the men from up north were doing what our people had always done. Moving in, and through conquest and marriage, changing the tribal make-up of the people. Our old people did not like this mingling of blood and warned against fraternising with 'those North Island Māori', those 'head-hunters', those 'Boongs'. I chose a descendant of Te Rauparaha, which went down very badly. I had no idea who Te Rauparaha was and was not moved at all by the objections of my old people. Later, I found that Te Rauparaha had had intentions of taking over the South Island – so no wonder they were against it.

My father became more and more involved with Māori politics and was voted onto the Ngāi Tahu Māori Trust Board, a position he held for over thirty years. I also became more aware of what it meant to be Māori and all that that entailed. As time went on, I began to read New Zealand history and non-fiction literature by and about Māori. I remember reading *Maori Girl* by Noel Hillard, and *Green Dolphin Country* and, for the first time, finding Māori inside the covers of books. I was hooked.

I listened to, and observed, my father at work. He was always available to people who came knocking on our door, or ringing on the phone, asking about who they were and if they were eligible for this or that grant. Dad was always off to the Bluff, or to Christchurch, for the trust board meetings. He used to attend the Titi Island meetings, which have always been the cause of bitter whānau quarrelling, to the point where people used guns to ward people – their own relations included – off their land. But from my father I learned about being committed to Maori and to Maori issues. I also learnt humility and respect for the past, for the old, for people.

I remember being taken to Ruapuke, our turangawaewae, for the first time with my parents. We spent a Christmas there with no power, no phone, no shops, no roads, no other people. It was really something and I got a real sense of what it must have been like to live on the island, two-and-a-half hours' steaming from the mainland. My father taught me how to catch weka the old way, with just a bit of bait and a piece of string. He taught me how to seek the pāua out on the rocks beneath the heavy swell of the mighty southern ocean. At night, he told me stories about Ruapuke and what it meant to our whānau, our hapū, our iwi. He took me over to the urupā – where he himself now lies – and showed me the graves of Topi Patuki, his mother, his brother, his father and sister and many more of our hapū. Standing on the hill, I looked back towards the Bluff and wondered about being stranded on the island forever. What would it be like? Would I miss school? Would I miss my friends? What would we eat if a boat didn't call in now and then?

When the time came for us to return to the mainland I felt very sad. On the day we were meant to leave, the weather came up rough. When it decides to play up on this stretch of water, believe me, there is nothing to compare with it. The huge seas and howling winds proved too much for my mother, who was petrified and cried to be taken back to land. My uncle's small fishing vessel was forced to turn back even though the men had no such concerns and were happily riding the boat as though nothing untoward was happening. The men who fish in these oceans know and respect the sea but have no fear of it. I too was very happy to return to Ruapuke.

We were forced to land at Caroline Bay, on the other side of the island from where we had been staying. When safely ashore again, my father told me the story of my great-aunt Caroline who lived on Ruapuke when she was young and after whom the bay was named. When she was only fourteen or fifteen, someone on the island fell very ill. Aunt Caroline rowed a dinghy all the way back to the Bluff by herself to fetch help. This story stayed with me for a long time. As had just been proved by our forced return, Foveaux Strait is notoriously rough, with the wind sometimes reaching cyclone proportions. I imagined her, struggling with gigantic waves breaking and washing over her tiny boat. I imagined her hair, wet and stringy, being swept wildly over her face, as she rowed the twenty-two miles back to the mainland over the roughest stretch of water in the Southern Hemisphere. This was a Herculean feat for a solitary teenage girl. I was, and still am, fiercely proud of belonging to the same whānau as her. When I met Aunt Caroline in real life, I found, instead of the brave young woman of the story, a frail old lady of over ninety. I still hold her and what she did in enormous respect.

With so many of my uncles and cousins at sea there were always stories of those who went missing, of people being washed overboard, of boats being found with no one on board, of the brave and courageous acts at sea. The sea is in our blood and I have no doubt that that same courage enabled us to travel from our island homes further north in the Pacific and to return with the stories of this long and beautiful country.

2.
July, 1996

Sitting on the plane gives me time to think. Too much time. Nothing seems real. I stare unseeing at people and things. I am not part of what's happening around me.

I know the next week will be hard and take comfort in the thought. In my ignorance, I think I won't have to think about Dad too much if I'm busy and have to keep up a public face. The thought that my beloved father is dead comes again and again and it's too outrageous, too overwhelming, to take in. Life without Dad won't work. I try, very hard, not to think about it.

I walk through the connecting tunnel to the terminal. The first karanga winds its swirling, liquid magic around me. I am to hear that beautiful, haunting cry many, many times in the following days. It calls me back to my past and heralds my future – a future without Dad.

My whānau drive me to the chapel where he is waiting. I know he is waiting for me. We enter the chapel and walk between the rows of pews. I am vaguely aware of people on either side. I am surprised, there are so many. Maybe twenty-five, maybe thirty people. All I have eyes for is Dad, lying there at the end of the aisle, on a slightly raised platform. He is covered to the shoulders with a white sheet. The need to cover him, to keep him warm, is uppermost in my mind. I tuck the sheet in around him. I touch him, he's so still. The shock of cold takes me utterly by surprise. This is death then. No warmth, no response to my kiss, my voice, my presence. This has never happened before. He was always overjoyed to see me. No more will those green eyes smile into mine. Vicious, gut-wrenching pain floods my being. I can't think. I am utterly lost. What do I do?

I am asked if I want to dress Dad. Of course I do. I must. It is my last daughterly duty. Marcia and Sally come with me, some men too. Who are these people? I don't know them. They are so kind, so firm. They know what to do. They have brought all Dad's clothes: his underpants, his light-brown suit, short-sleeved blue and white shirt (surely it's too cold for a short-sleeved shirt. It's winter in Murihiku), socks (one with a hole in it), and his fawn shoes. He needs shoes? Why? He doesn't need shoes. Where is he going that he needs shoes? Or any of it? The futility of what we are doing confuses me.

I uncover him slowly. I feel like a doctor preparing to operate. I expose his dear, dear body, so bruised, so discoloured. I see the pacemaker in his chest. Yet another shock. I see his fine, long-fingered hands, punctured and bruised. I am so used to seeing those hands folded over his carved tokotoko. He never made a move without it. I fold the sheet back further, slowly, exposing his chest, his stomach, thighs, knees, and lastly, his feet. Now I see, for the first time in my life, the true physical perfection that was my father. My beloved father. His long legs and arms, his finely shaped hands, so elegant and strong. This much remains of the truly beautiful young man he was. Our bones last the longest, our bones must be kept and remembered and loved and revered, forever. The rituals our tīpuna performed for their dead ensured that the bones were preserved. I understand now.

So, my whānau and I dress Dad. The men are strong and know what to do. I can only weep and help. His body is so cold, so very cold. No one prepared me for that, or for the dead weight (now the words have meaning).

We put him in the coffin and make sure he's comfortable. We fuss over this and that, making sure his tie is straight and his collar just right. Paitu and I stand by our beloved dad and Poua, our arms entwined. We are warned there will be very little time from now on to be alone with him. Those who have helped leave us. We say our private farewells, the first of many to come. We speak, but I can't remember what we say. The lid goes on and for a short time we are separated from him.

Paitu and I ride in the hearse, leading a convoy to the Bluff. It takes forty minutes for the twenty-five minute drive. For my Dad though it is too short. This is his last journey, the last time he will ride on the Bluff road, the road he knew so well, te ara a te rangatira. I talk to him all the way. I name all the places as we pass them: Clifton, where Aunty Naina lived (she too is now dead), Awarua (once the Awarua Radio Station), Greenhills and Greenpoint, where Mum is buried. *Now you will be forever together ōku mātua.*

We pass Ocean Beach where Mum worked in the dining room. Next comes Fowler's Oysters, probably both Mum and Dad's last real job. And then I feel overwhelming pain, the memories rushing in as we pass Shannon Street – this is where we used to turn up the hill for home when we lived at 231 Foyle Street. And on through the town, past all the pubs: the Eagle, the Golden Age, the Bayview, and the RSA, Dad's favourite place away from home. Dad knew all of them, had spent time in each. We continue past the new and old wharves, the old Town Hall and Picture Theatre, then a final turn up the hill to the marae, to Te Rau Aroha. This marae stands testament to the vision and determination Dad, Aunty Ngawara and Uncle Norman had. They dreamed all of this into existence.

We pull into the curb outside the old Māori House, and the reality of it all strikes home again. Out of the hearse, I am surrounded by kindness. People I don't know come to support me, help me, guide me. Paitu is beside me, Sally and Marcia too. They know what to do.

Dad is carried into the house. As we enter the light and warmth I see all the familiar faces of our whānau, waiting, turned to the door expectantly. My tears and theirs take Dad into the house. I can't believe anything, all this is happening but not to me. I am too close to see. None of this is true. It can't be true.

Then I see Sister Whaitiri, Mo, and Babe, so real and alive. Sister looks devastated. She recently lost her husband. She will be reminded again and again of this over the next few days. I grab Mo and Babe's hands and pull them to mattresses beside the coffin. We are the pani. These are my people, I know them and, like me, they don't know what to do.

Dad is placed in the centre at the back of the house, his feet facing the door. I take my place on his left. Here I will stay for the next four nights and five days. Paitu is on the right. We touch each other over Dad's still-handsome head.

The lid is taken off and Dad is covered from the waist down with a feather cloak and the New Zealand flag. When he arrives, Selwyn Pirini offers the family pounamu mere which lies with Dad until his burial. Later, I go to Dad's room at the Takitimu Home and find the particular photo of Mum he loved to have near him, and place it above his head along with one of him, Aunty Ngawara and Uncle Norman. They were all in their mid-thirties when it was taken and they look so young, so very beautiful. A recent photo of Dad in his green shirt in front of the blue and white New Zealand flag completes the gallery.

Dad becomes my treasure, my prized possession. I don't want to leave him, even for food and drink. I gaze and gaze at his beloved face until I am positive I see him breathe, see his eyelids flutter, see his lips form into a smile. (Now I understand King Lear so much better.) As I look at him I talk to him, about what is happening, about Mum, the boys, how sorry I am that he had to go without me being there. I tell him how much he meant to me. How much his being there was of the utmost importance to me. And now, he isn't there. This is so hard to accept, even to comprehend; how will life continue, how will the world keep turning without him?

Tari Bradshaw, Paddy Gilroy and other men I don't know sit on the paepae tapu for the entire tangi. They welcome the waves of people that come through from that first night. The beauty of the language, the words, the phrases, the stories, our history, repeated again and again becomes a blanket, a kākahu that wraps around me. The waiata too, they are a balm, stroking and lifting the spirit, so beautiful, so soothing. The men make each group of mourners feel welcome, important and respected. Paddy's Māori improves with each passing day. It all helps to carry the memory of the man. I'm sure Dad is enjoying it; in fact, I know he is loving every minute.

That first night, Lana and her daughter sleep with Paitu and me, beside Dad. The first night of my vigil will not be a lonely one. Lana gives me her sleeping bag. It is fabulously warm. It will cover our feet during the days and warmly envelop me during the nights. I appreciate her thoughtfulness. I had completely forgotten to bring blankets or a sleeping bag.

I sleep little the first night. Dad won't let me. He fills my thoughts, constantly reminding me of our past together, I remember the things he tried to teach me when I was growing up: our recent relationship, our squabbles, our long talks about Māoridom, education, and our relatives. But then, suddenly, the feeling of being alone floods in again, so deep, so acute. The pain is unbelievable, it leaves me stunned.

The first morning after Dad's death dawns brilliantly, crisp, clear, the ground white with frost. I remember mornings like this when I was growing up down here. Puddles tight with ice waiting to be jumped on by young feet, steam billowing out of mouths, and cold, so cold. Running up to the ablution block is a brisk awakener. The shower is good though. For the first time since stepping off the plane the day before, I feel momentarily relieved of the responsibility and the intensity.

Hana is one of the two youngest Bradshaw girls, sent up to Rotorua to be raised by their aunt when their mother, Aunty Ngawara, died. Hana was raised steeped in the culture and knows things. I ask her about having the photo of Dad, John Tapiata, and the others on the Matua Whāngai Committee, above the coffin with the others. 'No!' comes the emphatic reply. The photos must be only of those already dead. I'm glad she is there to warn me of such things. Hana is the organiser and the commander-in-chief of tangi operations.

Returning to the house is like returning home. Dad is there, the women have cleaned the house and made it ready for the day. Chairs are lined up for the manuhiri on the left-hand side of the house, and on the right, for the tangata whenua. The kaikaranga are stationed to the right of the door. They karanga to each group of mourners and are ready with waiata for the speakers. Mattresses with pillows and blankets are positioned on either side of the coffin for the pani. And so we are ready for the day's business. I clutch my tissues and tuck the covers around my legs and feet against the cold coming from the door directly opposite me.

Koro Wetere comes, the Mayor of Invercargill, a delegation from the Department of Conservation, Tipene O'Regan, Whetu Tirikatene-Sullivan, and many, many, more. A large contingent of Cook Islands people come with their straw hats and beautiful chanting. They sing for a long time, lifting our sorrow and pain, carrying it on their voices as their warm presence and song fill the small house.

Al arrives and I feel his support and his aroha. He must now contend with the cold and the strangeness. He discovers that the minister has spent time in Samoa, that he was a champion boxer, and played rugby for the Māori All Blacks.

The next morning Pita and Al are formally welcomed on with a group of Samoans from Invercargill. They present a fine mat and, contrary to Samoan custom, sing a waiata. Pita represents all those Pacific peoples who ended up working in Ocean Beach and who were made welcome in the very house in which Dad now lies.

This house is where it all began, where we re-established our Māoritanga, where I had my first Māori lesson and where all of us kids learnt our waiata, our kanikani, our poi and haka. Uncle Norman and Aunty Ngawara were our teachers. We came, every Thursday night, to meet, to dance, to sing. My mother, eternally in the kitchen, preparing supper: sausage rolls, sandwiches, sponge cakes filled with cream and Wattie's tinned peaches. Aulsebrook's biscuits, fresh scones, jam and cream, and lots of tea.

So sad that only one member of Mum's family comes, but I am so happy to see him. Denis Martin, son of one of Mum's brothers, Walter. He arrives with his wife, Margaret. He speaks for the family that had married into the tangata whenua of this place, of this land. He didn't know how highly esteemed his Uncle Bob was, didn't realise the status and mana of the man. Now he knows and his children will know.

On the Saturday night the delegation arrives from the Ngāi Tahu rūnanga. They arrive very late and much is made of this. Our speakers joke and say that they were so long and so late in coming because their waka must be laden down with koha. For this reason alone their lateness is excused. Tipene speaks, telling the history of the Ngāi Tahu Trust Board and the work which was Dad's life, and that is now bearing fruit. He tells of the struggles with friend and foe alike, of the eternal meetings, the arguments, the growth and development, the hard graft, that today makes Ngāi Tahu one of the most successful and energetic iwi in the country. The success is cause for much jealousy and resentment.

The following day many of the young people of the iwi come to mourn their Uncle Bob. Their skill with the language, their singing, their knowledge and confidence, are testament to the strength, depth, and vitality of Ngāi Tahu's renaissance. Dad can rest easy knowing that the future is in strong and secure hands. He would have been very proud.

Each morning I stand at the foot of the coffin and allow the pain and the loss to flood my being. How can there be life without Dad in it? The wonderful women who have stayed with me and have done the housework, they mourn with me. We stand, each alone but together, around the coffin. I am not given time though to indulge my grief. The first group of the day arrives, and with each, the tears come and come. When Mo and Babe come each morning just after breakfast, I feel relieved and comforted. They are my mainstay, and each morning I eagerly wait for them to enter the house and join me under the warm sleeping bag and blankets.

Paitu comes and goes. He is always on the way to doing something. He will feel it hard too. He was Dad's shadow, always there, driving him crazy.

Each speaker has something different to say about the man they knew, not my dad, but someone else. He was Mr Whaitiri, Uncle Bob, our upoko, our rangatira, our representative, a friend and confidante, a leader, the man who ... They have all had their special, unique relationship with him. I feel my pain is shared as I hear so many tell of their respect and love for him, as I hear of all the lives he has touched, all the things he has been involved in. There are moments of humour and humility, laughter sometimes. He was not a glum man, my dad. In his later years though, he was often bitter and angry about certain people who he believed had betrayed him or let him down. He was more outspoken in his old age too, the privilege and the right of all old people.

The minister is there first thing in the morning, to say karakia, and he is there last thing at night. He is a great comfort in a strange way. I have no Christian faith but I appreciate him and his wife, Heather, greatly. He is a good man to have on your side. Heather is there, always by his side, smiling and comforting. The minister warned me in the very beginning that the days ahead will be hard and to be prepared. He was right and I remember his words when the exhaustion sets in and the pain threatens to utterly engulf me.

After breakfast each morning, when I return to the house, I stand at

Dad's side and wash his hands with my tears. Paitu, and the women who have slept in the house with us, stand by me as together we weep our morning greeting to him.

Finally, the moment I have been dreading arrives. On the morning of the fourth day, they move to put the lid on the coffin. I must say my final farewell to his face, his dear, dear face. I can't bear to see him shut away. I will never see him again. This is hard, so hard. The men go about the business quickly and efficiently. The minister knows what to do. There obviously must be no nonsense about this part of the ritual. Reports of people throwing themselves on the body enter my mind but no, I wouldn't, couldn't do that. Things will move forward regardless of how much I want to keep my father with me. I stand back and allow things to proceed. I am exhausted and have no energy to resist anyway.

The coffin is taken to the church just down the road from the Māori House. I ride with Mo and Babe. Al comes with us. Outside the church we wait for things to be arranged. The crowd is huge, with the overflow accommodated in the hall next door to the church. Microphones have been put in so everyone can hear the service. I will be giving the eulogy. This will be my next trial.

Dad is carried into the church to the marching beat of the 28th Māori Battalion battle hymn. He will appreciate that. Paitu, Al, Babe, Mo, Aunty Naina, Kohowai, Rena and I move into the front pew, and the service begins.

The time comes for me to rise and walk to the pulpit to deliver my public and formal farewell to the most important man in my life. By some miracle I am able to hold back the tears and I get through most of what I need and want to say.

I briefly go over our early life together. I tell of how I learnt about honesty, loyalty and integrity from my father, and about love. He prepared me well for adulthood. I recount how he met Mum and that the general consensus amongst her large family was that she had made the best catch. I tell of the man who gave his life to his people and of the man who was my father, my mentor and confidante. I tell of all the things he loved in life: travel, for example, any excuse to get on a bus or a plane, a car, and off he'd go. He had a weakness for gambling and for alcohol. He loved having lots of people around him. And most important to him, his love, his absolute passion and commitment, to all things Māori. And most of all, his utter dedication to the people of Te Waipounamu. I tell of the enormous respect and love his very name elicited from people. My way was often made easier when people discovered I was his daughter.

My dad was a man. He was a woman's man and a man's man, and he was always a tātau tātau man, always including everyone. He tried to make people feel comfortable, no matter who they were or where they came from.

Now I address my father directly.

Dad, I hope that all the tears we have wept over the last few days will provide safe passage for your waka, the waka that will carry you to the other side. On that far shore, there will be a mighty host of our tīpuna waiting, Dad. They wait impatiently, because many times they have expected you but have been disappointed, as time and again you stepped back from the brink. But this time they will not be denied. And standing in front of that illustrious gathering will be your mother Effie, and father Bob, your brother George and sister Reina, and beside them will be Mum, Ida May, the woman you called Joe, your life partner. Take heart my darling Dad, you are nearly home.

If I have not loved you well enough in life, Dad, I promise I will make up for that now. I will raise your mokopuna, the boys you loved so much. One day I will bring them here to the Bluff and take them to Ruapuke for you to see. You will see the three young men, strong, beautiful and Kāi Tahu to the bone, who carry your blood in their veins. I promise to tell them all your stories; I will tell them all about you. They will learn from whence they came and what they have to live up to.

Farewell, Dad. Haere, haere, haere. I have had the enormous good fortune to be your daughter and to have known and loved, and been loved by, a truly great man.

The service continues for a short time longer but I don't hear anything, I notice nothing.

The body is carried down to the wharf, where two catamarans and the Department of Conservation's ship *The Renown* is waiting to carry us all to Ruapuke. This was always Dad's greatest and most adamant desire; to be buried in the soil that gave the Whaitiri hapū their beginnings. All our people are buried there, as will I one day be buried beside Dad. The newspaper claims there are one hundred and sixty people who make the journey but I claim it is more like two hundred.

The weather is rough, the seas high and there are strong winds. Just the sort of day Dad would have revelled in. As we make our way out of the harbour I watch the buses and cars full of those who chose not to make the rough trip to the island. They wind their way around the Bluff road to the Point where it ends. There they karanga us until we are well out of earshot.

The journey to Ruapuke is very rough; it is cold, the wind is blowing hard, with enormous seas. The catamarans are a very different mode of travel from the fishing boats I remember travelling in. They are fast and ride the waves well, and, in good weather, I can imagine the journey being a pleasure. The journey takes about forty minutes and I'm sure Dad enjoyed every minute of it.

On reaching the island we are taken ashore by motor-driven dinghies. Dad is brought ashore last and is welcomed by a haka. Things move very fast now, because of the cold, because we must catch the tide for the return journey. Immediately we move off up the hill to the urupā. The men carrying the casket change places often, as the weight of the man becomes too much. They change sides often, as they try to balance the strain. The weight is shared and there is always another strong, willing bearer waiting to step into the breach.

Women karanga the cortège all the way, their voices periodically being whipped away by the howling winds. One woman guides the other, who is backing up the hill and over the uneven ground as she throws her karanga into the teeth of the wind, challenging and defying the very elements after which we are named – Whaitiri.

It is freezing but I don't notice the cold; I concentrate on putting one foot in front of the other as I move in behind the casket. At the urupā we come to an abrupt halt around the grave. There is little time lost in putting the coffin in the ground. I hardly have time to touch the coffin for a final time. I have trouble focusing; I can't see. I can only think of Dad being in that box and being lowered into the cold, cold ground. Tommy Ryan plays the 'Last Post' and repeats those familiar words for old soldiers. I look around at the landscape which will be forever looking down on my Dad's resting place. The scene is exactly as I remember seeing in a photo taken some eighty years before, when one of our tīpuna was buried in this place. Dad will not be alone.

The most outstanding feature on Ruapuke is the rocks. They are huge, dwarfing the people below them, and white. I always see them as symbols of the strength and courage of our people. Like us, the rocks are here forever, growing up out of the very ground. When all the forces of both Māori, in the form of Te Rauparaha, and Pākehā, the colonisers, came against us, this island is where we made our stand. Tūhawaiki was preparing his resistance against the hated and dreaded Te Rauparaha. The rocks rise up out of the ground like teeth or bones, they lean against one another, supporting and pushing at the same time. They are scattered about in groups, thrusting up toward the sky but rooted fast. They will guard the resting place of my father as they have guarded all our dead for centuries past. I am happy to leave him here with the rocks frowning down on him. He will be warm in the ground that gave our people their beginning. For Ruapuke is where the Whaitiri hapū began and where all our tīpuna are buried.

We return to the Bluff. The sea is running behind us on our return journey and we go much faster, surfing the huge waves. There is no violent bumping and crashing and it is actually enjoyable.

The return to the land of the living is a happy occasion and my spirits lift as the beautiful ritual of lifting the tapu is performed and all the songs are sung again. The hākari is magnificent and the wharekai is filled to the brim. All the people who loved my father will remember his tangi as a great affair. Perhaps it will be the last of its kind, although I hope not. My father deserved every moment and I will be forever grateful to all those who made it happen.

Goodbye, Dad, farewell, haere, haere, haere. I know I will think of you every one of my remaining days. I love you more than I ever told you. I will make sure that your memory will be strong in your mokopuna.

Unuhia i te rito o te harakeke
Kei whea te kōmako, e kō?
Whakatairangitia
Rere ki uta, rere ki tai
Kī mai ki ahau
He aha te mea nui o te ao?
Māku e kī atu
He tangata, he tangata, ā, he tangata!

Draw out the heart of the flax
Where is the kōmako, e kō?
Move this way and that
Fly towards land, fly towards the sea
Ask me
What is the most important thing in the world?
I will say
People, people, people!

PART TWO

Post-Modern Māori

*Ko te waka hei hoehoenga mō koutou i muri i
ahau, ko te Ture, mā te Ture anō te Ture e
āki.*

The canoe for you to paddle after me is the
Law. Only the Law can be pitched against
the Law.

– THE PROPHET, TE KOOTI ARIKIRANGI,
AS HE LAY DYING (APRIL, 1893).

A BIOGRAPHY

We held them to catch
this. The glass shelves
are spotlighted to catch
green curves, green layering,
and prices – but I only want the singing.

The song is ancient. Flecks in the stones
show their breeding, which
is important. But turn the lights out
and there is only singing. This
stone is one of the singers.

I watch the top waters
flow – catching the spare light.
I lie here waiting
for you to hold me.

I am life and its shape,
shaped to you.
The song filling your heart,
Moving the blood of this stone.

Creatures flow in the space
around the stone, some control
the way they tumble. When
there is light the stone is here.
When there is no light the stone

is here. The presence of the stone
fills us, ribs our hearts as we tumble.
We have been tumbling a long time.
When we land, we land on other stone –
lining prison floors, reinforcing

citadels that launder
clothes and cheques.
But even in the gravel
that makes the grey stone,
there is greenstone.

What else keeps singing the song?
We hear it – yet there is nothing to see.
Our pounamu sings.
Even in the gravel there must be
flecks of pounamu.

We cannot leave, we came from here.
We cannot go back – this is our England.
We bring pounamu up from our rivers
The greenstones on our chests
are the life of this land.

Robert Sullivan

Body Parts

PHIL KAWANA

*Born in 1965, Phil Kawana is the author of the much acclaimed short story collection, **Dead Jazz Guys**, published in 1996. He is also twice winner of the Huia Publishers' Te Kaunihera Award for best short story by a published author.*

*Affiliated with Ngā Ruahine and Ngāti Kahungunu, Phil Kawana is a writer of increasing popularity and some notoriety – in 1998, parents of students attending Western Springs College asked the board to ban **Dead Jazz Guys** because of the 'graphic sex and violence content'.*

Phil Kawana lives in Masterton. He is working on another collection of short stories and a novel. In 'Body Parts' he shows his considerable flair for comedy.

One summer's day when I was six years old, on the way back home from the Argyle Street Dairy in Hāwera with one hand wrapped tightly around a vanilla ice-cream so that the dog wouldn't pinch it (vanilla was Rin's favourite flavour), I stubbed the big toe on my left foot. Layers of skin peeled back from the toenail like a damp magazine left to dry in the sun. Large droplets of blood formed and started to spill down between my toes. I noticed that the blood seemed darker and richer than it was when I grazed my knees or elbows. I looked up at my mother and howled at the top of my voice. 'Quick, Mum, I'm losing all my Māori blood!'

You see, I knew that my sisters and I were of mixed blood – Māori and Scots and, though we didn't like to admit it, English. Somewhere along the line I'd picked up the notion that it was the colour of the blood that determined the colour of the skin. Māori had dark blood while Pākehā had pale blood. That was why my mother could get sunburnt, peel and still be as white as she was before. It also explained why Koro could spend all day in the pub, never getting any sun at all, and still be the colour of the nugget my sisters used to polish their school shoes. Therefore, so my reasoning went, if you had mixed blood, then some parts of you had Māori blood in it and other parts had European blood in it. My bum had to be Pākehā, 'cos it always stayed white, and my ure *had* to be Māori because it was always the brownest part of me.

I had never thought of my feet as being especially ethnic, but the richness of the blood seeping from them was all the evidence I needed. The prospect of losing my Māori blood and only being left with the Pākehā terrified me. I can remember other times somewhere around the same age when I would squeeze the bright crimson blood out of my grazes, in the vague hope that I would subsequently get a little darker. Looking back at the stubbed toe now, I realise it was the first time I was consciously confronted by my dual heritage and the first time I became aware of having a preference for one over the other.

I guess I always wanted to be black. Not the stained-pine brown of my father, or the chocolate brown of some of my cousins, but black. One of my uncles was (and I think sometimes still is) known as Uncle Golly, as in Golliwog, because he is short with curly hair and very dark skin. That was how I wanted to be. But taller. As it was, I didn't even have the nose. Dad and his brothers all had the classic wide, flat nose. I figured their noses had been squashed into that shape through heaps of hongi-ing. For a while I tried to replicate it by hongi-ing my reflection in the mirror, but it didn't work. Even worse, one of my sisters caught me at it and thought I was kissing myself. Ever since I've been labelled the vain one in the family. Which I suppose isn't wholly inaccurate.

By the time I was eight I had resigned myself to the fact that, genitals aside, I didn't have a Māori-looking body. Perhaps, I wondered for a while, I had Māori organs. But then I wasn't sure there could be any real difference between one liver and the next, other than relative levels of alcohol. There seemed to be a definite Māori taste in food, and I could gorge with the best of them when it came to pāua and mussels and hāngi and Koro's fried scones. However, I never really cottoned on to mutton flaps or pork bones (I'd just scoff the pūhā and the potatoes and then say I was full), and I was about seventeen before I finally got past the smell of kina and tried some - they were okay, but give me pāua any day. So instead I started trying to find Māori traits in my behaviour and personality.

I started watching the Kawana whānau to see what common talents or traits they shared. I soon decided there were four things we were particularly good at. The first two were sport and fighting, and the two often seemed to be closely linked. The other two were drinking and fucking, and these also appeared to be closely connected. However, by comparison with my whānau, once I reached adolescence I didn't fare too well. I was lousy at sport and was far too shy to even ask a girl out, let alone get my end away. I *did*

Me at four, hoping my nose looks flat.

get the fighting bit down okay, and when my parents weren't watching I had the drinking sussed as well. But these did not seem to me to be particularly Māori traits. After all, wasn't vodka a Russian invention?

But at eight, I was not exactly a blushing innocent. There were only two or three Pākehā at the country school I went to, one of them a little blonde who followed me around like a puppy. She probably grew up to be a Rachel Hunter look-alike, but I ignored her. I only had eyes for the dark and lovely S. We used to sneak into this hideaway under the trees while everyone else was waiting for the school bus. For a while I was totally at ease with myself, because I could see how I was following the classic Kawana template.

It didn't last long, though. Our family moved a little further south, out of Hāwera and down to Waverley. Most of the Māori went to the convent school across the road from the primary school, so the racial mix at my school was predominately Pākehā. On top of that, we were now in an area belonging to a different iwi. I no longer felt as if I belonged, my self-assurance was gone and I once again started quest-ioning just where I fitted in the greater scheme of things. All this time I would be told by the Pākehā at school, both the teachers and the students, that I wasn't like a *real* Māori. In fact, I was *almost* like a Pākehā. The reasoning behind this was that I was into poetry and reading and so on – you know, stuff besides the *Turf Digest* – I was also able to say 'ask' instead of 'arks'. It seemed that as far as most people were concerned, I was neither one thing nor the other. Growing up in Waverley, it appeared that horis were only supposed to be semi-educated freezing workers. I think it stayed that way until the Pātea freezing works closed down. After that, people's expectations dropped somewhat.

Around Waverley, expectations were heaped on you according to your family. For the Squatocracy, a life of boarding schools followed by either Massey or Lincoln beckoned, and then from there back to the family farm. For the Natives, life did not bode quite so well. It was very much Us and Them. The surname our family was known by at the time was the English equivalent of Kawana, Governor. This placed me somewhere between the Us and the Them, whoever they may have been. Every day of my school life, some little dickhead insisted on calling out, *'There goes the Governor-General, tee hee hee!'* Yeah, like I'd never heard *that* one before. Legally, we were always Kawana, but Dad had been known as Governor all his married life. Most of my childhood I just took it for granted that the choice of surname had been made for me. Still, even when I was at primary school, I always felt much more like a Kawana than a Governor.

So I had a Māori name, even though some people didn't realise it. At least I knew. And so maybe my skin wasn't as brown as I wanted it to be. Having brown eyes and brown hair was some kind of consolation. Eventually I was even able to cope with not being fluent in te reo, contenting myself with being able to put down a hāngi. Well, okay – *helping* to put one down. At sixteen I finally got around to learning how to play the guitar. Do you get any more Māori than that?

And so, at sixteen, as I stood on the edge of adulthood, I was able to resolve that burning childhood question. Maybe it had taken some years, but no matter. I was able at last to understand just where my Māori blood manifested itself. It had nothing to do with my feet, or my nose, or my white bum. It made sense out of my taste for pāua and rewana and watercress.

I was Māori on the inside.

Snapshots from a Boyhood Album

MOANA JACKSON

Moana Jackson is the Director of Ngā Kaiwhakamārama i Ngā Ture, the Māori Law Service. Born in 1948, his iwi affiliations are with Ngāti Kahungunu and Ngāti Porou. He is one of the most influential Māori legal thinkers of his generation.

Moana Jackson went to Mayfair Primary, Hastings Intermediate and Hastings Boys' High School. He graduated in Law from Victoria University of Wellington and did further study in the United States – at Arizona State University, where he worked with the Navaho Legal Service – before returning to New Zealand in 1984.

In this piece on growing up Māori, Moana Jackson offers us snapshots from a family album.

Snapshot 1

FOR MY generation, the Second World War took a long time to end. But, in a sense, for our fathers who fought as part of the Māori Battalion, it never ended at all. Their experiences shaped the rest of their lives – and those of their children.

Like many of my friends, therefore, I grew up to a certain extent with the legacy of war. This was in the 1950s when Māori held dear the pride and memory of war exploits in faraway places. The names of uncles buried in North Africa whom we would never meet. The faded photographs in family albums or on the walls of the meeting house. The unveiling of gold-lettered rolls of honour on the marae. The musty smell of uniforms in an old tin trunk. Most of all – for it is the living who keep the memories alive – I remember the tears we shed for those who came back from the war when *they* died. They were buried in urupā with poppies tossed on their coffins.

The war impacted in other ways. Our father came back with terrible wounds to his body and spirit. Our mother had to raise a whānau with no benefits of any kind save her own strength and compassion. If Mum rarely spoke of tikanga and seldom mentioned aroha, it was because she *lived* it. That we managed to grow up at all, let alone grow up as Māori, is a tribute to Mum and the wider whānau which nurtured us all.

Snapshot 2

Apart from the war, what shaped us *most* as we grew up were the attitudes, the behaviour, the joys and sadnesses of our whanaunga.

For instance, there were times of what seemed to be non-stop tangihanga at Korongata – and not all of the memories are of wailing and tears. The kui made wreaths as they sat around the tūpāpaku. The young women overfolded different coloured paper for the tablecloths. On the marae, the old uncles enjoyed and relished the speeches, whaikōrero, between tangata whenua and manuhiri who had come to mourn. Sometimes the speeches were delivered not with great flourishes but considerable humour. The koha would be laid down and sometimes it wasn't money but newly dug kūmara or freshly caught kaimoana. And Aunty Matekino was always there, speaking on the marae as well. I remember her framed at night between two fires that spat sparks in the air as she joked or berated the dead as well as the living.

There were also other hui where the paepae stretched in a circle around the marae. Each whānau had its own kāuta behind the whare and took turns in preparing the meals – and that *kai*! Tables with raised platforms sagged with the weight of the food. The cooks knew nothing about cholesterol but a great deal about manaakitanga. Their generosity showed itself in the freshly bled meat, kaimoana, multicoloured trifles, and dumped clusters of lollies and fruit that lay waiting to be eaten. In between were huge jugs of sweet cordial. The artificial colouring stained your lips.

Among the hui, I have a special memory of the weekend card schools at Whakatū. Mum cooked as the aunts played cards with a fierce intensity. There were all night parties around beer kegs. Sometimes there'd be a flaring of violence. And always a guitar, where the uniqueness of the Māori strum was matched only by the unparalleled ability of my uncles to make up their own lyrics.

In the mornings after the card schools, I loved listening with others, wrapped in blankets, to the radio. The static-filled rugby commentaries of the game of the day would make my uncles remember the glory days, when Dad had been an All Black, of seeing him play.

Then there were the marae hockey competitions. My old aunties played their nieces. They told us what a flyer our Mum used to be.

And in quieter times there was our koro, a staunch Kahungunu who told us about our land, our relations and our history. At his house, I used to watch him while he cooked on a shiny wood-burning stove in a kitchen that had only two pictures on the wall. One was our Nanny who had died young and before any of us were born. The other was a photo of the 1924 All Blacks – there was a special inset of George Nepia. At his house, and then at ours when Koro came to live with us, he spun tales of the past. He was a reassuring strength, adding to the reality of who we were.

Snapshot 3

All this made up the warmth of our lives. But beyond the whānau was another world, a colder world, where paid work at the freezing works or in the orchards was only seasonal. There, in that other world, card games were necessary as well as fun because, who knows, Lady Luck might give you a winning hand. As well, Māori food like pork bones and pūhā was fun too, but the reality was also that it was the only food that could be afforded.

In that other world, we sometimes had to get permission from a Pākehā farmer to go across his land to forage for karengo at the beach. As well, although travelling with Mum in the shearing gangs was fun it was a necessity, because Mum was working as the cook. Sometimes, an uncle working on a sheep station was one of the only full-time jobs in the whānau.

For a while we were sheltered from all that life *really* meant. Presents on birthdays and hakari at Christmas were wonderful moments that just seemed to happen. But sometimes I would catch an inkling of the world out *there*.

I heard talk about the latest attempts by Pākehā to close off part of the beach. I saw my parents and their generation joke about the rent they were getting from their last posthole at Māhia. Even before I had even heard the world 'colonisation' I was reminded that there was another world where the land through which we travelled was no longer ours.

Snapshot 4

In those boyhood years, going to school was perhaps where the real understanding of that other world began. The irony was that school was the place where both our parents felt lay the key to our future.

So at primary school in Hastings we would march around the quad while 'Sussex by the Sea' blared out over the tinny loudspeakers. We sat in class beneath a big bright picture of the young Queen Elizabeth. Once a year we made a pā out of matchsticks.

Later, at high school, anything Māori – even a matchstick pā – was gone. In its place were French and English history texts like *1066 And All That*. The history we were taught was nothing like the history I learnt at home. My classmates and I were 'streamed'. I ended up in the 'professional' class but all my relations were streamed away into the 'trades'. Nobody explained why.

As my schooling continued I became a compulsory military cadet. I went to Linton Camp for NCO training. I was also playing rugby and had the ultimate honour of being selected for the first fifteen. In Hastings Boys' High School's big annual game against Gisborne Boys' High, most of the opposition were my own Ngāti Porou relations.

My years at high school were part of a life where things were done *differently*. The school world personally wasn't difficult or too strange but, culturally and politically, it invisibilised Māori.

I doubt, however, if I would have survived the seductive power of the Pākehā world had it not been for my whānau. They were always there in good times and in bad. And the marae was there to nurture me in those Māori values, philosophies, kaupapa and histories not taught at school.

So it was that I grew up within the whānau as a Māori. The wider community of those who weren't us was simply *there*.

Then I left the whānau and headed for university. I felt the dull ache of homesickness.

Only then, as the years at university burgeoned, did I realise what that *other* world had done to our people.

That's when I realised that growing up had also been a triumph of survival as much as it had been a joyful boyhood.

Fair-skinned, Blue-eyed

MAKERE HARAWIRA

Makere Harawira was born in Christchurch in 1945. She attended Christchurch Girls High School, then married and shifted to Auckland in 1971 at the age of twenty-three. She began university studies at the University of Auckland seven years later. Her MA thesis was about the impact of colonisation on the Māori whānau, and she is now completing her PhD thesis. She is currently a part-time lecturer at Te Whare Wānanga o Awanuiarangi, Whakatāne, and the School of Māori and Pacific Development, University of Waikato. She also tutors at the School of Education, University of Auckland. She has been a keynote speaker both in New Zealand and overseas on the impact of globalisation on Māori.

*Makere Harawira wrote the piece reprinted in **Growing Up Māori** under the name Margaret Stewart-Harawira. It was a cry from the soul. Almost immediately after its publication she discovered that whakapapa actually confirmed her Māori identity and gave her back the whānau which had been wondering why it had taken her so long to find them.*

Within my family, my maternal great-grandfather was one of those who changed his name, and whose descendants, in common with many Ngāi Tahu, attempted to bury their Māori ancestry. Of his wife, also believed to be Māori, there is no trace. Growing up in Christchurch in the 1950s meant, for my sisters and me, that we had little contact with Māori. At that time Māori were virtually invisible in Canterbury. At school, we learnt that Hone Heke was a bad Māori who chopped down the flagpole, and that Māori lived in pās and wore grass skirts. Beyond this, Māori did not exist. At the age of sixteen I had a Māori boyfriend whose first question to me was to ask which tribe I came from. It was difficult for me to reconcile my mother's expressed concerns with either her Christian beliefs or my own feelings of Māoriness that had been with me since very early in my childhood. Conflict between seeing the reactions of my mother to my father's teasing that she was Māori, and my own inner sense of being Māori in some way led me to a vague notion that if indeed we were Māori it was because someone, somewhere, had 'done something wrong'. At the same time, if we were indeed Māori then it seemed that apart from my mother, I was the only one. My sisters and brother, wanting no part of things Māori, continued to hold firmly to their identity as Scots/European.

Nevertheless, my own experiences continued to affirm otherwise. Over and over again, both in my childhood and adult life, other Māori (but not all) have recognised me in some way as Māori. Despite this, it was not until my mother's death that it became clear to me that she was indeed Māori. I can no longer ignore what I know in my heart to be true but my sisters and brother continue to disassociate themselves from anything Māori, preferring to deny their Māori ancestry. And without the crucial evidence of whakapapa, it is difficult to irrefutably prove otherwise. For these reasons, during my early years I was also denied the benefits of Māori community life, being brought up within a totally Pākehā, middle-class environment. Yet on the rare occasions that opportunities to associate with Māori (such as with my cousin's wife, and when friends met in obscure places) arose, I instinctively gravitated towards those amongst whom I knew myself to be 'at home'.

Can I, a fair-skinned, blue-eyed person, whose Māori genealogy is uncertain, claim myself to be Māori, have the right to speak as a Māori? Colonisation succeeded in assimilating my forebears into the race of 'the Britons of the South Pacific'. On the basis of upbringing and genetic determination, I am unhesitatingly constructed by the majority as being non-Māori. Nonetheless, identifying myself for most of my life as a non-Māori whilst experiencing within myself an ever-increasing sense of being Māori, of being recognised by other Māori, of being haunted, if 'haunted' be the word, by dreams, by visions, by my unquestionably Māori tīpuna from the other world, I too have found it difficult to survive in either world. Why then have I in recent years had such a strong need to identify myself as Māori? And to what extent does my upbringing, appearance, and uncertain whakapapa matter?

For some authors identifying oneself within a particular ethnic group is to take a political stand. David Pearson in *A Dream Deferred:*

the Origins for Racial Conflict in New Zealand (1990), examining the 'ethnic' resurgence of the 1980s sees the reconstruction of individual and collective identities as a response to the processes of colonisation in which iwi become minority populations in their own lands. According to this argument, says Pearson, having moved from communal groupings and the experience of minority subordination, Māori are now in the process of developing an emergent ethnic group status. For many Māori, the key to their cultural or ethnic identity as Māori lies in whakapapa, that mystical element that forever links Māori, through their tīpuna, to this land. The deeply spiritual nature of the relationship of Māori to the land is seen by some as the single most unifying and meaningful factor in the development of a pan-Māori identity. The alienation of Māori land by the colonisers has been for Māori the main source of inequality within society. The Land March of 1975, the occupation of Bastion Point in 1977 and the following eviction, during which the unforgettable beauty and extreme dignity of our old people was outstandingly displayed, were, for myself and many others, key points in the development of our consciousness. Land as tūrangawaewae, a place to stand, is for Māori the source of both physical and spiritual wellbeing. It is the reason, says Terry Ryan of Ngāi Tahu, that people come through his door to discover their ancestry. Despite Pākehā constructions, whakapapa is not about what you inherit, but about who you are. As far as categorisation by blood is concerned, Ryan has this to say:

> A person with 128th-caste is just as much Ngāi Tahu as half-caste. I don't like those terms. You either have this thread of ancestry in you or you don't. You can feel it...

My involvement in issues of Māori education and in affirming my own Māori identity is not a denial of my other sources of whakapapa. It is a response both to the present-day needs of my people, and to the crying of my own soul for its identity. I have had to discard much of what I have been conditioned to accept and to take responsibility for my own learning. Nevertheless, doing so has quietened the struggle within, has eased the pain of years and brought peace in its place. It has permitted that which has been recognised in me by others of my own people.

Tīhei Mauri Ora

APIRANA TAYLOR

Apirana Taylor was born in 1955. In his biographical note he has written he is 'of Ngāti Porou, Te Whānau ā Apanui, Ngāti Ruanui and Ngāti Pākehā descent,' and that he tries to earn a living as a writer and actor.

*Apirana Taylor has published two books of short stories, **He Rau Aroha** and **Ki Te Ao**, two poetry collections, **Eyes of the Ruru** and **Soft Leaf falls of the Moon**, and a novel entitled **He Tangi Aroha**. A book of his plays is about to be published. He is presently writing more plays and thinking about writing another novel.*

> *Tīhei Mauri Ora. Tīhei i te tai ao.*
> *Tīhei i te whai ao. Tihei i te ao marama.*
> *Ā ka puta ko au he tangata. Tīhei Mauri Ora.*
> Long live the breath of life.
> The dawning of the light.
> *Tīhei Mauri Ora!*
> I am born.

The breast at night. That is what I'm sure I remember first. The ūkaipō. But I know that as I came down the path to be born there was a light on the horizon to which I made my way, though I may not have seen it. I was born a man.

I remember running into my mother's lap and curling into her warmth in the mornings as my parents lay on the bed like mountains. My mother's name was Reremoana, which means sea spray or flying over the sea.

I was born at the time of the turning of the tide. In the curved lap of the wave between high and low tide. Tai timu, tai pari. My star sign is Pisces, which is represented by two fish swimming in opposite directions. One swims upstream to the old world and the other heads downstream to the new world. This symbol is a description of my life and an apt portrayal of the times in which we live.

My mother was of Ngāti Porou, Te Whānau ā Apanui, Ngā Puhi, and Ngāti Ruanui descent. The blood of the Spanish and Portuguese and some English ran in her veins. Her maiden name was Shelford. Her mother was Te Aowaina Kirikiri. Some people called her Te Aowaina pōrangi. Which means crazy Te Aowaina. Te Aowaina spent a lot of her life riding on horseback between Gisborne and Ōpotiki. She stayed at many of the marae along the way where she had relations.

Mum told me that when she was about three she and her older brother, Charlie, were taken by Te Aowaina around the coast on horseback from Te Kaha and left in Waiomatatini, to be raised by a lady who was tough on the children. She sometimes beat them with a spade.

The elders rode over and took my mother and her brother and gave them to another woman called Riwia Fox, to raise as her whāngai. Whāngai is the Māori term for adoption or to adopt. Riwia Fox had no children but raised eighteen adopted children on her own. My mother was fond of Riwia Fox, as were all those adopted by this old lady.

After the Second World War, Mum moved from the backblocks of Ngāti Porou to Wellington. This was the time of the great Māori urban migration and she was part of it. She shifted to Pōneke, as Wellington was known to Māori in those days, in search of adventure, work and a better way of life. This urban migration is part of the pull between the old and new world which has affected Māori, and it was one of the great movements of the time in which I was born.

My mother met my father, Melvin Taylor, and our family began. Dad's parents were Salvation Army officers. My childhood was alcohol-free. Many writers and actors come from that side of the family.

We lived in a huge ramshackle house in Khandallah. In winter, wallpaper billowed out from the walls like sails filled with air, in this case, the Wellington wind. There were water stains on the ceiling and walls. The roof leaked like a shower. My father was no great handyman.

Dad worked long hours and was seldom home. When he was at home we spent a lot of time looking after him because he had terrible asthma.

Mum had a health problem although she never once complained. When she was a child someone gave her caustic soda to drink. This poison burnt inside her and her mother Te Aowaina wouldn't take her to the doctors at Te Puia because she felt the incident was the will of God. By the time someone managed to sneak Mum off to the hospital most of her throat was burnt. Consequently a lot of the inside of her throat was replaced by plastic tubing. When Mum ate she poked at her neck with her fingers and made swallowing motions, and noises, as she tried to get her food down.

A happy memory that I have of my childhood is one of our house being often filled with Māori. Many of these people were relations and were Ngāti Porou or Te Whānau ā Apanui people coming to the city as part of the Māori urban migration. There were flocks of old Māori ladies that stayed with us for a time. These old kuia were endearing characters. Some of them had traditional Māori moko on their chin. They had a sense of humour that leaves me with the memory of their wrinkled smiles and their hoots and cackling laughter.

Riwia Fox, the lady who raised my mother as a whāngai, was one of these beloved old ladies. We called her 'Nana Posh' because of the many hats she wore. Once she put on one of the hats and paraded about the room like the Queen. 'Ooo, Nana Posh,' she said, laughing at herself. From then on we called her Nana Posh. She liked lollies known as blackballs. She had a packet handy whenever we were around and if we swung off her arms and legs long enough her hand went into her pocket and out came the lollies. Nana Posh was a favourite with us.

Sometimes Mum's brother, Uncle Charlie, came to see us. He was a favourite of Mum's. He became a legend in the Māori Battalion. He got two citations and was recommended for the Victoria Cross. Charlie Shelford was a tough man. This family has produced its fair share of All Blacks, and some fine artists. As children, my brother and sisters had some strong role models to follow on both sides of the family.

During the day, when Dad was at work, my Māori relations often spoke Māori. They talked a lot about the land. I remember sitting under our kitchen table and listening to them. I said, 'Mum, talk Māori to me,' but she mainly spoke English to us children. Mum thought of

My first book opening, twenty-three years old.

herself, firstly, as Ngāti Porou. Secondly, she thought of herself as a Māori, and she probably thought of herself as a New Zealander as a poor third. At school she was smacked for talking Māori and she was taught that you had to learn the Pākehā way in order to get on in life. This was the future she probably had mapped out for us. However, Mum couldn't help but think and act Māori. We were surrounded by Pākehā culture but our house had Māori culture within it. Mum brought it with her. Our house was the only house in the street with kina soaking in the washhouse. Mum took us to many Māori hui on the marae. These hui were great occasions for huge feasts and hangis, followed by lots of talk and sporting and cultural competitions. They were sociable occasions which at times filled my life. I'm of Māori, English, Scottish, Irish, Spanish, and Portuguese descent. I've lived in palaces and gutters. I am familiar with many societies. I identify myself as Māori. That is the world I understand and love. When Pākehā people die they say they have gone to heaven. When I die my spirit will go to Hawaiki.

Sometimes Mum got a distant look in her eye and she recounted tales of the previous century's raids by the musket-bearing Ngā Puhi raiders. When I was about from four to seven years old I often thought about raising an army of revenge when I grew up and going north to destroy the Ngā Puhi. I'm glad this never happened as I'm related to many Ngā Puhi.

I became aware that I was different from many of the Pākehā children when some of them crowded around me at school. They jeered at me and chanted, '*Māori Māori do a haaaka for me. Māori Māori do a haaka for me.*' This ended by me exploding into tears and charging at my tormentors with my fists and feet flying as I tried to pummel these bullies into the ground.

The haka is in my blood. The haka is my dance and I love it. I feel driven to dance the haka.

My brother Rangimoana lived in a fantasy world during his childhood. He daydreamed about being a circus director. Once he invited other children from the neighbourhood to come and see 'THE SAVAGE MĀORI'. He persuaded about a dozen Pākehā children to come and see the show. He charged them threepence. He lined them up on the drive in front of our palisade-like gate and whacked the fence with his stick, which he wielded like a baton. This aroused three-year-old me, seated on the other side of the gate. I climbed the gate and shook it and growled *grrrrr* as I shook my fist at the petrified audience who were mortified to see me reach through the gate and try to grab them as I poked out my tongue, rolled my eyes and growled. The terrified audience gladly paid up again for another show.

Caroline, the oldest of my younger sisters, who we've always called Riwia in honour of Riwia Fox, also lived in a fantasy world for a lot of her childhood. Her room was crammed with hundreds of dolls. She played with them for years, enacting roles as she played with them. I think she was doing the best she could to hone her skills for theatre because she has gone on to be a successful director, writer, and actor. She wrote the screenplay for *Once Were Warriors*, and various successful plays.

This is what is good about my childhood. My brother and sisters played and played, and by doing this we developed our skills. We have all developed into artists – writers and actors. My youngest sister, Haina, has written one or two beautiful pieces.

My brother was one of the first Māori to graduate through the New Zealand Drama School, as it was then known. It was a monocultural drama school in those days, with nothing Māori in it except my brother. He learned theatre skills there and a few years later he brought his knowledge back to many of our people. About twenty years ago, theatre was mainly a monocultural institution, but my brother was one of the first to bring the Pākehā world to Māori theatre and vice versa. He directed a lot of plays written by emerging Māori writers, when this had seldom happened before.

After my mother died our nuclear family drifted apart. I was sent to Te Aute College. There are good and bad aspects to boarding school, but Te Aute College was good for me.

Te Aute was a small and impoverished boarding school with a brilliant and justified reputation. Trying to live up to the school's tradition forced us to seek excellence and survive and strive against the odds. At the end of my time at Te Aute it was decided I should go to university.

My siblings and I excelled at art. In about 1974 I heard Alistair Campbell read his poetry. I opted out of university the next day, for the poetry made me remember a childhood dream. I'd loved writing and that's what I wanted to do with my life. I decided to make my way through life as a poet. Materially, life has been a struggle since then.

> Nō reira, e hoa mā. Tīhei mauri ora!
> Tīhei winiwini, tīhei wanawana
> Tīhei ki te waitaki hua o Kupe.

> Friends, long live the life breath,
> the power and the force within
> the fruitful waters of Kupe.

The Politics of Contemporary Identity

JENNY TE PAA

Jenny Plane Te Paa was appointed Ahorangi of Te Rau Kahikatea at St John's Theological College, Auckland, in 1995. She was the first Māori woman and lay person appointed to such a position and, through the appointment, became one of the most influential Māori women in New Zealand.

Throughout her career, issues of social justice have been Jenny Plane Te Paa's passion. She has been a key speaker both nationally and internationally on feminist and Māori issues and on matters relating to the spiritual, economic and political position of minority peoples. Her PhD at the Graduate Theological Union/University of California (Berkeley) is on race politics and theological education. Last year she caused great debate with her outspoken challenge to the popular Māori discourses surrounding the perpetuation of stereotypical warrior images for Māori men.

1.

When I was asked to write on growing up Māori, I was confident that I could deliver. As the weeks went by and I began to think more deeply about what I could write, it became obvious that I was more preoccupied with thinking about what I should write, rather than what I could.

I recognise that this self-consciousness is symptomatic of our time and generation. It has to do with a heightened awareness of just how complex issues of race, culture, and identity politics have become. It is no longer unproblematic to simply self-identify as Māori or Pākehā. Because contemporary identity politics have become inextricably linked with economic and social justice arguments, there is, I believe, much within our popular discourse on who and what is 'authentically'

211

Māori, which now demands careful consideration and ongoing critical examination.

While I do not wish to become pedantic about true meanings, I suspect I am not alone in wanting to say at the outset that I believe myself to be still very much in the process of growing up Māori. I have not yet, by any means, arrived.

2.
E tipu e rea mō ngā rā o tōu ao ...

I was born in Kaitaia in the early 1950s. My father is Pākehā. At the time of my birth, he was working as a meteorologist at Kaitaia Airport.

My mother is Māori. Prior to my birth, she had worked as a nurse in Kaitaia, until she met and married my father and she began to have babies. I have one older brother and one younger sister. My mother is the eldest daughter of Hariata and Ephraim Te Paa from Ahipara and she has one older brother and fifteen siblings below her.

Because my father was a public servant, his work enabled him to shift around Aotearoa in pursuit of promotion and greater opportunities, so, as a child, I experienced shifting house quite regularly. All of our shifting also took us all, as a family, far away from my mother's whānau, hapū and iwi in Ahipara. Before I was eight years old, I had lived in Kaitaia, the Chatham Islands, Auckland and Wellington. My first school was May Road Primary in Mt Roskill. My second school was Kura Street Primary in Titahi Bay, Wellington.

In those early childhood years, I had no contact with marae, tangi, or hui. All I recall is having my Māori mother, and from time to time, either my Māori grandparents or many of my mother's younger brothers and sisters who regularly came to stay with us, as part of my world. The experience of having whānau to stay allowed me to develop a conscious awareness of significant difference in terms of values over money, preferences over kai, socially acceptable behaviour, language differences, and the fraught task of establishing priorities over family relationships and commitments. I began thus to develop a tentative sense of my bicultural heritage.

When we returned to Ahipara for visits with our grandparents and our aunts, uncles and cousins, we would always stay at each other's houses and, in this way, we had no need or reason to go to the marae. For most of my early childhood and virtually throughout my teenage years, I had little or no marae experience.

When I turn to consider my parents' role in nurturing me into some kind of self-awareness in terms of who I was, a number of poignant memories are evoked. Firstly, I recall that my father was always respectful of my mother as a Māori woman. My most profound emotional memory is that of witnessing my mother's deep, deep grieving every time we left Ahipara. As a little girl I could never reconcile how leaving those you love so much and who in my mind, would always be there, could be so difficult! My father always seemed quietly stoic, and yet always so reassuringly present, on those occasions.

One other important nurturing memory I have is that of my father always insisting upon the proper pronunciation of Māori words. Whenever we came across names of towns or important sites in our travels, he would tell my brother, sister and me the history as he knew it to be, and he would ensure we took special care to pronounce Māori words carefully and correctly.

My mother is very beautiful and my abiding childhood memory is of being reminded lovingly by all who encountered her, of just how beautiful she always appeared. Instinctively, I associated her beauty with her being Māori. My younger sister is very much like my mother and my older brother is physically and emotionally more like my father. As for me, I hope that by being 'in the middle' I have inherited an equal share of both my parents' looks and talents and genetic predispositions.

3.
Ko tō ringa ki ngā rākau a te Pākehā ...

Throughout my primary and secondary schooling years, although I was never taught by a Māori teacher, I recall my mother encouraging me to take pride in any school-based activity which sought to celebrate Māori language, song or history – and she also made sure I took my Māori badge for Brownies! I excelled in all I did at school, whether in sports or academic pursuits. I loved to learn, I had many, many friends, and my childhood was also rich with travel experiences throughout Aotearoa. I now realise that it was probably through this mobility that I was, in turn, blessed with regular contact with both my whānau and my Pākehā family.

When I was twelve years old my idyllic childhood was painfully disrupted. My mother was diagnosed with cervical cancer and she was unable to receive proper medical treatment in Kaikōura where my father had landed a job. My father struggled bravely to cope with raising three young children as best he could, while continuing to work full-time in order to support us economically. He insisted upon maintaining twice-weekly visits (by public transport because we had no car) from Kaikōura to Christchurch so that my brother and sister and I could all continue to be close to our mother.

On reflection, I realise that it was during this time that the cultural dichotomy represented in my bi-racial parentage became problematic. In response to my mother's illness, my Māori grandparents and a number of my Māori aunts insisted on caring, as *whānau*, for my father, brother, sister and me – they indicated a willingness to move into our home and live with us until my mother was capable of returning to full-time 'mothering'. My Pākehā grandmother also took care of our material needs by sewing and knitting clothes which she would duly deliver to us. In the meantime, my father insisted proudly and with fierce independence that he was quite capable of raising his children alone until my mother was well enough to return home. And so it was that, as a pre-pubescent girl, I recognised a longing for whānau, for the daily love of an aunt or grandmother, and for the fun-loving presence of my Ahipara uncles. Instead, because of the dominant cultural preferences of my father, I became pseudo 'little mother' to my older brother and younger sister, and together with our dad, we managed to struggle our way through the difficult years of our mother's illness.

My early teenage years were marred by the absence of my mother from my day-to-day life, and so it was, not unexpectedly, that I turned to those young people who appeared similarly bereft for solace and support. All of my best friends throughout secondary school were Māori. Kaikōura was then a small rural community whose population was clearly stratified – you were either a member of the landed gentry or 'squatocracy', or you were a 'transient'. In this latter category were, firstly, all the civil servants (police, Ministry of Works, traffic officers, meteorologists, railway workers). Second in the 'transient' category were teachers, nurses, doctors, and social workers. These were professionals who were posted to rural communities or who applied for short-term relieving positions in order to escape the increasing pressures of city life. A high percentage of railways and Ministry of Works families were Māori and thus, not surprisingly, many of my school friends were the sons and daughters of either railway workers or workers for the Ministry of Works. By and large it seemed that they were all raised in homes characterised by alcohol abuse, gambling and violence.

Although I shared nothing of the home experiences of my friends, what we had in common was an extraordinarily naïve commitment to political protest and struggle, as we understood it to be in the late 1960s. By the time we were all fifth formers, I was at a watershed point in my life; school was a site of incredible oppression, but I had no clear idea of any alternative vision. So instead, at sixteen years of age, I became 'petulantly' radicalised but without any real idea of what I sought to do or to become.

My father became very disenchanted with my increasing wilfulness, and it seemed to me that I had two choices in life: to be loyal to my friends (and therefore reject the advice of my parents), and opt for a life of limited social and economic potential; or reject my friends, take the well-meaning advice of my parents and concentrate on gaining School Certificate and University Entrance, thus being able to exercise some kind of choice about a future career, whatever I might have wanted that to be.

At sixteen years of age I found both choices impossible to reconcile and so I ran away from home in a desperate and misguided effort to strike a compromise between betraying my friends and hurting my parents. I sought to be able to pursue both a career option and to retain and strengthen an increasing sense of personal identity as a young Māori woman, who by now simply longed *to know* and *to belong*. I found it very easy to obtain work and enjoyed varied employment in Dunedin and Christchurch. My mother's brothers and sisters variously cared for me and tolerated me during my first year away from home.

A serious miscalculation in terms of naively agreeing to an intimate relationship resulted in my first pregnancy during my seventeenth year. Not unexpectedly, the father of my son soon abandoned me. Initially, I was also so deeply ashamed of my situation that I became afraid of approaching my parents for support. In the early 1970s, the social stigma attached to 'unmarried mothers' was cruelly judgemental and I greatly feared parental rejection. My fears were totally unfounded. My mother was ecstatic at the prospect of her very first mokopuna, my grandparents were enormously proud of their first great-mokopuna and my father simply 'melted' at the sight of his tiny grandson, in spite of his best efforts to assert his stern sense of English moral propriety. The birth of my son was celebrated in my whānau Māori in terms of his special status as the first-born in his generation and he remains precious in the eyes of his elders and his whanaunga because of the whakapapa position he undeniably holds.

4.
Ko tō hinengaro ki ngā taonga a ō tīpuna

As I began to be reconciled to my position as a young mother, my teenage wilfulness was strangely moderated by a powerful urge of wanting to be a model for my son, something of a life of pride – I wanted my son to be bicultural and bilingual. Out of respect for my parents and whānau I agreed to marry the father of my son, and within two years I had given birth to my beautiful daughter; my ambition to establish and sustain a 'life of pride' was thus doubly reinforced. Sadly, my first marriage was not built on any sense of shared cultural, political, social or spiritual understanding and so it ended within a few years.

In the 1970s, the impact of the Land March, the rising tide of Māori consciousness over te reo Māori, the emergence of gangs, and the inescapable presence of urban Māori protest, all contributed to an overwhelming national surge in Māori cultural pride. My own life became passionately focused on pursuing knowledge and understanding of those things Māori which I felt I had experienced only superficially as a child. To my surprise and delight, my mother joined me in learning to speak Māori. Together we joined the Māori Women's Welfare League, we began to work with our local marae committee, and we began to ask our kaumātua and kuia questions about our whakapapa, our own tribal background, the history of our marae and the history of our own hapū and iwi. It was only much later that I realised that my increasingly profound sense of cultural loss was an experience also shared by my mother, and that it had arisen for us both out of a complex web of social interactions and political decisions *within* which we had participated as individuals and *to* which we were both inevitably subjected, as members of our most socially, politically, culturally and economically marginalised minority group – Māori women.

I enrolled at university and began to study Māori as an academic subject, I moved to Auckland in order to be closer to my whānau, hapū and iwi base in Ahipara, and I have maintained very close involvement in marae and Māori church work in Auckland and around the country. I secured employment in a range of positions – each one specifically focused in one way or another on Māori development. I worked as Māori Social Worker, Advisor to the Vocational Training Council, Māori Advisor to the Labour Department, Māori Counsellor at Auckland Polytechnic and Māori Advisor to Auckland City. I was appointed to various statutory and community-based positions in order to represent Māori interests. These included the Lotteries Board; the government's first Women's Advisory Committee; the Parole Board; the Medical School Admissions Panel; government working committees on Tertiary Education and Justice Reforms – the list is almost endless. The experience was utterly invaluable in terms of the extensive range and depth of knowledge I was able to gain, the relationships I was privileged in establishing and nurturing and, above all, in that these multiple experiences enabled me to develop and sustain enormous personal and professional confidence in all I was asked or expected to do.

The focus of all my work throughout this time was on redemptive justice. I always saw my role as being educative of both Pākehā (who needed Treaty information and knowledge in order to reconcile an understanding of why Māori grievance at historic injustice was so prevalent and so insistent) and Māori (who also needed Treaty information and knowledge in order to ensure Treaty grievances were addressed fairly and realistically, and were able to be settled in a way that was respectfully cognisant of the past but was appropriate to contemporary circumstances). It seemed to me that in order for restorative justice to work, there first had to be a factual understanding of past injustice, an acceptance of responsibility for that injustice, a gesture of repentance, a seeking of forgiveness and thus a freeing of the bonds of guilt and oppression which would allow a movement toward negotiating a collective or mutual commitment toward restorative justice.

5.
Ko tō wairua ki te Atua ...

Since the late 1980s I have worked mainly in tertiary-level education; for the past eight years I have worked in tertiary and community-based theological education. I completed a Bachelors degree in Theology and a Masters degree in Education and am currently working on my PhD through the Graduate Theological Union in Berkeley, California.

Over the past five years or so, I have become increasingly concerned as an educator at the way in which 'Māori issues' are now popularly and, in the main, rhetorically represented throughout mainstream, private and alternative forms of education. An unhelpful oppositional discourse informed and sustained by racial rhetoric is now prevalent and the resultant polarity between Māori and Pākehā (and between Māori and Pacific Island people and other later migrant peoples) is a direct and inevitable result of this uncontested ideological development. I yearn for the introduction of a more balanced and more deeply considered moral discourse to the 'race' debates which now pervade the public arena.

6.
Nāna nei ngā mea katoa

Throughout these past five or so years I have noticed a certain 'mellowing out' in terms of my own perspectives on what it means to 'be Māori' and an increasing willingness to evaluate myself in terms of my original desire to live a life of pride. I realise that more than anything else I want to be able to live my life as a decent citizen of this land of my birth. I believe myself to be as equally precious and deserving as every other person in the world. I want to live my life in a worthy and dignified manner – to be generous to my neighbours (whoever they happen to be), to be compassionate enough to care for those who suffer in our communities (whoever they happen to be), to be willing to take a stand for justice (for whoever it is who is being oppressed), and to do all of these things with boldness (if my actions are to indeed make a difference) and yet with humility, because I recognise it is the gift of being fully human that enables me to be so alive and so active in the world. It is my secondary defining characteristics of being Māori, of being Pākehā, of being woman, of being 'straight', of being single, and of being young, which are of peculiar, rather than significant, importance.

I have found it easiest to describe something of my story by thinking of the most profound memories I have of growing up Māori, though, in doing so, I recognise that I have of necessity, and doubtless for self-protection, been selective in my choosing of what information I wish to share and what I choose to withhold. I have also described some events somewhat more superficially than I might otherwise have done for such a 'close' community of readers. I have not struggled with any piece of writing quite as markedly as I have with this one, but I offer it without reservation in the hope that what is familiar to readers might prove reassuring, and that what is provocative might be a source of renewed conversation among those of us who seek not to dominate others but to establish and to nurture loving human relationships of mutuality and interdependence.

He aha te mea nui o tēnei ao hurihuri? – he tangata, he tangata, he tangata.

Post-modern Māori

ANTON BLANK

Anton Blank was born in 1962 and is of mixed Swiss and Māori ancestry. His Māori affiliations include Ngāti Porou, Ngāti Kahungunu, Rongowhakaata and Te Aitanga ā Mahaki. He attended Birkdale College, North Shore, and has completed a BA at the University of Auckland.

Anton Blank has spent most of his career in social services. He is currently employed doing media work for the Children, Young Persons and Their Families Service in Auckland.

I've lost count of the number of workshops and tutorials I've survived where the question *du jour* has been, 'What is culture?' It is a question that seems to bring out the worst anxieties and resentment in Pākehā, and sends Māori running for tradition so that we can say, 'We're still spiritual, we've still got these superior values despite what you've done to us, keha.'

I'm still amazed at how few Pākehā have a good grip on their culture. They seem to have a fundamental resistance to recognising a collective identity. Perhaps it is because there are parts of their culture they don't like, so it's easier to say, 'That doesn't represent me.' Maybe they are fearful of losing their right to individuality. Even when they reach some sort of agreement on what makes their culture tick, it is provisional, so that when they feel fucked off with it they still have the option of disowning it. They treat culture like a thing.

As for Māori, we are still trapped by romantic notions of an authentic Māori identity – as if there ever was one – failing to recognise how many of our own we alienate when we talk like that. I'm no more sure about Māori traditions than any Pākehā is about their customs of yore. I've willingly rubbed shoulders with the oppressor too long to claim

With Mum, Dad and my sister Marino.

that it's all been imposed, that I haven't made any choices, that my culture isn't hybrid.

I was born in 1962 to a Ngāti Porou mother and a Swiss father. Those were the days in which people came up with ridiculous equations to measure their Māoriness, and an indigenous great-grandparent meant you could proudly claim you were an eighth Māori. Kids like me spent most of their childhood being called half-caste.

My main reference point for being Māori is Mum. She is Arapera Blank, née Kaa, and she was raised in Rangitukia, which is a small village at the mouth of the Waiapū River. Rangitukia probably catches the sun before Mount Hikurangi, and a few high profile Ngāti Porou come from there – so, despite its size, it is a significant place. With typical Ngāti Porou conceit, Mum never tired of reminding us when we were young that we had an impeccable pedigree, and the Kaas were nothing less than venerable and colourful role models.

Mum and Dad were teaching at Panguru Area School when I was born, so Ngā Puhi was also there during my early years. Dad used to love telling the story of how the matron at Rawene Hospital announced my arrival. Alluding to my size, she told Dad over the phone that his wife had given birth to a rugby player. Matron made a resounding misjudgement – my sissy childhood was spent playing hopscotch with my sister Marino, and wishing I had my own dolls to play with.

Mum worked almost immediately after I was born. I still bump into Ngā Puhi who were taught by Mum and Dad, or who had a hand at baby-sitting. We lived right next to the school, and the students used to collect Marino and me during their breaks and cart us around the netball courts. There were lots of warm kitchens with wood-fire stoves that we treated as our second home. We felt like the community's kids, and there was always someone looking out for us.

Our parents' liberal views, and their status in the community, also set me and Marino apart, however. The Catholic church and convent gaze down on Panguru, but Marino and I were the only children who didn't attend religious instruction at our all-Māori primary school. Our parents wanted us to make our own choices about religion, and during God's time we went to the teacher's house for a salad lunch. We were labelled Pākehā by the other kids at school, and I don't think it was supposed to be a compliment. That is my first and most vivid memory of thinking about being Māori. I felt like I was and I wasn't.

When we moved to Beach Haven on Auckland's North Shore, Marino and I became more aware of our bohemian parents. They were both creative. Mum was the first Māori to win a Katherine Mansfield award, for an essay she wrote on capitalism and Māori, and she continued to write when she came to the city. I remember how, one frosty morning, when Mum was taking Marino and me to school, she burst into a recital of Keats's *Ode to Autumn* as we turned the corner from Beach Haven onto Birkdale Road. My favourite piece of hers is a poem called *He Koingo/ A Yearning.* It is a sexy, erotic ode to my father I suspect, and it aches with desire. Mum and Dad were passionate about one another.

Dad was a photographer when he met Mum. He and a friend

promised each other that they would never marry Swiss women – a story which I once rudely recounted to a dining room table full of stony-faced Swiss hosts. I suspect that Dad was enchanted by the romantic idea of a Polynesian bride. The family home is still cluttered with black and white photos that Dad took many years ago, including the odd nude of Mum. Mum could be quite prudish about that. There was one nude silhouette of Mum that Dad swore no one could recognise, and visitors would inevitably ask when they saw it, 'Is that you, Arapera?' I think Mum's conservative rural upbringing meant she would have preferred that people remained clothed – but honeymoon photos reveal a blissfully happy couple frolicking on a Coromandel beach without a stitch.

Dad bought a tiny cottage overlooking the sea, and spent almost every weekend making or planning alterations. He was obsessive about it and there were always 'things to do'. The house eventually rambled in different directions with rooms that were panelled with teak or rimu. There was a sauna in the master bedroom, and a Swiss flag fluttered at the front of the house. Dad never truly assimilated. His Germanic accent is thick even now, and on a good day he sounds like Victor Borge. Eric and Schiscka Schwimmer used to come for lunch.

Marino and I delighted in Mum and Dad's eccentricities. There were always stories and letters from our Māori side and our other tūrangawaewae in Europe. Our parents helped us look at the world in different ways. The home was alive with ideas, and we were taught to have a social conscience. Mum and Dad may have been fringe but they were also moral people. 'That's not on' was one of Dad's many over-used expressions.

As the tables of our relationship turn and Marino and I begin to take more responsibility for both of them, I've realised how they instilled the importance of family into us. It may be about whānau but those values are as much about Dad as Mum.

There was almost no validation of being Māori at high school. There was no one on the radio telling us it was 'cool to kōrero'. When I was a senior pupil, the school built a marae, and began to offer te reo. I was in an academic class with one other Māori classmate, and had been learning French and German since Form Three. Once a year there would be a survey of students and I would dutifully answer the questions as a Māori student. I felt ambivalent about this responsibility and hated being singled out in front of my Pākehā classmates.

In and out groups were determined by sport, and I suffered the weekly humiliation of being the last to be picked for team games. I was also painfully aware of the fact that I was queer, and I spent lunchtimes gazing longingly at senior boys in grey drill shorts that were tight around their thighs.

When, many years later, Mum and I confronted my sexuality together, I discovered that for Māori whānau every sperm is sacred. 'It wasn't uncommon for men to sleep with one another before the colonisers came,' Mum declared. When they went to the trenches to fight, they were tapu and had to remain untainted by women, she explained. 'Be that as it may, they all returned to the village to procreate,' Mum pronounced like a full stop as she peered at me over her glasses. I've never been too sure where Mum got that fable from.

Mum has always been a funny jumble of the old and new. She taught with gay men and lesbian women for years, and I think she garnered their respect. But my coming out was more painful for her than it was for me. There was a point at which I had to say to her, 'I've explained as much as I understand, Mum, and now it's up to you.'

Dad became increasingly reclusive as he got older – a trait I've noticed in Europeans. My *tantes* in Switzerland virtually never leave their flats. Someone comes to collect their mail for posting, and they have their groceries delivered – it's as if the outside world becomes too much for them to cope with. It is almost the opposite for Māori, who want more people around them as they get older. As Dad retreated, it became increasingly difficult for Mum to express herself at home. She could not have whānau there. That was tantamount to spiritual starvation, and the conflict was at times unbearable.

Mum coped by living her life away from home. She was involved in the Māori Women's Welfare League and the Māori Writers' and Artists' Society. She would attend whānau gatherings unaccompanied, leaving Marino and me at home with Dad. We were unwittingly caught up in his isolation. On those occasions when Mum did take us with her to different events, I felt awkward, and resented the way in which she would expect us to know the rules and perform. I still feel my back arch when at thirty-five I'm told, 'Say hello to your aunty.'

I think I understand how Mum's generation suffered -- the messages they were given about the power of White education, and the way in which they were forbidden to speak te reo. Like many Māori who went to the city to be educated, our branch of the Kaa whānau has favoured mixed marriages. But it still seems strange that they didn't just fail to pass tradition down to their children: they actively excluded us from it. At our house te reo was used for coded telephone conversations and secrets. I know virtually no middle-class Māori of my generation fluent in te reo, and yet our elders delight in taking the piss out of us for our honky ways.

If I have implied any regret at missing out on things Māori, it is momentary dissatisfaction. I don't feel like half a Māori. I get bored with the authenticity debate, and that simplistic search for an equation of values that equals Māori. Tradition doesn't own my generation like it does our parents – those days are gone.

My whakapapa means that I am Māori, and from there I determine what it means for me. It is an intellectual and political exercise, and I am informed by values and beliefs that circulate outside Te Ao Māori as well as within it. I feel powerful and free because my definitions are not finite.

Māori have made, and continue to make, conscious and considered choices about who we are in this post-modern context. We have resisted and adopted other cultures and that means our Māori-ness has become more enigmatic, more confusing in a way – a blend of authentic and inauthentic representations.

I don't believe that our identity is innate: rather, we construct it. There is no truth about Māori any more. There is only discourse.

Growing Up Half-caste

ALAN DUFF

Alan Duff is the acclaimed author of **Once Were Warriors** *(1990), surely one of the most important novels ever to come out of New Zealand; its sequel,* **What Becomes of the Broken Hearted?** *(1996) won the fiction section of the Montana Book Awards and confirmed Alan Duff's status as one of New Zealand's leading writers. His other books are* **One Night Out Stealing** *(1992),* **Māori: The Crisis and the Challenge** *(1993) and* **State Ward** *(1994).*

Alan Duff is also a newspaper columnist and scriptwriter. **Once Were Warriors** *(the film) became a national and international hit. Alan Duff is working on future film projects.*

Of Ngāti Rangitihi and Ngāti Tūwharetoa descent, Alan Duff lives in Havelock North.

1.

I DIDN'T grow up Māori, I didn't grow up New Zealander (though I thought I was); I grew up half-caste, and half-caste Māori at that. Born in 1950 to a country with a seeming fixation with grading its people into measurements of one-sixteenth bits of Māori blood – you were never asked on official forms to state the amount of European blood – it rapidly dawned on us at school that there was a separation, even though it wasn't at all plain in the playground. I was actually seven-sixteenths Māori, which put me near enough to the halfway mark. Kids exchanged the number of sixteenths they were and certain Pākehā kids proudly proclaimed they were 'pure'. The part-Maoris of various divisions of sixteenths had no choice but to retort with physical assertion that they were 'tougher'. Which they generally were. (Except,

226

I later found out, being physically tough is not remotely the same as being successful.)

I didn't grow up Māori, even though in all my school classes, at primary level in particular, I was considered one. I just grew up as I thought I was, another New Zealander, with a Māori mother and a Pākehā father. We all ate roasts and loved lamb chops and had weetbix or porridge for breakfast, marmite or meat paste in our school lunch sandwiches; we played rugby, softball, did athletics together; we were New Zealanders together. That my own household was proving to be dramatically different to most others still had little bearing on my perception of what I assumed I was growing up as.

At school, on official forms, a seven-sixteenths Māori. In real life, just another kid.

I do have a distinct and hurtful memory of having Pākehā twin brothers as my standard four playmates and going to their house to play for the first time. Their mother blocked me on the footpath and informed me coldly she didn't want her children playing with Maoris. I trudged home feeling the heaviest hearted Māori in Rotorua and wishing I wasn't one.

At the end of that year I was awarded school dux. I was a straight first in virtually every subject, these twins in the top ten somewhere. That night my European father received a telephone call from the twins' mother, inviting me to a pre-Christmas party, throwing in her congratulations that I was dux. He knew of my incident with her and he told her that if I wasn't good enough back then, I wasn't good enough now. And he hung up on her. So racists were alive and well back then but of course my father being the same race as this woman, and several of my best friends, it was reassurance that my country didn't all hate Maoris or part-Maoris.

That incident aside, racism was hardly a factor in our growing up. There were social differences, so the doctors' and lawyers' kids probably played with their middle-class own and they were definitely white. But the country was overwhelmingly egalitarian then, so the professional class were in the tiny minority. Besides, enough of these perceived 'rich kids' played rugby in our teams for it to hardly matter. In fact, I have memories of poor whites in our area who were teased more than anyone just for having no money when the rest of us had little.

I grew up in a parental situation of such contrast it bothers me that I might not be as objective as I would like. Links could be made and were made to the differences between Māori and Pākehā outlook. My father was a university-educated man of logic and highest order rationality and a man of non-violence. He never hit us as I recall. His brother was a renowned museum director and internationally respected anthropologist. Another brother was a university lecturer. His father was a famous former newspaper and journal editor, having held the first *Listener* editorship and, by the time I was old enough to appreciate it, recipient of an OBE for services to journalism in times when an "Oh Bee Ee" meant serious achievement.

My mother, on the other hand, was her husband's stark opposite: volatile, unreasonable, a bad drunk, violent, a gambler, a partyer, an altogether selfish and irresponsible wife and mother who didn't, in her own legendary words, 'give a fuck' – meaning about whatever responsibility you tried to thrust upon her, if she so chose. She had sisters who had more than their share of being as bad as she was, especially with the drink. And all of us cousins saw that their Māori parents had in common a virtual total dismissal of children unless the child was in the 'pet' or 'favourite' category.

We saw that Māori kids got regular hidings where Pākehā kids hardly knew of the word, let alone the experience. In my household, we half-caste children couldn't help growing up making comparisons between the two races' differing attitudes to alcohol and children. Nor could we help noticing that our Māori relatives were violent and explosive as a matter of daily life whilst we did not see a single incident of violence nor explosive outburst by any of our Pākehā relatives. Which is what bothers me about my objectivity. It at least means I have to fight hard to find truth.

But I happen to have lived the years in long and careful observation, experiencing life on 'the other side' first-hand, the life that I saw around me as my downward spiral continued, dominated by Māori faces. If the majority of inmates being Māori in the range of penal institutions I served custody in can be read as an undeniable Māori social and behavioural indicator, then my experiences and subsequent observations have validity. An avid newspaper reader, I have been unable to deny the glaringly obvious fact that Maoris are more prone to violence, more likely to commit crimes, more prone to educational failure, and therefore more likely to figure in every poor statistic – almost as if it is a pre-ordained fate.

I happen to have written the novel that begat the superb film adaptation, the story of a dysfunctional Māori family that got read by hundreds of thousands and seen by probably two-thirds of the country, that gained me the feedback from everyone, including Māori, that this story was all too tragically true and typical for too many Maoris. So some of my observations must have been right: that some people grow up in a certain manner that is hard-wired to almost certain failure; and that those people are prevailingly Māori, is simple fact. Simple awful fact if you're a child born into this legacy. And it needn't be. It *musn't* be.

2.

But of course I have memories of my Māori relations singing in beautiful harmony and being loving to their children. Of course I have memories of Māori humour, Māori self-deprecation that has you splitting your sides with laughter. I treasure my rugby memories of extraordinary natural Māori talent turning defence into most exciting, innovative attack. I have funny memories of a lighted cigarette being slipped to our fullback during a game and him taking a catch with a fag in his mouth! I remember every tangi as if for the first time, those ornately carved surrounds, the dignity of the people, the proud male elders taking their turn to rise and orate, the senior women joining their elders in a waiata, the loving embrace of the bereaved and the sharing of grief, the brilliant and subtle martial movements in an elder's speeching posture, and the uplifting experience of an entire funeral gathering singing hymns that remains one of life's most vivid memories for me. One day the same shall resonate at my tangi.

But I would not be telling the whole truth if I did not mention my concern that, as the years have gone by, so many of my people, so many of my peers, have not come to much in life, when as youngsters they had no equals. Not on the rugby paddock or at any sport or at singing and at simply being freely expressive beings. And most had intelligence enough to suggest they could have gained and aspired higher occupationally. But where are they occupationally? Where are they in this modern life? Why have they been left behind?

There is a stark and fundamental difference of thinking, of outlook, of life attitude that few are honestly addressing. One race, the European, has in its entrenched thinking, job, money, material goals, more clearly defined values, a better desire for life satisfaction and quite frankly more drive. The other, Māori, has far less specific and too few goals, Every occupational trade and profession is covered by Europeans, whilst Maoris dominate manual labour and the unemployed ranks. We have a new breed of Māori that has emerged from the welfare and hand-out periods; places like Waikato University are churning out Māori graduates (in Māori Studies, too many?) with their heads stuffed full of angry, 'We're victims' rhetoric. Bristling with wounded indigenous people's anger that we have been hard done by. Modern-day so-called intellectual warriors trained and ready-primed to add their thrusting hands, demanding the country pay its tithe to the tangata whenua for simply being Māori. This breed will take us nowhere. This is not what we want to become. It's an outcome of my generation, more than any, growing up being what we shouldn't. Our leadership is an extension of our lazy thinking, of wanting much for little and being precious while they're at it. Too few Maoris are looking at their problems with an honest and necessarily brutally frank eye. A race that has little regard for analysis, and an aversion to criticism, is a race that cannot solve its own problems.

I want the Māori Fairy Godmother to bless her people with some fundamental values: a reverence for knowledge, for education therefore. A work ethic. A set of life goal values. And keep the love, retain the natural dignity, glory in the humour, delight in the lateral thinking, keep as much of the culture as possible – but throw out the oppressive, the sexist, the elitist attitudes. Be proud to be Māori, but more proud to be New Zealander. That's how my children are growing up.

Finding a Place in the World

CLIVE ASPIN

Clive Aspin (Ngāti Maru) was born in Waiuku and brought up in his tribal area of Hauraki. He was a teacher for twenty years, working in Sydney, London, Paris and Algeria, as well as New Zealand. He returned to university in his forties and completed postgraduate studies in Applied Linguistics. After working as a Māori policy analyst for two years, he moved to the Wellington School of Medicine and took up a lectureship in Māori Health. He is currently living in Nice with his partner and son where he is completing his PhD in Public Health.

My grandmother always used to tell me never to marry a Māori. My mother told me never to marry before the age of twenty-eight. And when I went off to boarding school my aunt insisted that all the brothers were 'queer' as she put it, and I should always be on my guard in case one of them tried to have his way with me. When I look back now it is obvious that there were powerful forces at work trying to turn me into a pale heterosexual replica of the Pākehā side of my heritage. The unspoken message was that the Māori side of our heritage should be downplayed so that future generations would eventually be able to put it firmly behind them.

Throughout my childhood I received a multitude of confusing messages about the two most important strands of my identity, the cultural and the sexual. It would take years of torment, a string of broken hearts and thousands of miles of travel before I was able to untangle the confusion and accept myself fully as a Māori gay man with every right to stand proud as a member of my whānau, Māori society and the wider community. For most of my adult life I have struggled to find my rightful pace within society and now, as I approach my fiftieth year, I have a clearer understanding of the special ways in which I am able to contribute to the development of our community.

I grew up in a family of four boys, one girl, two parents and numerous aunts, uncles and cousins. Overseeing all this were two strong matriarchs, my grandmother on my father's side and my nana on my mother's side. Occasionally they would meet but most of the time each of them reigned separately and imposed their own particular characteristics on proceedings. My father's mother, Grandma, was serene and much admired. She went to church regularly and encouraged her children and their children to do the same. Holidays at Grandma's always involved weekly attendance at church, the part of the holiday I enjoyed least.

Nana was a totally different kettle of fish. Although no one really spoke about it we all knew that she'd had three husbands. And then, years later, someone let on that she hadn't actually been married to the last one even though she'd had two sons to him. It seemed that there was a lot of shame around Nana's life. As a child, whenever I went out with Nana, I could see people staring at us from all directions. She had lost the use of her left eye when she'd looked at an eclipse as a young girl and I was convinced that this was why people looked at us. Her eye was the physical manifestation of all the things about Nana that made her appear to be different.

But most important of all, Nana was a Māori. For me as a child this was the most difficult thing to understand. She was proud of her own Māori heritage but, like everyone in those days, she believed the way to success was to be found in the Pākehā world. The Māori dimension could serve no possible value and she, along with all my other relations, impressed upon us the need to emphasise the Pākehā side of our heritage and to forget about the Māori side.

Nana had lived in Auckland most of her life and only came back to her ancestral land of Hauraki in her latter years. Even though she was in her seventies it was as if she had found a new lease of life. She loved going into Thames, where she would always run into old friends from her past, people she had known when she was growing up on the Coromandel, when the only connection with the big city was by boat or horse. She used to talk about the time when she'd ridden a horse all the way from Coromandel to Auckland. In her lifetime, Nana had witnessed the first aeroplane flight, as well as, years later, the landing on the moon. I often marvel at the changes that she had seen in her seventy-odd years. And on top of all this she had to adapt to all the changes within Māori society. One of my greatest regrets is that she wasn't around to see the development of the kōhanga reo movement because I'm sure that she would have become thoroughly involved in it. Towards the end of her life she seemed to seek out opportunities to use te reo. Whenever she ran into her friends from the past they would immediately turn to Māori as their language of choice. For her, it was the most natural thing to do, especially after years of city living where she hardly ever came across anyone with whom she could speak Māori.

In her latter years, however, she did find a passion which became all-consuming. She dredged into the recesses of her mind and recalled the locations and names of land that had been in our family and which had been occupied by our forebears. And then she took her information to the Māori Land Court and got them to record her name on legal deeds so that future generations could identify with ancestral land. And it was during this process that her skill in the Māori language came to the fore. She struggled with the bureaucracy and did it all in the Māori language. Although she may not have passed the language on to her children, she did use it to leave a legacy that is of equal importance and just as enduring. If it had not been for her efforts, our rights to live on ancestral land might have been lost forever.

Before she died, Nana arranged to be laid to rest with our ancestors on the pā that overlooks our river, the Waihou. Her actions throughout her life emphasised the importance of our links with the land, the greatest message that she has left for me personally. I was brought up in this area and it is to this part of Aotearoa that I feel most attached. Because of her example, I can now say with confidence that this is where I belong. During all the years that I have travelled around the world it is to the land of Hauraki that my mind turns when I yearn for home. And I know that that is where I will rest, along with my Nana, when my time comes.

Nana gave me the confidence to identify as Māori. I regret that I didn't learn the language from her but, with hindsight, I fully under-stand the social pressures around me that allowed that to happen. As an adult I have made efforts to rectify that shortfall. I often wonder what it would be like to be able to converse with her in Māori. I grew close to her in her latter years and I'm sure that being able to speak Māori with her would have brought us even closer together.

As an adult I have sought out opportunities to deepen my understanding of my Māori ancestry. Over recent years, my professional work has brought me into close contact with other Māori people and this has had a profound effect on my personal identity. I have received boundless amounts of support from my Māori friends and colleagues and this has given me the strength and confidence to persevere in my chosen work within the area of Māori health. Above all, it has helped me to feel more and more linked to the land of Aotearoa.

Just as I had to leave New Zealand to discover how important this land is to my identity as a Māori, so too did I have to leave home to understand fully the other important strand of my person, the sexual. Throughout my life the cultural and the sexual have been closely intertwined. But growing up in New Zealand in the 1950s and 1960s wasn't really ideal for developing a sense of self-worth, either from a Māori point of view or a gay one. Like many others in the same situation, I left New Zealand in the 1970s to escape the prejudices and narrow-minded attitudes that sought to impose tight parameters around the way that people lived their lives. The anonymity of places like London, Paris and North Africa provided the perfect context in which to explore my sexuality without having to face the scrutiny of family, neighbours and colleagues.

I returned to New Zealand in the early 1980s after almost ten years of travelling the world. I tasted the delights of romantic Paris. I danced at Heaven in London where I was seduced by music, men and drugs. And I sampled the Maghrebian pleasures that I'd only ever read about in chronicles written by the likes of André Gide and Oscar Wilde. My Māori identity had taken a back seat but my sexual identity had been given full vent. I returned home determined never again to hide my true identity from anyone.

And now I can't help feeling that my timing was impeccable. Like thousands of other gay men who'd left home to find their way in the world, I had no idea at all that the communities we were creating were slowly becoming contaminated by a deadly virus. In 1983, I returned to New Zealand and to a gay community that had the strength to take on the responsibility of spreading information about how to remain safe from AIDS. In contrast, Paris, from which I had returned, has been ravaged by the AIDS epidemic and I wonder what the consequences would have been if I had stayed longer.

Now, in the 1990s, I have become a father and my greatest hope is that my son will grow strong and sure of his rightful place in the world. Essential to this is a full understanding of his heritage. As he grows into maturity, I want to ensure that he has the confidence to choose from all the options before him. My greatest hope is that he will be surrounded by love, acceptance and tolerance, so that he will never feel the need to leave home in order to find himself.

Made in Hamilton

JOANNA PAUL

This one's for those among you who don't speak Māori, can't swing a poi properly or who aspired to but never could do the haka.

Joanna Paul was born in 1962. She is a household name, having been for many years one of New Zealand's leading television presenters and a correspondent for 60 Minutes, One Network News and 3 National News. Behind the cameras, Joanna Paul is an accomplished producer and director of national and international documentaries and dramas, with sixteen years' industry experience. This includes the highly acclaimed **Te Manuka** *series, a wildlife series for the Natural History Unit in Dunedin and more recently* **A Work of Art** *written and directed by her.*

Among other achievements, Joana Paul has spent the past two years writing freelance for the **New Zealand Woman's Weekly** *and on the Internet. She has published her first book, lectured in media studies, fronted media campaigns, and is a public relations consultant with her own consultancy.*

Affiliated with Ngāi Te Rangi, Joanna Paul now lives in Auckland.

Well, the first thing to say is that I'm *still* growing up Māori. A lot has changed since it was first and rather cruelly pointed out to me that I was 'different, coloured and apparently dirty' because I was a hori – a not so nice term out of the mouths of some kids in my home town. I've felt unclean and ashamed, then confused and wondering; I've been angry and proud, envious, struggling – and now I'm just starting to feel a little more comfortable. I guess at thirty-six it's about time I felt more comfy with the colour of my soul. Nevertheless, the question of growing up Māori has sent me ricocheting back to a shaky past.

Hamilton in the 1960s was a funny town, a city bristling with its own pride and self-importance. It was pretentious, really puffed up by the consequence of developing a brand new university, a place of higher learning and intellectual greatness on one of its very few hills. It had turned its back on the mighty Waikato River and glared inwards on itself. Its inhabitants suffered much the same fate. At the age of five I was suffering mostly from ignorance.

My neighbourhood was made up of plain squat houses set on wide streets. Almost every house seemed like a replica of the one before: single level dwellings, in realty-speak, with three bedrooms, a modest lounge, separate kitchen that oozed into the dining room, and large flat sections broken up with whatever took their owner's fancy. Anything more could be considered ostentatious and spelt bouts of whispered gossip about what really went on in richer folks' homes. The petty politics of the street meant everyone knew your business. Well, most of it anyway.

My parents would harp on about the white trash across the road. Or the scum up the street we were only to go near if we wanted to catch some incurable, and at that time, unnamed disease. Or the dirty little Māori kids around the corner we weren't meant to associate with at all. My parents had *standards* and went to great lengths to have us girls done up right. Early photos show three little poppets all dressed exactly the same. Their hair is either pulled so tightly back off their faces it left a sheen on their taut skin, or tortured into long ringlets. Our shoes wore a similar gloss and our dresses bore the handmade-with-love mark.

By the time I was six the only thing I ever really noticed about myself was the gap where my two front teeth should have been – and the freckles liberally spread from bed to breakfast across a round and strange face. I knew it was my *face* staring back at me, but it was still mysterious. After all, I had really only started to get to know it.

Ironically it was the part-Māori boy who lived behind us who first set me to notice more about my face. On the way home from school one day he taunted me as usual by trying to push me off the footpath and yanking my dress up. Suddenly his parents jumped out of his mouth: 'Ya dirty little Maari. Don't touch me, ya blackie.' I'd heard them shout that sometimes when all hell broke loose at their house and knew it was an offensive thing to say. It spelt mean voices raised in anger and booze. It meant trouble – and here it was being spat out of his mouth at me. I felt stung, and although stings are sharp and

Five years old, Hamilton, 1967.

temporary, this just *stabbed* at me. It went straight through my clothes and my skin and even the layers I had built up to withstand an over-bearing real world. Then it wound itself around my heart and squeezed it hard.

What did he mean 'Ya blackie'?

I wasn't black at all. I was *Joanna*. It was *me*.

I was too stunned to cry.

Another lesson came my way at Intermediate School. I learnt French. All the top stream kids did. And why, you might ask, way down here at the arse end of the world, were the bright young things learning a foreign language? That's the question I asked myself when I got to high school and, without an adequate explanation, I opted out of French. I asked to be enrolled in Māori Language instead.

What a turnaround. I went from a class of lively, popular, inquiring little minds, where my skin colour waved like a flag before me each day, to a class of the same colour, only most of them had been told they were dummies for so long they'd started to believe the education kit PR. If you were brown and you couldn't make your mind up about the subject choice you were handed Māori. After all, it's got to be one subject you can pass, right? You *are* that colour, right?

This ignorant piece of logic saw many struggle through a new linguistic field, confirming their deepest fear that even when they were the 'right' colour for a subject, they were still going to flunk it. Being Māori wasn't getting them anywhere. I watched the hurt develop over my five years in high school. It turned into anger, then resignation, then defiance – and who can blame them. Even now my head throbs just to ponder on the injustice of those arrogant and insensitive people in charge. What made them think a skin colour could make it easier to learn a language most of us had only heard in snatches from parents and kin who had been beaten for speaking their mother tongue? Stupid, stupid people.

That was the start of my angry phase.

I got 'divorced' many times over at that high school. The separations were partings caused directly by growing up Māori. At Intermediate School I had formed some friendships with children who could happily overlook my colour because of my intellectual abilities, coupled with an unhealthy need to be liked, but in High School my Māori subject option was irrefutable confirmation of my skin colour and much too hard to ignore. With some friends the parting was polite and I knew they were uncomfortable with it. With other kids it was a swift and painful alienation. For instance, I was put firmly in my place repeatedly by one thoughtless hormone-inspired boy. In a packed play quad he kept asking me if '*That's* what happened on a pā?' or tell me to, 'Go home to your pa.'

I still hate that boy.

Ironically, I suppose I'd hoped to find new *real* friends within the Māori group. Sadly, I made only two, both of whom were more like me – a little alienated in their own ways, with dysfunctional families and a foot in other worlds. If ever I tried to muck in, it was inevitably a disaster.

For instance, the first time I joined the school's Māori cultural group turned out to be the last.

Sweating and shuffling into the gym where every word echoed like a tomb, we set about learning the first poi song. I wasn't quite like the other girls – they all wore their uniforms rakishly because, I guess, there was no other way to wear third-hand clothing. Their socks had holes in them and their black hair sprung from their heads untamed by brush or comb.

The bigger boys all fought for a place on the sporting fields and those ones looked down on their own Māori girls, preferring to hang a white chick off either bulging bicep. The stouter, shorter, brown boys all looked like jail bait and acted as tough as one could in High School, in the seventies.

Then there was me, a short, brown, fresh-faced girl, still desperately wanting to be liked. I was anal and uptight, well groomed and, after years of ballet, poised and pompous. I may as well have been green, not brown.

The murmurs started the moment they called 'wiri', a call for a delicate quivering motion of the hand, and a cornerstone of waiata-ā-ringa. Except that I couldn't do it. As hard as I tried, my hand would *not* quiver. It shook in a slow and disconnected way, back and forth like a naughty uncontrollable piece of blubber. This was not a 'wiri' and my colleagues knew it.

The final humiliation came the moment the pois were raised. I had seen the other girls practising at lunchtime, twirling and giggling and swaying their hips. I couldn't join them though because they weren't my friends, so I walked stiffly by, barely catching their eye, stealing the odd envious glance.

Well, my poi rose like the others – but with the first twirl it flew out of my hand and shot off across the room. The laughter was no more deafening than the roaring in my ears. I felt burnt all over and through false smiles braved the rest of my final Māori cultural class.

It is with some irony then that I note here that in my twenties I went on to play Princess Te Puea in a television play – a woman renowned for her performance group who would tour and raise money for her good causes. Once again, in rehearsals, I lost control of my poi, only to spike the eye of Queen Te Atairangikaahu's daughter.

It took me a long time to realise that pois don't make or break a Māori.

I used to think that without the reo you couldn't be a Māori. I used to believe you had to attend every hui on offer and always let the kisses through – even from the slobbering drunk old men, who'd grab the chance for a quiet grope too.

I used to think I was the only one who felt like me. But now I know it isn't so. There are other half-castes who know they are Māori just by maintaining the ahi kā. We labour at keeping our fires burning and settling into the soul that is ours.

Although stained by time, I am still growing up Māori.

Ko taku Whakaohonga

ANDREW VERCOE

*Andrew Vercoe is a lecturer in Māori Education at the University of Waikato and the author of **Educating Jake**, published in 1997. He has tribal affiliations with Whakatōhea, Te Arawa and Tūhoe, and maintains a high profile on Treaty issues, parliamentary representation for Māori, the Whakatōhea land settlement and other matters of concern to Māori.*

Born in 1960, Andrew Vercoe's life and attitudes reflect the experiences of many of those who were raised during the years of urban drift and the penetration of Māori into Pākehā society.

My father was a Māori chaplain for the Anglican Church and so, as a family, wherever Dad was sent, we went. This meant that we were pretty well urbanised and educated and, being physically separated from our iwi and whānau, we grew up different from them. As a boy I can remember my country cousins mimicking the quaint yet sophisticated language my brothers and I had grown up with and taunting us, 'You're townies, eh.'

I must admit our visits back home were fleeting and most likely had all the appearance of an alien invasion. To my cousins, we probably appeared as curiosities blown in by the summer holiday urge – here one day and gone the next.

On top of this, when Dad was sent to Singapore, my older brother and myself found ourselves growing up in Terandak military camp. By the time my family returned to New Zealand and were stationed at Burnham, just south of Christchurch, the Māori part of my identity had been fundamentally undermined. The education curriculum wherever we went was Anglophile and without any comprehensive exposition of Māori society. And, as I have already stated, our geographical isolation from our Māori roots meant we were separated from any appreciation of whakapapa and a cultural Māori standard that might have opposed the European one I was brought up with.

Nor, to be frank, did I protest. The reality of childhood is that because it is the only one you know, you just live it. There were no reference points from which to assert a different world view and, therefore, life – to an impressionable little fellow – was as it should be. This was it.

Despite the best efforts of my parents, I became an Anglo young boy and I developed an Anglo-provincial view of myself and the Māori world. One day I remarked to a friend, 'I wish I was White.'

Then, in 1970, Dad left the Army and in 1971 he was appointed Principal of Te Wai Pounamu Māori Girls College – Te Wai – as it was known then. So our family packed up and moved again – and it was only then that his second from the womb began to comprehend the Māori in him.

My first impressions of Christchurch, the South Island's big smoke, was that it represented the dark side of the industrial revolution – pollution, overcrowding, miles of concrete and not enough friendly faces. It was my father's desire to shunt me off to Christ's College, but upon viewing their school uniform, I promptly and stridently protested on the basis that wearing stripes would make me look like a mobile pedestrian crossing. His hopes dashed, Dad relented and allowed me to attend the neighbourhood Intermediate in Linwood. It was here that I was introduced to the rigours of the timetable and the superfluous attention paid by the teachers to the rules and codes of conduct. Male teachers were predisposed to this zealousness, venting their frustrations on twelve-year-old backsides. The school was like some sort of tragic wilderness. Even the buildings portrayed a clinical manifestation that made me think of Charles Dickens' magic character, David Copperfield, and the stark reality of the Victorian era.

During my schooling Māoritanga was non-existent and French and German were given considerable status as the preferred alternative languages. No doubt the school's excuse for not addressing the centrepiece of what makes New Zealand unique was most likely, and ironically, that there weren't enough brown faces to warrant the inclusion of it – fostering the parochial mentality that Māori stuff was only for Māori people. In my classroom the study of ancient Greece and the struggles endured by the people of India were deemed more important than learning about how our nation developed or indeed why it developed the way it did. The student-teacher relationship that I had the misfortune to encounter was not that impressive either.

I can remember an experience of being dressed down by my form teacher, who also happened to have the duty of supervising the school's tennis teams. I had misunderstood his instructions about when and where we were to meet on sports day. Despite the fact that I had been innocent of any discretion, hanging around at the wrong place for close on an hour, the teacher publicly humiliated me the next day in class. He insisted that I had lied about my whereabouts and as such lacked integrity, was 'sly', unreliable and really didn't deserve to represent the school. Of course, he couldn't resist the proverbial jab in the guts, belching out, 'This is typical of you Maoris.' He did this while I was waiting in line to have my spelling checked off.

A deathly silence fell upon the room as he methodically riveted all the characteristics of a common thief upon my shoulders. The next thing I can remember was breaking down – tears flowed. My high-pitched voice rang out, somewhat embarrassed, vigorously objecting to this fellow's false allegations. All the while his lips pulled themselves into a tight snarl that seemed to say, 'Got ya, Māori boy!'

I never said anything to my parents. I was petrified by the thought of the payback that could have followed if I'd opened my mouth. Twenty-seven years on, I can still remember my tiny size that day, my mates with their heads down and the impression that school was something that I was not going to enjoy – at least not with that neanderthal teaching me. As the gods would have it, I was to endure his disposition for two years. Going home, then, was something that I really looked forward to, relishing the last school bell on Friday afternoons and wishing that the weekends would last longer.

Te Wai Pounamu, where Dad taught, literally became a cultural shelter, a place where I learned that being Māori was something one should aspire to – and I tried desperately to do so. While it provided Mum and Dad with the opportunity to exercise their leadership and teaching skills, it allowed me the space to develop a sense of self-worth and of revelling in the process of learning about who I was. The social discourse that I shared with the young women who studied there, introduced me to a range of thinking I'd never experienced before, especially a feminine mentality that at times left me flabbergasted.

They became my sisters and often evoked the matriarchal spirit whenever I stepped out of line. Thus, Te Wai ushered in a new personal dispensation, one which opened my eyes to the rich textures of my culture and the nobility inherent in us – Ko Ngāi Tāua.

On many occasions I would join the girls in kapahaka, for the first time putting a big dent in an otherwise impenetrable, shy exterior. Sometimes the local boys' hostel, Te Rehua, would combine and I'd observe with fascination the intricacies and timing of the haka, and the way in which the men would carry themselves. The only aspect about the whole experience that caused me some consternation was that I didn't know what the hell I was singing or saying. The language became the cultural barrier to a holistic understanding of what being Māori meant, and it was to remain so well into my adult life.

I did, however, make an enthusiastic 'youthful' attempt to address the lack of knowledge I had about the language. I surprised my mother once when she discovered me intensely studying the pages of Hoani Waititi's book *Te Rangatahi: The New Net Goes Fishing*, and of my passion to not only acquire the language in a fortnight but to also become an accomplished exponent of mau-taiaha as well! Mum was kind enough not to erupt into an uncontrolled fit of laughter and lovingly encouraged her son to continue to cultivate this noble attitude.

The annual kapahaka events attended by Te Wai Pounamu College, the field trips we made to the bastions of Māori significance and the sweet chord struck with the local tangata whenua, made life bearable. My five years spent in Christchurch helped rekindle the link with my tūrangawaewae, somehow easing the life of a schoolboy who at times struggled with the demands made on him by an environment that was, generally speaking, destitute of any Māori offering.

Despite my ignorance of te reo, my esteem for who I was developed. I gradually learned to appreciate more the brief excursions to Tōrere and Ōpape, at times wishing Dad could find a ministry in the rivers and valleys of Ngāi Tai and Te Whakatōhea – I was sure that even the whitebait and the rabbits would appreciate his personal sentiments concerning the gospel.

As I ponder upon these early encounters with my culture, I can truly appreciate the battle that our rangatahi face today. While we now have a significant number of kōhanga and kura kaupapa Māori, more than eighty percent of our tamariki are exposed to a world view that marginalises their history and fervently encourages the marketisation of the human experience. Our future as Māori people lies in our adherence to the fundamental principles of life that complemented the strong sense of community fostered by our tīpuna. I believe that is what I discovered all those years ago, as a young man learning to grow up 'being Māori'.

My Name Helped Me Grow

RIWIA BROWN

*Riwia Brown is one of New Zealand's foremost playwrights and screenplay writers. Her two early plays, **Roimata** and **Te Hokinga**, were made into short films, and she subsequently became the scriptwriter on **Once Were Warriors** and other feature films.*

Born in 1957, Riwia Brown maintains a busy career in the theatre and film. A writer of sensitivity, she offers an insight into how names can shape identity.

Riwia Brown lives in Wellington.

I spent most of my early childhood living in a large old house in Khandallah, a suburb of Wellington. My mother, Reremoana Shelford, was Māori. She died in January 1966. From this beautiful woman I claim my Māori ancestry. I have two older brothers, Rangimoana and Apirana, and a younger sister, Haina. Up until my mother passed away my childhood memories are largely happy.

I remember times when my mother's sisters would come down to Wellington. My mother was part of a large extended family and at these reunions the house would resound with her infectious laughter, the sound of our language sweet to my tender ears. The kitchen would be filled with the delicious smell of rewana bread baking in the oven.

Sadly, my mother was not well. When she was a young girl of about eleven somebody had put caustic soda into a drink bottle which she mistakenly drank. It burnt out her throat and stomach lining. In the end this tragedy crippled her and ended her life prematurely. She was advised by doctors not to have children. However, she had other ideas and gave birth to four of us. She was a brave and courageous woman.

My mother died when I was nine. I remember her as a hard-working woman and certainly one of the most fastidious people in our affluent neighbourhood. She was very, very particular about what we wore and how we presented ourselves; we had to be seen as the cleanest children in our street. When she was at school she was strapped for speaking Māori. This, I believe, had a profound influence on how she thought to bring us up, her children, into a world that she had witnessed become increasingly Pākehā. It was important to her that we all possess the skills necessary to survive the fast pace of change. I reflect on the *aroha* she must have had, to sacrifice her very nature to make our transition into the world of the Pākehā easier than her own.

In fact, it was my father, Melvin James Taylor, who insisted my name be Riwia. My mother wanted to call me Carolyn and this name still appears on my birth certificate and passport. In this small way my mother got her way. However, my father told everyone that my name was Riwia, after Riwia Fox, the gentle old lady who had a loving hand in bringing up my mother. She was a real character. She wore thick, thick glassess which made her old eyes large and endearing. We used to call her Nanny Posh because she always dressed immaculately, with matching hat, coat, shoes and handbag. Her handbag seemed to be always full of one pound notes which were eventually dished out to her grandchildren.

Over the years I have learnt to respect my name, but as a youngster growing up with it, it was hard! For a start, nobody could pronounce it. At primary school I was sometimes called 'Wee Wee' or worse, not only by my classmates but by those who were responsible for my education. So I learnt from a young age that my name, Riwia, somehow made me different. But it wasn't only my name – I looked unlike the other children at school. I was brown and had larger features. This was also true of my brothers who were even darker than my sister and me. We lived in Simla Crescent but we were known as the Māori family from 'Similar Crescent' – which I suppose we were. As far as I remember we were the only Māori children in the immediate area: certainly at the school we attended.

The real confusion came when we went to visit my mother's family up the East Coast of the North Island where we were known as the Pākehā cousins from Wellington. Not even my name or the fact that I had similar features and skin tone would convince them otherwise. In my case I thought it was because I had lighter coloured hair. So from my early childhood I was forced to make sense of who I was.

This issue followed me well into my adulthood. There was a time in my early twenties when I had a job in a very 'well-to-do' employment agency. The American owner couldn't be bothered getting her tongue around my name and felt sure it would put her clientele off doing business, so it was easier for her and all concerned to change my name. She named me Lisa and, sadly, I wasn't confident enough at that stage to say or do anything.

There have been occasions when I have considered resorting to the name on my passport so I wouldn't always have to justify myself and continually be confronted with the hard issues of being Māori. This is what my mother wanted to protect me from. She had offered me a hiding place, but in the end my own reflection would have given it away. My name has helped me grow.

Now, as a mature middle-aged woman confident in my Māori-ness and secure in my career, my name means a lot to me. Sometimes it can even open doors. I think of my mother often and wonder how she would view the world of her children and grandchildren and how we have managed our lives. I think she would be very proud.

Excuse Me While I Kiss the Sky

MIKE SMITH

Those who know Mike Smith will not be surprised that behind the public face of the man who put an axe to the tree on One Tree Hill is strength, determination, wit and intellectual rigour – all of which are on display in this piece written for **Growing Up Māori***.*

Mike Smith was born in 1957. He is a staunch supporter of all kaupapa Māori concerning land rights, Treaty rights and other sovereignty issues. He lives in Rotorua.

Over the last couple of years I've been subjected to some fairly intense media scrutiny. I've seen how cults of personality can be manufactured by the news media. While on one hand this may present opportunities to push the kaupapa into the realm of public debate, the downside is that the message can sometimes be subsumed beneath one-dimensional portrayals of the messenger.

Therefore, contributing my childhood experiences initially triggered the following reaction: *'I'm* not the issue. What's this got to do with the development of us as a people?' However, following eloquent reassurances that our collective histories help to explain our social condition in far more intimate ways than dry impersonal political commentaries, my initial reluctance has been overcome. But at what point are we 'grown up' and what does Māori mean exactly?

My view is that life is an 'on-growing' process, so that's easy to deal with. The second question, however, is a different matter. My dad's younger brother once told me that when he was a kid the only context he heard the term 'māori' used was in relation to fresh water: 'Tiki mai he wai māori' ('go and get some water from the creek'). In this sense 'māori' refers to water and other things in their natural state. In reflecting upon my childhood experiences, this state of natural grace would be hard to find, not because it wasn't there, but because its expression was either outlawed or transformed. Yet it existed, humming in the background like a subliminal harmonic, out of tune with the Western world.

Welcome to the twilight zone.

I was born on Pukeroa Pā on Christmas Day, 1957. On face value that sounds pretty staunch. Pukeroa Pā, the stronghold of the Ngāti Whakaue people of Te Arawa, standing sentinel over the whare tūpuna, Tame-tekapua, protecting the village of Ōhinemutu. Pukeroa Pā, site of the Rotorua public hospital, where my afterbirth went up in smoke.

My dad's people are Ngā Puhi. During the urban drift of the late-forties and fifties many Ngā Puhi families left the enforced poverty of Taitokerau to seek employment in the cities and provincial towns. So we grew up as a generation of exiles, far from our hapū and marae. However, the bounds of whanaungatanga remained strong among our parents, and the Taitokerau whānau would meet at the local Buffalo hall to maintain our ties and support each other.

I grew up in a state-housing suburb known as Ford Block – destined to become transformed into Pine Block in Alan Duff's *Once Were Warriors*. But for me it was a place of good memories rather than bad.

I toddled off to a State kindergarten and then a State primary school. I fed the chooks in the morning and then smashed the ice puddles on the way to school. I marched around the playground to the tune of 'Colonel Bogey' on the Tannoy speakers before assembly, with maybe a bit of American square dancing before lessons. I suffered a half-pint of curdled milk with a green striped straw at playtime, followed by a literary diet of *Green Eggs and Ham* and *The Donkey's Egg* before lunch. I learnt that Abel Tasman discovered New Zealand – and other fundamental truths – with a token bit of Māori mythology thrown in now and again. I helped Mum in the garden after school, and had brisket, rīwai, and doughboys for tea, you know, Māori kai. The weekends were spent playing sports, helping around the house, swimming and fishing the rivers and lakes, patching the nail holes in our corrugated iron waka with tar from the streets and hanging out with the kids from the block: 'Half-caste dirty arse'.

That's me on the far left.

Puberty kicked in during my Intermediate School years and being cool was top priority. Boss Bellabrava jeans with 24-inch flares was the look and our heroes drove Mark One Zephyrs with Squeegee (a type of soft drink shaped like an orange) bottles impaled on the aerials, along with triangular felt pennants listing the local towns in which hell was raised. The Soundshell was the local music venue where Eddie Lowe, Howard Morrison and the local showbands would perform. We were a bit short on international heroes until Hendrix came along. Black, bad, and ice cool. Afros were in and black consciousness began to surface in the neighbourhood.

Our local boys' high school was modelled on an English private school. Caps, blazers, institutionalised violence, Victorian attitudes and Afros. The school motto was 'Ad Astra per Aspera' ('To the stars through hard work'). Excuse me while I kiss the sky. In our third form year the students staged an uprising at the school that was subsequently hushed up, apparently to prevent similar occurrences around the country.

I left Rotorua in the early seventies to begin the rites of passage into adulthood. Subsequent years have been spent mainly in Taitokerau working in the field of community development and social justice.

These snapshot images from my childhood describe how the process of colonialisation and subsequent urbanisation has not only sped up the process of assimilation but also transformed the popular culture of the people in the process.

To this extent, being Māori has added a number of dimensions to our identity: firstly, being ethnically Māori; secondly, being tūturu Māori; and, thirdly, being part of the transformed popular Māori culture with all the subsequent inconsistencies and tensions.

The right of Māori self-determination guaranteed in te Tiriti o Waitangi has the potential to reconcile these tensions. This can be done by the empowerment of a constitutional framework for our country that enables Māori to express ourselves, according to our own ways, in all aspects of our lives – while retaining the ability to cross over into Te Ao Pākehā if we so choose. This opportunity is not limited just to us. It also provides an option for Pākehā to adopt new values, priorities and a renewed commitment to a system of social, economic and political justice envisaged in Te Tiriti.

I need look no further than the love and warmth of my own family and upbringing for evidence of the goodwill among our different peoples required to initiate positive change. The challenge of our nation is to harness this energy into effective, focused organisation and action. At the same time, we must resist the shallow attempts of the economic and poltical elite, both Māori and Pākehā, who seek to subvert this agenda to maintain the status quo for their short-term individual financial gain.

In this vision, anyone can grow up Māori if they want to. It doesn't mean that they will be Ngā Puhi or Te Arawa or whatever. The vision will provide you, however, with a sense of identity and a positive framework to express your humanity in accordance with a worldview that extends beyond the Western consumer culture.

More importantly, it will ensure that never again will systems of institutionalised racism be allowed to dispossess our people.

We cannot allow another generation to fall between the cracks.

None of Us is What Our Tūpuna Were: When 'Growing Up Pākehā' is 'Growing Up Māori'

JACQ CARTER

Jacq Carter was born in 1974 and is currently completing her Master of Arts at the University of Auckland. Her thesis critically considers the politics of constructing Māori identity in Aotearoa New Zealand – a colonial society. She is also tutoring in the Department of Māori Studies and teaching Māori at Auckland Normal Intermediate. In her spare time she works as a facilitator for Ngā Moemoeā a Te Rangatahi, a group who use drama, song and dance in their work with young Māori. Her interests include decolonisation as the praxis of our liberation and theatre as practice for revolution. Last year Jacq studied Creative Writing with Albert Wendt and Witi Ihimaera and intends to publish a collection of her poetry.

> *Ka hoki au ki te mauri*
> *o tōku waka o Mataatua*
> *ko Putauaki ki Ngāti Awa*
> *ko Tawhiuau ki a Tangi-haruru*
> *ko Te Rae-o-Kohi, ko Awatope*
> *ko Te Mānuka-tū-tahi*
> *ki Whakatāne, ko Apanui*
> *ko te mauri rā i haria mai nei*
> *hei whakaoho i taku moe*
> *ko-ko-ko-koia e ara ē!*
> *ko-ko-ko-koia e tū ē!*

It might be misleading for me to begin with the above tauparapara in so far as you, the reader, might assume mine was a 'traditional' upbringing. But I want to begin with this tauparapara because I want to begin by talking about the Mataatua waka.

It was, as many of you will know, one of numerous waka upon which our intrepid tūpuna made the journey from distant Hawaiki to the island identified by Hine-i-te-aparangi with the words 'Ao-tea-roa!' (otherwise known as Te Ika ā Māui). When the waka made landfall at Whakatāne its crew included Wairaka, her father Toroa, her aunt Muriwai and her uncles Puhi and Taneatua. Toroa was the waka's captain, Tama-ki-hikurangi its navigator. They were searching for a place that fitted the description given them by Irakewa, the priestly father of Toroa and Muriwai (although there is one account which records Irakewa, or Wairakewa, as being their *mother*). And sure enough they came upon the waterfall, Te Wairere, and a cave which Irakewa had spoken of as a home for Muriwai, both of which still grace the environs in what is now the township of Whakatāne.

Many of you will already be familiar with the events surrounding the Mataatua's arrival at Kakahoroa (the ancient name for Whakatāne). You will have heard how the men went ashore without having

Voyaging with my father on his boat in 1987, aged thirteen.

properly secured the waka and how, according to Ngāti Awa, it was Wairaka who saved it from drifting out to sea. I like to suggest the men were in such a hurry to get ashore and name various pieces of land after themselves they forgot to anchor it properly(!) but I am also aware that Wairaka herself is responsible for the naming of several places in and around Whakatāne (and as far afield as Tamakimakaurau). Indeed, the name Whakatāne commemorates her words as she performed that infamous feat – '*Kia whakatāne ake au i a ahau!*'(often translated as 'Thus I make myself a man!').

Some say it was Muriwai, not Wairaka, who performed that great deed. Muriwai is also credited with establishing a tūāhu in a place marked by a lone-standing mānuka tree, Te Mānuka-tū-tahi, which later became the repository of the waka's mauri. Taneatua is said to have taken the puhi of the waka and deposited them in various places further inland for safe-keeping. And Puhi – well, some of us like to say he *stole* the body of the waka, but really it was only natural that when Puhi and his followers migrated to the North they should have travelled on the Mataatua. Which is how the waka came to be anchored where it remains to this day – near Te Tīheru o Mataatua at Takou Bay.

I was seventeen when I first heard that story. I was in the seventh form at Epsom Girls' Grammar School and was accompanying a group of fifth form history students on a trip to Te Tī. It was the requisite 'marae experience' for a group of mostly white, middle-class young women – only in my case it was white, middle-class and Māori!

As part of our stay our hosts took us to Takou Bay. It is a place where Papatūānuku hardly breathes and is silent so that she will not give the hiding place away. It is the place where I came to *know* I was Māori as opposed to being *told* I was Māori. It is the place where I first heard the waka's story and its kōrero brought about a lot of sadness and shame within me. The next day I was given the very great honour of thanking the people of Te Tī and I had hardly said anything before my words were tears and I was crying. I will never forget what Whaea Erana Wineti (Epsom's first teacher of te reo Māori) said to me: that was your wairua speaking. I like to think that was how I entered te ao Māori 'ā-hinengaro' or consciously (remembering that for Māori the hinengaro is the seat not only of the thoughts but also of the *feelings*). Talk about out of the frying pan and into the fire! Sometimes it seems no sooner was I aware I was a Māori than I was a Māori feminist, a Māori activist, and, dare I say it, a Māori writer!

But the transition from being a woman who had only been told she was Māori to a woman in the process of 'becoming more Māori' was not easy. Did not knowing I was Māori mean I was *not* Māori? Did realising I was Māori mean I had only *just* become Māori? How could I suddenly consider myself Māori when there had been very little about my upbringing to suggest I was Māori?

It seems to me that talking about 'growing up Māori' is a bit like talking about *who* is a Māori. Indeed the two are inextricably related.

Just as we might ask the question: 'Who is a Māori?' (or perhaps more pertinently: 'Who decides who is a Māori?'), we might also ask the question: 'What is growing up Māori?'

If we answer that question according to the predominant and indeed popular constructions of Māori identity then we might come up with something like this: someone who grows up the daughter of a Pākehā mother and a Māori father is 'part-Māori'; someone who 'grows up Pākehā' is 'un-Māori'; and someone who doesn't know or realise they are Māori until they have grown up or are in the process of growing up is a 'born-again' Māori. Ultimately we might find ourselves suggesting it is only the 'real' Māori who 'grows up Māori'. So 'growing up Māori' might include being born of a Māori father and a Māori mother; growing up on or around your home marae; growing up speaking te reo Māori; growing up surrounded by your kuia and koroua; growing up in a world where you know you are Māori. We might say 'growing up Māori' involves all those things which we conceive of as being authentically and/or traditionally Māori.

If I were to construct my own identity according to these notions I would be a part-Māori, un-Māori, born-a-bloody-gain Māori! What does this mean for me as a descendant of my tūpuna in Aotearoa today – a colonial society? How valid is – and who legitimates – my way of being Māori?

It was my mother who first told us we kids were (part-) Māori. She seemed far more knowledgeable than my father when it came to things Māori. Much of her life's work has been devoted to arguing that the Treaty of Waitangi is the supreme law of this country. I used to joke she was more Māori than my father and thought that was terribly funny. It is a sobering thought when we consider the circumstances which have led to the perception that there are Pākehā in this country who know better than Māori what it is to be Māori.

But Mum thought we were Tūhoe, so for a while there (and after some rapid research) I was carried away by the thought of my being one of the 'children of the mist' descending – I wished! – from a long line of staunch (Tūhoe moumou tāngata ki te pō) warrior women and warrior men. When I found out we weren't Tūhoe I felt terrible – I had already been to a number of hui and proudly proclaimed Tūhoe as my tribal identity in my mihi! Such are the pitfalls of my way of growing up Māori.

It was not until I published a piece of writing very much like this one that my grandmother found it necessary to discuss our being Māori. She said as much as she'd rather I let bygones be bygones I should know her mother was Ngāti Awa, not Tūhoe. Same waka, different iwi. This small admission on her part is very important to me – it's probably the closest my grandmother will get to saying Ngāti Awa is the greatest tribe in the country. My grandmother's experience of 'growing up Māori' was one of such great shame she consciously chose to *not* be Māori. To my way of thinking that is the ultimate triumph of colonisation in this country – to convince people it is so shameful to be Māori they do everything in their power to make sure they and their descendants *believe* they are not Māori. Some would say that by the time it got to my father there was no doubt about it ... *but saying that suggests he isn't Māori.*

Most of us don't have a choice as to whether or not we are identified as Māori because skin colour and appearance are made to be markers of identity in a racist society. The notion you can tell, and thereby discriminate against, a person by the colour of their skin, the flatness of their nose or the thickness of their lips was introduced to these shores by Pākehā, not Māori. Prior to that we knew people by their river, their lake and/or their mountain. I am privileged by my ability to *choose* – I have white-skinned privilege in a racist colonial society. Couple this with the fact that I didn't grow up in poverty, and that *both* my parents were tertiary educated, and my way of growing up has very little in common with the upbringings of most Māori. Which has often led me to think I'm not *as* Māori ... a feeling intensified by other people's expectations of what constitutes Māori identity.

We tend to locate what is authentically and/or traditionally Māori in a past that is pre-European Māori ... or in post-European experiences that are common to many Māori (like eating pork bones and pūhā and living in poverty). The closer someone gets to growing up in this colonial society in ways we consider authentically and/or traditionally Māori the more we regard them as really Māori – or less contaminated by contact with Pākehā. Which is how we've come up with the idea there is such a being as a 'real' Māori and others in comparison are somehow *less* Māori – whether we think of them as part-, or un- or born-again Māori.

I remember when I first read 'Being a Māori' (published in Ranginui Walker's *Nga Tau Tohetohe* with acknowledgements to its Tūhoe originators). At the time I read it like a kind of checklist for the qualities and characteristics of *the quintessential Māori*. When I came to the end of the list I was somewhat dismayed – I had, if you like, scored very badly! That reality was not my own and I cringed when it came to 'knowing the difference between a Māori, a Māori-Pākehā, a Pākehā-Māori and a Pākehā *and to beware of the last two.*' Imagine if I became the 'Pākehā spouse' whom my husband got to go and ask the landlord for the flat! Imagine if I went to some whānau's house and they hunted for their best china for me – the Pākehā – to eat off! I felt sure I must be seen by other Māori as being – at best – a *Pākehā*-Māori and this was obviously not a desirous category of Māori-ness to fall (or to be *made to fall*) into.

Much of my experience of being Māori tends to revolve around what happens when I meet other Māori and whether or not they think I'm Māori. I don't blame people for thinking I'm Pākehā because, like I've said, I look like a Pākehā ... but every time I'm treated like a Pākehā it has grave consequences for my being Māori ... *it feels like something dies within me.* Like when I'm with friends and we meet another Māori who says 'Kia ora' to everyone else and 'Hello' to me. Or when I'm in the hongi line and I get a sense some people just don't want to hongi me ... I used to give them the option of just kissing me and we'd end up doing one of those half-nose half-lips jobbies... and then I'd think that'd really convince them I was a *Pākehā*-Māori because it seemed I couldn't even hongi properly!

But there is one experience which really stands out for me. I had just joined the Auckland-based activist group Te Kawau Maro, formed in 1994 to raise awareness about the fiscal envelope, and we had gone to support the occupation at Pakaitore (otherwise known as Moutoa Gardens). Our kaikōrero had just finished speaking and because I had come with them I stood with the other members of the rōpū to sing our waiata tautoko. When I realised I didn't know the words it was too late to sit down because I was standing already – I felt highly conspicuous and somewhat vulnerable. Then a voice behind me said, 'She's got guts coming on here.' And another chimed in, 'She may be white, but she's definitely a hori.' Those words were ringing in my ears all day – especially when that fulla with the tino rangatiratanga flag kept flying it over me!

I was not at that stage 'known' to the movement. When I first started going to movement hui I thought if there was anybody they'd suspect of being a 'D' it would have to be me – precisely because it was too bloody obvious! But no, the movement was quite *au fait* with ones like me ... I remember at one of the Hirangi hui standing right in front of a well-known activist and hearing him say to his friend: 'The movement always seems to attract the pale ones.' (It would not be fair to not say here that the person involved swears he has no recollection of this occurrence!) Contrast that with the words of his cousin: 'You look more Māori than me, I'm just browner, that's all.' I used to consider that in order to make up for my physical appearance I could go out of my way to act like a 'real' Māori... but it's hard to look like you really love kina when all you want to do is ruaki!

The fact is there is no *unitary* Māori reality, no *one* Māori identity, no *single* way of growing up Māori. All of us have been subjected to colonisation and colonisation has affected us all in different ways. Some of us identify as 'part-Māori' and others lay claim to being 'full-blooded' Māori. Some of us grow up speaking te reo Māori and some of us grow up not even knowing we're Māori. Indeed, such is the legacy of colonisation that 'growing up *Pākehā*' is one of the ways in which many Māori 'grow up Māori'. The thing we need to appreciate is for every Māori who grows up in this society *there is another way of growing up Māori*. None of us have grown up like our tūpuna did and the way in which we do grow up is our particular reality. We must accept that despite the difference in the ways we grow up *all of us were born with the potential to be Māori* ... and it is this potential which makes us Māori.

Some people refer to me as 'part-Māori'. Or – even worse – say I have 'Māori blood in me'. The coloniser would have us believe the amount of 'Māori blood' in me determines the extent to which I am Māori. Being Māori for me means I descend not only from Ngāti Awa but from people who are not tangata whenua in this country – but that doesn't make me any less Māori because it is *not* blood that determines my identity. No matter how much Pākehā blood flows through my veins there is something else ... like a karanga inside me ... or a fire burning deep within me. It is a fire lit there by my tūpuna. This fire began when my mauri brought together my tīnana and my wairua. *It is my mauri which called forth my potential to be Māori.* As Nelson Mandela said in his inaugural speech:

We were born to make manifest the glory of God that is within us. It is not just in some of us; it is in everyone. And as we let our own light shine, we unconsciously give other people permission to do the same. As we are liberated from our own fear, our presence automatically liberates others.

I believe what Mandela refers to as 'the glory of God' is what our tūpuna referred to as tapu. This kind of tapu is our inherent potential which, according to our tūpuna, resides in *all* things as well as in people. There are constant meetings of tapu with tapu and because these meetings are never neutral it made sense to our tūpuna that there be restrictions relating to these inherent tapu which are themselves referred to as tapu. These restrictions are some of our tikanga Māori – practices that make sense to us as human beings who are Māori.

Those who manifest their inherent potential with regard for other intrinsic tapu are the individuals most likely to inspire other people; it makes them capable of weaving people together, which is the meaning conveyed in the Māori word for 'leader' – rangatira. Tino rangatiratanga then is 'letting our own light shine' – it is the activation of our inherent potential to relate to our world and other people in ways that make sense to us as Māori. When we develop our potential to a state of excellence the feeling we get is what our tūpuna called ihi. When we are recognised by others as having achieved excellence they may describe us as possessing mana. This is the relationship between mana and tino rangatiratanga.

The ability to assert one's inherent potential is *the ability to become more fully human.* Paulo Freire describes this as a human vocation and that which distorts this vocation is oppression. If oppression prevents us from being more fully human then colonisation prevents us from being human beings who are more fully Māori. In making us less Māori it seeks to dehumanise.

Only Māori are born with the potential to be human beings who are

Māori – but the extent to which this potential is realised is restricted by (our endurance of) the limitations imposed by a colonial society. No matter the way in which you 'grow up Māori' in this particular colonial society, 'growing up Māori' is about growing up in the midst of spiritual warfare and political struggle – regardless of whether we perceive and/or engage in that struggle. Our tūpuna were trained from a very early age to be highly skilled in the arts of war – the coloniser works hard to ensure their descendants are ill-prepared for colonial warfare. The coloniser uses every means at his or her disposal to keep us submerged in our own oppression. The education system alone has been responsible for misinforming and disempowering successive generations. The casualties of this war include all those committed to penal and mental institutions and all those kept *out* of tertiary institutions. And all those who limit their potential to be Māori.

The field where we fight for the right to construct our identity is one of the most critical battlefields in the war between Pākehā and Māori. The more Māori who believe that being Māori means being dumb and lazy – *and it's therefore best to not be Māori* – the better. The more Māori who believe that being Māori is dependent on the amount of Māori blood in your body – *making people half-Māori, part-Māori, or only a bit Māori* – the better. The more Māori who believe there is only one way of being Māori – *and that depends on growing up like our tūpuna grew up in pre-European society* – the better. Because all these notions accept the limitations imposed upon our potential to be Māori in this particular colonial society. Which means more people submerged in the fact of their oppression and less people who are ready and willing – or even able to perceive the need – to engage in the struggle against the coloniser. This struggle is not just for ourselves but for our world and for our tikanga.

The question before us is this: how do we bring about our total liberation from the physical, mental and spiritual effects of colonisation? How do we arm ourselves for colonial warfare and how do we ensure that we win? Moreover, how do we ensure the change we bring about is not in turn oppressive?

One of our tūpuna's military strategies was pretty straightforward: *know your enemy*. If there's one thing we need to know about the coloniser in this country it's that he and she will never put down their weapons. They will never relinquish power and control. It is not in their interests to bring an end to oppression because they are the beneficiaries of the ongoing process of colonisation. The coloniser fails to consider that if *having* is a condition of *being* then it is necessary for everyone. It is for this reason that the coloniser cannot find it in him or herself to recognise that Māori are fully human – nor do anything that might enable us to perceive the fact of our oppression and that this 'fact' is a changeable one. Doing so would mean bringing about a situation in which they would have to *share* the benefits of cohabitation.

As Freire says, 'Liberation is a task for the oppressed.' Māori must take responsibility for the totality of the struggle and we must begin on a personal level. When we say tino rangatiratanga begins with ourselves it is because we recognise the progress of the social struggle depends on the progress of the struggle which is personal. Which makes our task necessarily more difficult. We need to bring about the conditions in which each of us can perceive how our respective realities are oppressive and we need to empower ourselves to believe that those are realities we can change. We need to realise the oppression we suffer is *the oppression we endure* – meaning we deserve the best but *we get what we settle for*. If we allow the coloniser to call us *part*-Māori then we limit our potential to be Māori. If we settle for $170 million then we fail to intervene in the oppressive reality that sees our people swelling the ranks of the unemployed, the under-educated, the institutionalised, the incarcerated. We need not wait for them to recognise our humanity but recognise it ourselves and act accordingly. And in settling for *nothing less than our liberation* we will be in the process of becoming more fully human. This is the process of decolonisation – the praxis of our quest for liberation.

If I wanted to I could choose to not be Māori. I could *get away with* being or 'passing' for Pākehā. And while this may prove useful on certain occasions (like going on pre-protest reconnaissance missions), I have to be honest – the idea horrifies me. It amounts to a negation of my potential to be Māori. *It amounts to a negation of my tūpuna Māori.* It is for this reason that I cannot describe myself as *part*-Māori, *un*-Māori and/or a *born-again* Māori – regardless of the fact that I also descend from, look like, grew up like and maybe sometimes still *act* like people who are not tangata whenua in this country (and who are not only my friends but also my family). If I identify as any of the above then I negate my potential to be more fully Māori; I act as if my reality is not the product of colonisation in this country; and I negate my ability to *change* my reality. I must take responsibility for the totality of my identity and the only way I can do that is by *not* allowing myself, let alone anyone else, to limit my potential to be more fully Māori. It is a potential put there by my tūpuna – like Whaea Erana said, *'It is the tapu inherent in my wairua.'* How can I negate my tūpuna Māori when they continue to live and breathe in me? When I am because they were and because I am they are.

Many of us say the one thing you must have in order to be Māori is whakapapa – *because whakapapa records the passage of our wairua.* This wairua has divine origins which is why it is often translated as 'soul' or 'spirit'. When the mauri binds the wairua to the body there is a meeting of tapu – the physical and the spiritual. If my Irish descent has limited my potential to be more *physically* Māori then part of my struggle is in the *spiritual* overcoming the *physical* ... because in this particular instance the mauri bound my Ngāti Awa ancestry to my Pākehā-looking body! I *choose* to be able to relate to my world in ways that make sense to me as a woman who is Māori – and I *choose* to be able to do that fully. Even if it means risking everything in order to validate my reality. All of us who descend from other Māori (regardless of whether we know our whakapapa) have a choice when it comes to *the extent to which we negate we are Māori.*

Earlier I referred to a fire which my tūpuna have lit within me. When I assert my potential to be more fully Māori I feel this fire burn ever more brightly. When I am relating to my world in ways that make sense to me as a Māori I feel my potential being realised. I am one more vessel for the mauri of their line ... watch how the mauri leaps with fire ... at the making of something, at the telling of some story, at the singing of some song.

When I left Epsom Girls' Grammar School I decided I was going to university to learn how to speak the reo. I was naïve enough to believe that I would emerge after three years not just with a Bachelor of Arts in Māori Studies but also as a fluent speaker of te reo Māori! Those three years were drawing to a close and I was well on my way to getting another C + when I went to my first wānanga reo – a week-long marae-based total immersion Māori language hui – run by Te Wānanga o Tuakau ki Waikato. It was one of the hardest weeks of my life. I felt like a fish out of water – not just because I couldn't speak the lingo but because I didn't look like those other ika either! That first night I lay in my bed just wishing I had the reo so I wouldn't have to go through what I knew was going to be a long and hard journey ... I felt if I had the reo I would have fitted in immediately. I felt like I couldn't express myself at all ... I was unable to show anybody that this was someone they might want to get to know! I wanted to be able to make jokes in Māori so I could be like those ones who entertain the whole hui .. because in the English language I was one of those (at least, I thought so!).

So when it came to the end of the week I was really quite relieved to be going home. And then as soon as we left the marae things started to dawn on me. I noticed street lights and shops and cars filled with other people. I realised that for a whole week I hadn't thought of anything other than what had been happening on Te Awa Marahi marae. By the time we got to my house I didn't want to go inside. Because I was living with three Pākehā mates at the time, and as much as I enjoyed their company, I didn't want to have to speak a word of English! It was the first time I wished I was living with just Māori ... I think appreciating that feeling and its having come to fruition have proved to be somewhat difficult for many of my Pākehā friends.

Like when I moved into 'The Whare' above the shops in Grey Lynn, It was a big warehouse space just like the inside of a really big wharenui. When you came through the door you walked right into the 'living room' ... you turned around and you could see all the 'bedrooms' – we had our beds spaced at intervals along the walls up until just before you reached the kitchen. There were eight 'tangata whenua' (me, another wahine and six tāne!) and a constant stream of manuhiri. None of my Pākehā mates came to see me for ages after I moved in. When I asked one of them why they said it was because they hadn't been invited. I had never had to invite them to any of my other homes. Negotiating my way between my Māori friends and my Pākehā friends is a journey I still don't make with very much ease.

One of the best things about 'The Whare' was the kōrero – whether it was in English or in Māori. The talk got so revolutionary we even had the place done for 'bugs' ... and there were some ... of the you-fullasneed-to-clean-the-place-up-more variety! If there is one thing I regret about 'The Whare' it is that it was a wasted opportunity – too much talk and no action. Now I try to make sure there's a healthy combination – walking the talk and talking the walk. I try to take responsibility for the totality of the struggle because, despite the progress of my personal revolution, if my tikanga and my world continue to be colonised I am yet unable to be fully human ... while learning te reo and tikanga Māori may have the effect of making us 'more Māori' *they will not restore our lost humanity*. Because we will still be living in a colonial society.

One of the most exciting things that has been happening to me lately is the rediscovery of my tribal identity. It is the activation of my potential to be Ngāti Awa (which for someone who hasn't long known she was Māori is even more recent than my becoming more Māori). Just as there are things that make sense to me as a Māori there are things which make sense to me as a person from Ngāti Awa. For example, now that I know about the death of Irakewa it is impossible for me to eat the fish we call araara. It makes sense for me to begin this kōrero by talking about Wairaka and the waka Mataatua. And when I came across the whakataukī '*Ngāti Awa wareware*' and '*Ngāti Awa tiko rau raha*' it totally made sense to me that I am Ngāti Awa – because I *am* forgetful and (in what is a somewhat Pākehā-fied translation of the second one) I *am* transient.

All of our illustrious ancestors – men and women – are people who activated their full potential to become more fully human. *Every single one of us has that potential* – we tell ourselves stories about such legendary figures in order that they might inspire us to act on this potential. Which brings me back to Wairaka and the words she spoke when she saved the Mataatua. It took me a long time to come to terms with the words: 'Kia whakatāne ake au i a ahau.' It always bothered me that she had to 'make herself a man'. Now I understand it like this – the only reason Wairaka said she was acting like a man was *because she was doing what they told her only men can do*. Wairaka's story is about a tupuna wahine who liberated herself from a particular instance of oppression; in doing what she did she demonstrated her potential was not necessarily less by virtue of her being a woman.

One of the first things that inspired me when I 'entered' te Ao Māori (it was a while before I fully appreciated the significance of Wairaka's story) was the whakataukī '*E kore koe e ngaro, he kākano i ruia mai i Rangiātea.*' I understood this as meaning that no matter the way in which I had 'grown up Māori' I would never be lost *because I was Māori*. It didn't take me long to question the truth with which people utter that whakataukī when they also refer to part-Māori, un-Māori and born-a-bloody-gain Māori. To paraphrase Irihapeti Ramsden, if aroha is the force that enables us to understand and accept other people's realities then aroha might be something we're not feeling very much of these days. Nō reira, I would like to end this kōrero by anchoring my seed to the soils of my reality, by activating the Wairaka in me, by naming my world in order that the coloniser is not the one who names me: *Kia whaka-Māori ake au i a au!*

Identity crisis

I'm sick of being
a Pākehā-Māori
not a real one
but still a hori
sick of being
middle-classed
(as if poverty is
traditionally Māori)
sick of hearing
the same old thing
I'm the whitest Māori
you've ever seen
sick of people
who have to ask
am I eighth
a quarter
I couldn't be half.

But if I chose
to be Pākehā

I'd be turning my back
on my tūpuna

when I am
because they were
and because I am
they are.

Colour

I'm not a white woman
wishing I was brown
I'm not a white woman
pretending to be brown
I'm a white woman
who descends
from men and women
who were brown
who unlike others
married white
and made that the colour
they handed down.

None of us is what our tūpuna were

Dedicated to Irihapeti Ramsden
on coming across 'borders and frontiers'

Who do I think I am
with that top-knot on my head
that pounamu in my ears
that taonga around my neck?
Anyone'd think I was a *real* Māori
not a lowly 'born-again'!

Bunga in a Bucket

MIKA

Mika, born in 1962, is one of New Zealand's leading performance artists, actors and cabaret personalities. He was the hit of the Edinburgh Fringe Festival in 1997 and has engagements to perform throughout the world. He's gay and proud of it, and in your face and proud of that, too.

I wasn't born in an alley, I was born in a hospital bed. Born to a woman who gave me away at birth. She never even saw me. As if my being born wasn't worth even a look in. Now she never will see me I suppose.

I was born Terence John Pou to Witoti Winiki Pou and Elizabeth Halkett, but I was given into the arms of Evelyn Hazel Dawn and Bill Gudsell to be renamed Neil William Gudsell. Happy, yes. Mum always told me I was the special one, I was chosen. My brother and sister weren't adopted but I was the special one.

When I am asked, 'Do you want to find your *real family*?' this always aggravates me. My *real family* were the ones who raised me, who held me when I cried, who paid for my clothes and sang happy birthday to me. My *birth parents* only had sex and made a baby. God, even I can do that! So if you ask me what it was like for this Māori baby to be raised White, I can only reply, 'Damn fine'. My mum (who is Kāi Tahu, Kāti Mamoe descent – which I only found out when one of the aunties decided she wanted to claim the family land at Akaroa!) didn't like me playing with other Māori kids or learning anything Māori. Not cos she didn't like them – God, she adopted one, and lost friends for doing so! No, she did it cos from 1968 to 1978 you still didn't do Māori things. But even though I may never have a fluent grip on where I came from and where I'm going in relation to the Pou whānau from Kaikohe, at least

I had a mum and dad who loved me, who supported me and who allowed Neil to be special. Somehow if they were alive now I think they'd like Mika as well.

He iti taku iti

TAINUI STEPHENS

*Tainui Stephens was born in 1958, and lives in Auckland. His iwi is Te Rarawa, his hapū are Ngāti Moetonga and Te Rokekā. He worked in the Race Relations Conciliator's Office before becoming one of New Zealand's leading television executive producers and directors. His documentaries include a commemorative visit of the Māori Battalion to Europe, the **When the Haka Became Boogie** series and a profile of pianist Michael Houstoun, **Icon in b Minor**. He recently completed the major documentary series, **The New Zealand Wars**, fronted by historian James Belich.*

In this piece for the anthology, Tainui Stephens tells his story in a dual text, English and Māori, moving easily and bilingually between both. He reflects on the fact that growing up is a lifetime process; indeed, many Māori consider you are still a young man in your fifties and only begin to enter your maturity during what are considered, today, as being your middle years.

1.

*Ka pū au, ka whakaaro noa. E kapo nei ko te mahara
e kapo nei ko te kupu.*

Vince Stephens was a 'gun' boner, a bright young Māori man working at Ocean Beach Freezing Works, Bluff, in the mid-1950s. Originally from the Far North, he had sought escape from family abuse and public racism in Auckland. He was supremely talented on the chain and just as smart when it came to making money out of the drinking habits and gambling of his mates. He never drank himself. He made a heap of bucks.

Adrienne Watson was a smart, vivacious, young Pākehā woman from Wellington. She was escaping her own difficult life. She was attracted to Māori culture and thought, and one Māori boy in particular. She loved Vince with a passion.

Vince and Adrienne moved to Christchurch. Adrienne spoke to house and flat owners about a place to live. When the landlords saw that her man was Māori the accommodation was suddenly unavailable. Eventually, however, Vince and Adrienne found an elderly Pākehā woman who had never met any Māori before and had no hang-ups about them. She owned a flat in Slater Street.

My mummy and daddy moved in. They were blissfully in love and looked forward to a bright future together. My birth reinforced their optimism and love.

I WONDER whether anyone can truly say that they have ever grown up, for this seems to me to be an ongoing process. At the age of forty, only now am I beginning to feel (at last) comfortable with who I am and what I am not.

An overwhelming reason for this sense of comfort is my ever-evolving understanding of what it means to be Māori. Identifying as Māori is not something that I was born into. It is a part of my life that I have actively pursued.

The pursuit of it has given me my life.

I was born and grew up in a working-class family which aspired to upper middle-class security and comfort. Dad showed a talent for business and figures. My mother was smart at real estate deals, and adept at a wide range of jobs. They were a team. The butcher shops Dad set up grew to become an impressive chain of factories and outlets throughout the country. But he still called himself a butcher and continued to keep his hand in on the factory floor.

I know now that one reason why Dad was so driven to achieve success was to simply do better than the white man. His earliest memories seemed to revolve only around the shame of being Māori. On the Ōtāhuhu bus and in his Avondale school he was taunted by the dimwits of the day, saying that he and his beloved Nana stank.

In his business activities, Dad went out of his way to employ Māori and to identify his company as successful and Māori. In those days this was not an easy task. Then he decided he wanted to base himself back in Auckland. One reason was so that he could involve his whānau in the business.

Mother wanted to stay in Christchurch. She and Dad grew apart and then stayed apart. It hurt. A lot.

Then the business collapsed. Dad ran away to Aussie.

We lost everything.

The year was 1970.

2.

Gladys Stiles was my standard two teacher. She was keen to instill a sense of Māori pride into the boy known as Brent (Bless her!). She called me by my middle name, Tainui. She meant well, but I didn't like it. Whenever my classmates called me Tainui it sounded like an insult.

I recall standing at the front of the Pākehā class and poking my tongue out. I bloody hated it. I wanted to be like them. I didn't want to be different. By and large, being Māori was simply not part of my life. I bore the occasional racist joke with good humour but wanted to melt into the crowd. It may have been white but at least it appeared happy.

Māua ko Paraima e piri ana.

Even so, by the time I got to the seventh form, I figured that I'd better do a good job of the school rugby haka. I did – only later did I realise that the haka the school was taught was embarrassingly bad.

My school-life figures prominently in my childhood years. My mother believed that the pursuit of education had to be uppermost in her children's minds. Although I was a solitary sort of kid, I had a good all-round education. In particular, I revelled in music – choir, Highland pipe band and piano. School was also a sanctuary from a difficult home life.

When my parents separated, my brother and I were halfway through a private school education at St Andrew's College. The school wanted to ensure that our education was kept safe from this trauma. They sympathised with our domestic plight. They also felt that there were too few Māori enrolled. For these reasons they allowed us to complete our education at half price with no deadline for payment, costs which we eventually paid ourselves.

School became challenging and sometimes fun. There, I was one of the crowd. Home, however, was hard work. I bore the responsibility of being the oldest male and helped tend my baby sister. I also saw that Mother was working hard and scheming harder to ensure that we were loved, well clothed and well fed. She succeeded but at great personal cost.

I grew into a serious sort of young fella. At the same time I was also starting to grapple with what being Māori meant.

My mother, whilst admiring aspects of the culture, knew relatively little about it.

Neither did we know much about Dad's family.

They were from up north and we'd had limited contact.

That's all we knew.

Then, at the end of my secondary schooling, I dutifully meandered into university to do a degree in English, French, German, Russian and Music. At my mother's suggestion I applied for a study grant from the Māori Education Foundation.

John Bennett and Elizabeth Murchie were on the interview panel. They were gracious and kind, and most interested in my academic record. They asked me to take them to the student common room to play them some Beethoven.

During the interview John Bennett asked me, 'Do you belong to the university Māori club?'

I said, 'No.'

John became silent but I was given a grant.

Then, as I left the room I met another candidate for a grant, a young Māori woman, who was far darker than me and more culturally oriented. Although I was Māori by blood alone, I had got a grant; but she had been unsuccessful at getting anything at all.

I felt a sense of guilt – and remembered John Bennett's silence.

Because of this incident, I decided to go to the next Māori club practice. The friendly camaraderie was genuine and welcoming. When I got in line to learn 'Haere mai' I felt a physical and spiritual electricity grab my spine. I knew this was for me.

The following day, I switched my English course for Māori.

3.

I te tau 1977 kua tū tētahi o ngā hui-ā-tau a Te Huinga Rangatahi.

I puta ngā rangatahi Māori o ngā whare wānanga puta noa ki roto o Ōtākou ki te kōkiri i ngā nawe nunui o taua wā.

I reira hoki mātou te Rōpū Māori o te Whare Wānanga o Waitaha. Engari i te mutunga iho, ehara taua hui i te ngāwari ki a mātou o Waitaha.

I taua wā, he kūare mātou ki te reo, ā, he paku noa tō mātou mōhio ki te tū o te marae. Tētahi take i pēnei ai mātou, kua kore he kaumātua hei ārahi hei tohutohu i ā mātou mahi. He rerekē anō te āhua o tō mātou noho ō roto o Te Wai Pounamu, rerekē noa atu ki tērā o Te Ika ā Māui. Pai kē atu rātou ki i te whiu i te reo Māori. I waihotia mā mātou e ngaoki tonu ana.

Ka pā mai ko te whakamā i tō mātou kaha kūare.

Tua atu i tērā, ka tāwaia mātou e ētahi o ngā rangatahi matatau nei. He nui ngā kupu taunu i utaina ki runga i a mātou . Kīhai hoki au i te tino mōhio he aha te pūtake i pērā ai rātou. Tērā pea kua nā te kakī mārō i te mea i tupu tahi ake me te reo. Koia i whakararurarutia ai mātou. Aua atu!

Heoi. Kua tau nei ko te rikarika, me te aha, me te whakatakariri hoki i roto i a mātou – Yeah well fuck you too! Ehara rawa i te mea nōku ake tēnei mamae, nō mātou katoa.

Nā. He nui tō mātou hiahia kia akona ki te reo – engari, ki a mātou, pai kē kia oti ai i runga anō i te pai me te aroha ki te tangata ahakoa ko wai.

Hāunga tērā, kāore e kore he hui whakahirahira inā he nui ngā kaupapa Māori kua whakatōkia iho nei ki roto i a mātou. A tōna wā ka titi iho nei, ka mau.

At university, being Māori suddenly became important to me. A capacity for leadership evidenced itself in my busy activities with the varsity Māori club. We spent a lot of time working in and with the small Christchurch Māori community. I was also able to identify with people outside the confines of Christchurch's smug comfort. Up to that moment, my interests in the Māori world were more cultural than political. I threw myself into learning te reo and tikanga. This was my antidote to my loneliness.

Meantime, I was also having a wonderful time as a student. Bonking and boozing were as important to me as study and self-discovery. Being at university meant having interesting stuff to learn, interesting people to mix with and great parties.

It was during the holiday periods, when I worked as a waiter or barman around the country, that my Māori interests began to become politicised. In particular, I was a barman at the South Pacific Hotel, Auckland, at the time of the Bastion Point protest. I remember trying not to tangi as I watched, on the television set in the public bar, the police assault and forcible eviction of the protesters. At that time, many patrons were not sympathetic to Māori causes. A few cheered the cops on as they marched onto Takaparawhā.

Then, back in Christchurch, the university Māori club instituted a programme teaching te reo and waiata at Paparoa Women's Prison. At one hui we met Dr Pita Sharples, who told us all about his work at the Race Relations Office. The man's charisma, intelligence and wairua turned me on – big time – and I knew then that my future was to be connected in some way with Māori.

From that moment on, I wanted to do something to support kaupapa Māori. I didn't know what it was to be, but Pete showed me that you didn't necessarily need a degree – as it turned out, I ended my academic career badly with straight Ds and Es. What Pete showed me was that I needed to know my people and be known by them.

This instilled in me the desire to spend more and more time with the Māori community and I asked my lecturer, Bill Te Awaroa Nepia, if it might be possible for me to spend holidays with his iwi at Tokomaru Bay. I wanted to surround myself with reo and understanding of tikanga.

Bill agreed, but then asked me, 'Wouldn't it be better, though, if you did this amongst your own iwi?' Good point, Bill. But who the hell were my iwi?

At that moment, a series of ironies and coincidences happened.

I also discovered that my grandfather was alive and living in Ahipara.

It was time to find my iwi.

4.

I tēnei wā kua tū au hei waewae takahi ki roto i te rōpū kapahaka o Te Kotahitanga. E kore e mutu noa ngā mihi ki te rōpū nei me ngā kaiārahi pou ako a Tihi rāua ko Willie Puanaki, me Lu rāua ko Joy Hau. Kua pau nei ō rātou kaha ki te hāpai ake i ngā kaupapa Māori o taua wā. He tino kapa tēnei ka mutu i hiki ai te whatumanawa Māori i ā rātou mahi katoa. Otirā, he manaaki i te tangata te tino kaupapa.

Heoi anō, he uri aua kaiārahi nō te Tai Tokerau. Nā, ka taka ki te wā i kōrero tahi mātou mō taku rapu i tōku ake rahinga. He paku noa te mōhiotanga i riro mai i a au ki te taha ki taku Pāpā.

Ko te wāhi i whānau mai ai a ia ko Waihopo. He kāinga tērā hore kau kē i tino tawhiti mai i Houhora ki Muriwhenua. Ko te ingoa o tōna matua tūturu ko Bobby Roberts.

I tau mai te whakaaro ki roto i a au, me āta nuku atu au ki te kāinga o tōku Karanipā. He āwangawanga nōku ki te nuku tata atu ki a ia. I pēnei ai au nā te āhuatanga o ngā kōrero i whakarerea mai e taku Pāpā mō tōna whānau. Hei tāna, i mahue ia i tana matua tūturu hei mōkai noa iho mō tana matua Pākehā atawhai. Koia te take i tūkinotia rawahia ai taku Pāpā i te wā i a ia e tamariki ana.

Heoi. Ka karanga mai a Lu rāua ko Joy, pai kē kia hoki atu au ki roto o Hokianga, Whakapau Karakia ki te taha o ō rāua whanaunga, ki reira noho mārika ai. Atu i kō, ka māmā ake pea te whātoro atu ki tōku tūpuna e noho mai rā i Ahipara.

Nā, ka tae ki te wā Kirihimete, ka piki au ki runga i taku motopaika

BSA, ka tika rawa atu ki te raki. Engari ka tae atu au ki roto o Whanganui, heoi anō he māuiui kua pā kino mai ki taku hōiho. Kāore i roa, mate atu ana. Auē! Nā, ka tū au ki te taha o te rori, ka hikihaiki au, tae pai noa atu ki roto i ngā whāruarua, ngā raorao o te Taitokerau.

Otirā, i tau atu au, ki roto o Hokianga, ka tūtaki atu ki ngā whanaunga o ōku hoa a Lu rāua ko Joy. Ka manaakihia mai au e rātou. Ka rapu mahi au, ka noho, ka noho, kāhore i kitea.

I te mea kua pau haere taku pūtea moni iti nei, i oti i au me haere tika, ki Ahipara.

Nā, ko Joe Murray te āpiha o te Tari Māori. Ko ahau i Broadwood ki Hokianga, i reira hoki a ia. I mōhio ia ki tōku tūpuna, ki a Bobby. Nāna au i kawe ki te kāinga o te koroua rā.

Nā, ka tika au ki te huarahi, e torotika atu ana ki tōna kāinga, me taku āhua ohooho i roto i ahau. Kia ahatia ake. Tae atu au ki te kūaha, ka pātōtō atu i te tatau.

I made my way from Christchurch to the Far North – to the Hokianga. It was a journey filled with adventure, excitement and trepidation and, by the time I got there, being a student, I was flat broke.

I hadn't grown up among Dad's whānau, hapū and iwi. When I knocked on the door to my grandfather's house, I guess I had harboured visions of what he would be like – what *they* would be like – which, in retrospect, were too romantic to be real. When Bobby Roberts opened the door the romantic and the real came together in the old, very real, man standing there with an enquiring look on his face.

'Tēnā koe, I'm your grandson.'

I began the voyage of discovery into my Te Rarawa ancestry and, through that voyage, I discovered that the reality was much better than I had dreamed of. Āe, he tika anō hoki ko te kī, ko te mea nui rawa o te ao, he tangata.

There was another piece of the puzzle, however, that I had to find and, on my return to Christchurch, I told my fiancée, Poto, that I wanted to be with my father in Australia. I eventually located him. We then moved to Sydney and began the typical Kiwi OE experience. During the course of our stay I got closer to Dad. We talked, I asked questions, he told me all the *whys* of all the decisions that had led him to leave

New Zealand – and us and me – and the various pains of youth were put into a perspective I could begin to understand.

But the pull to return home to New Zealand became too strong to resist. I had come to some further confirmation of what I wanted to do with my life. I wanted to be more closely reconnected to my iwi, and spend time with my elderly kaumātua.

This also happened to coincide with Poto's own wishes. Like me, she needed to find her own whānau and roots. (When she did, it turned out that she was my cousin!) We flew to Auckland.

5.

Nā, i roto i taku hinengaro me taku wairua ka rapu ka kimi i ngā mātua tūpuna. Ahakoa rā kua mate, kei te ora tonu. Ko Ephraim Te Paa, ko Mereana Kerehoma, ko Vivian Gregory. Nā rātou ahau i tino atawhai kia pakari ai taku tū i runga i te tika, i te pono, ā, me taku heke mai i a Te Rarawa iwi.

Auntie Mereana taught me my whakapapa and corrected me when I talked.

Viv Gregory shared with me his phenomenal knowledge of iwi history and taught me to view it without nostalgia.

Ephraim taught me about faith.

Nā, i Tamaki Makaurau ahau i tētahi wā ka patu mai te waea a Auntie Mere Williams me tana kī, 'E tino heke ana tō tāua matua a Paraima.' Nā, maranga tonu atu ana, kātahi au ka haere kia tae wawe atu ki tōna taha. Tae kau atu kite iho, āe, kua mōhio pū au he poto noa te wā mōna. Kua tino heke rawa tōna tinana, ka pupuha noa ana te manawa.

Kua tata atu au ki a ia. I roto i ā māua mihi mutunga, ka tukuna mai e ia ēnei kupu: 'Tūwheratia mai ngā tatau onamata. Ko wai te Kīngi o ngā Kīngi? Ko Ihowa o ngā mano, piringa mō te iwi.'

He ōhākī, he kupu whai mana, he wai aroha.

E kara e Ii, kourua ko Nani, hoki wairua mai.

Poto and I settled in South Auckland. Poto gave birth to a son, Aotea. We all became firmly ensconced in the fertile Māori cultural life of the city. I began to strengthen my links with my whānau, Te Rarawa iwi, and with many Māori throughout the country.

It helped that, in 1980, I was fortunate enough to secure work at the Race Relations Office. At that time, Hiwi Tauroa was the Race Relations Conciliator.

For four years I busied myself in the important work of the Office. I investigated many cases of racial prejudice. I travelled the country exhorting the benefits of cultural difference and of respecting human rights.

The work was an eye-opening experience. In the future, historians will look back and realise how turbulent the 1980s were as a period in New Zealand's history. The Springbok Tour happened and became symptomatic of the country's ambivalence about what constituted good race relations.

On the cultural side, Poto and I became involved with kapahaka.

We joined Manawanui, a Manurewa-based kapahaka group led by Archie and Maidey Tamanui. Manawanui was not a competitive group; we did performances at school fairs, rest-homes, charity gigs and hui Māori. We had a wonderful time.

After a while though, I guess you could say that some of us started to get itchy feet for the thrill and excellence of competition perform-ance. He pono mārika te kī, he iwi whakataetae te iwi Māori nei. Kāore e kore, he hua kei roto i tērā hanga tangata, ka mutu e anga whakamua ai te iwi. Inā kore pea, ka noho noa iho hei roro more. Because of this, some of us in Manawanui joined Te Waka Huia, the group set up by Ngāpō (Bub) Wehi and his wife Pīmia (Nen) when they moved from Gisborne to Auckland in the early 1980s. Te Waka Huia displayed all the hallmarks of the 'supergroup' that Bub and Nen had belonged to in Gisborne – Waihīrere – and was a great showcase for Māori lyricism, melody and haka. Very soon, I found myself on the Te Waka Huia circuit performing at the Auckland Museum, in restaurants, on cruise ships and anywhere the club was wanted – including competitions.

And, of course, along the way, Bub and Nen added much more to my understanding of being Māori. They were, and still are, two of the most naturally gifted teachers I know. Not only was their knowledge of waiata, haka and tikanga profound, but they taught and practised a brand of pride and humility which still inspires me. In addition, their type of leadership taught me more about the effective management of people resources than any professional training I've had. Bub's wisdom was always brief but it went straight to the point.

'The world revolves around respect,' he'd say. Or, 'If you look good you are good.'

Nen, on the other hand, wouldn't say much at all. But when she did, ka mau te wehi!

Apart from this, in Te Waka Huia I came to understand fully the catharsis of haka and the simple joy of singing – when you know what you're singing about, that is. My seventh form school rugby haka was a distant and slightly uncomfortable memory.

Although my work in the Race Relations Office was fulfilling, I decided it was time for a change of job. On April Fool's Day, 1984, I started work with Television New Zealand as a reporter/researcher for *Kōha*, then the most significant deliverer of Māori news and cultural programmes to New Zealand.

From that very day I knew that television and the film/video media would be my vocation. Through my work I discovered a chance to explore my creativity, and an opportunity to advance kaupapa Māori.

In 1987, Poto and I separated. Our son went to stay with Dad while Poto and I sorted things out.

On 14 January 1988, Aotea, who was then six years old, was hit by a car.

He died from his injuries soon after.

Nothing really prepares you for the death of your child. The death of my son was the sweetest tragedy of my life – tragic because any child's death is a tragedy, but sweet too because the death of my boy helped me to achieve a better understanding of life and what's really important about having it.

Poto and I brought our son back from Australia to be buried at our home marae in Ahipara, Northland. It was a long journey. Kua mātua tīraha mai a ia i roto i te kāinga o taku Pāpā i Poihākena. Kātahi ka whakawhiti mai ki Manurewa nei ki tō māua ake kāinga takoto ai. Ahu atu i kō, ka whakaritea te marae o Kōkiri ki Maungarei i Tāmaki-makaurau nei hei wāhi tangi, tuku poroporoaki. Te otinga ake o tērā wāhanga, kua whakatika rawa atu mātou, kotahi atu, ki te hau kāinga, ki raro i te keokeo tapu o Whangatauatia maunga tutuki ai i te tikanga mate. My overriding memory of those awful days is simply a feeling of gratitude for the efficacy of tikanga Māori in assisting me to cope with death, and humility in the face of those many hundreds of people who came to tangi and to shed and share pain.

A year later came Aotea's unveiling.

Whānau and friends came up to Northland and paid their respects at our hapū urupā of Ngātotoiti. After the ceremony I turned and looked at our mountain, Whangatauatia. Years earlier it had seen me come to Ahipara as a teenager looking for my grandfather and my roots. It had seen me come back at Aotea's birth, as a new father, to bury his pito. Now it had seen me bury my son.

Looking at the mountain, however, a great sense of aroha and understanding came over me. I realised that the mountain, the maunga, had seen not just my story but the stories of countless others who had lived in joy or sadness, laughter or tears, season after season, year after year. Countless thousands over countless years.

I was overcome by a sense of place, of belonging, and my place in it. My story was one of many stories and it would join with them and go on forever.

It's good to feel small. To know that sense of place historically and tribally.

I te tau 1977 i taku hounga tuatahi atu ki roto ki tōku tūpuna whare a Te Ōhākī, terā ko ōku wheinga e kitea ana hei whakaāhuatanga mai, hei whakaataatatanga mai. He hononga tāngata e whiria ai e te taura mana o tuawhakarere. Heoi anō i taua wā tonu he kanohi tauhou katoa ērā whakapakoko ki au.

Tōmuri rawa mai, i ngā wā e tū ai au ki mua i tō rātou aroaro. He rerekē noa ake nei taku tirohanga. Ināianei tonu e mōhio pū ana au ki a rātou. Ehara rātou i te tauhou. He whānau kē. Ko tōku rahinga ake terā e iriiri mai ana kei nga pātū o te whare, ā, ko taku uri a Aotea Daniel Te Aewa hoki terā.

Haere koe e taku tama.

E tama piki atu ki Whangatauatia
Whakarongo ā tai
Kariri Kura ē
Tiro haere kimi haere ē

E tama uia nō wai tāua
Nō Te Rarawa iwi
Pōroa me ngā ture
Hei kahu iho nei

E tama uia ko wai tāua
He wairua tuku iho
Nō ngā tūpuna
Kāti rā, whakarongo ē

E tama uia mā wai tāua
Puritia te aroha
Hutia te rito
He tangata he tangata ... Moe

6.

Kua roa au e mahi ana i roto i te ao pāoho. He tini ngā whakaaturanga kua oti nei i a au te hanga, ahakoa Māori, ahakoa Pākehā te kaupapa. Me te mea nei i kaha waimarie au, koia te take e taea ai e ahau ngā iwi maha, nga hapū maha te whakapā atu, tae rawa mai ki te reanga tamariki mokopuna. I te mea he kanohi ora ēnei me kī ko rātou mā, he taonga.

Heoi anō kua mōhio atu kua mōhio mai. He hōnore nui tērā e whaka-whanake ake ai ko taku tū Māori.

He hokinga mahara tēnei nōku ki ngā wā i noho tahi ai au me ngā kuikuia, koroua o taua ao. Ko te nuinga, kua nunumi atu ki te pō. Hāunga anō rā te taha ki ngā mahinga pāoho o taua nohotahitanga. Tērā he pito-pito māramatanga i riro mai i a au i te āhua o ngā kōrero kua kōrerotia e rātou. He ākoranga, he tohutohu i roto i ā rātou kupu. He mea tuku mai ki a au i runga i te aroha mutunga kore.

Koutou kua moe, haere, whakangaro atu. Pikihia ngā whetū, te marama, kia rere ko te ata e whāia nei.

I met my darling Lee, a Pākehā woman, who has been with me now for eleven years. Our relationship is a reflection of biculturalism – its many dilemmas and its many fruits. Our respective points of view are often so different. We are often torn between the Māori and the Pākehā sides of our lives. When we are able to reach a decision which melds both, however, we achieve what I call 'the magic that can result when you marry the Māori mōhio and the Pākehā clever'.

Seven years ago, Lee and I had a daughter, Ariana Jo Te Ripowai. She is now older than Aotea was when he died. Getting her past that age was important to me.

Today, I have a large and very spread-out family. My mother still lives in Christchurch and my father still lives in Sydney. I've got brothers and sisters in both countries and love them all to bits.

My whānau in Auckland is a large one. On my grandmother's side the cousins are innumerable. Their kids are everywhere. Our kaumātua, Auntie Clare and Uncle George, reign over it all from the kitchen of their home in Papatoetoe. Auntie Aloma is in charge of her lot over on the North Shore. Denis and Sonia, out West Auckland way, are also the Te Arawa and Hāmoa connection. Richard, Grenville, Walter, Dennis and Stephen are spread around South Auckland with their tribes. Barry gets around all the rohe. Lee, Ariana and I are bang in the centre.

On my grandfather's side, the grand old lady of the clan is Auntie Hera Waitai, who still lives up at Waihopo. She might be eighty-four but she still swings her legs around to get outside and do her work. She might irritate her many mokopuna sometimes but we all respect her. We know her, what she's like, and what her place is in the whakapapa. She's a living legend.

Up in Ahipara there's Isobel and her whānau, who live in the old homestead, the same one whose door I had knocked on those many years ago when I was trying to find my grandfather. Auntie Mere Nu is still up at Wainui Junction, offering her boundless aroha to all.

Across from Mere's place in the Ngātotoiti cemetery – where my boy, Aotea, lies – are our tūpuna of Ngāti Moetonga and Te Rokekā. Among them are Uncle Sam, who died in his brand new gumboots, delivering a mihi during a whānau fundraising event. Uncle Graham and Auntie Hera are also there, two kaumātua who were so good to their 'tamaiti Pākehā' – although they couldn't afford it, they used to slip me twenty-dollar bills when I visited them on holiday from Canterbury University. Too young to die, Scotty MacPherson, a principal of Tīpene College and a man of great mana and vision, rests in the cemetery. So too does Whangatauatia Williams, who was as big as the mountain and had a heart to equal his considerable girth. Ā, me te nuinga noa atu.

And next to Aotea's grave is my grandfather, Bobby Roberts. When I found him, all those years ago, I was the first of his uri he had met. He'd never known my father, his only natural child. Grandad was a hard but fair man. He took me into his care and loved me. I, in turn, needed him. He was my link to the land and to the people that I belong to. He made it possible for me to find myself and, in doing so, I know that I have a place prepared for me in our whānau urupā.

I once managed to get my grandfather together with Dad in Australia. There was too much bitterness, regret and difference between them, so the meeting never worked out. I never really did get the chance to see four generations – grandfather, father, son, and grandson – together. Inā taku mamae.

In that little urupā are people who have been good to me and people who have been pissed off with me. People who lived the usual gamut of life's slings and arrows and aroha. They are my people and I am proud of them.

As for the rest of life, the Māori experience of existence is as full of variety and difference as the Pākehā – but I place a greater trust in the Māori. It is linked to nature and to the human reality in a way that has been forgotten and discarded by Pākehā. It also embraces the ironies of existence.

The more I learn about my Māoritanga, the less I see it as a clue to my Māori-ness than as a means for realising my humanity. Tikanga Māori represents a map of the human condition. We disregard it at our peril. None of this makes life any bloody easier. But at least it gives some clues to help me along the way.

I'm a lucky bastard. I've seen the ups and downs of life. I've been around this country and much of the world and sampled many scenes and situations in the process. So much so that it sometimes seems to me that I've been from the gutter to te rangi tūhāhā! I'm endlessly fascinated by people, and the good and bad that they do.

In many ways, I'm still the quiet loner of my youth. I like to do things that allow me to think and ponder. I love my music and my books – a koha from my mother. I'm fascinated by history.

Shakespeare was right. The past is our prologue. He whakaaro Māori tūturu tēnei.

I'm arrogant to the degree that I like to think I have a certain capacity to be visionary. I am often good at what I do. People look to me for leadership. But I believe too in a sign I once saw in Pita Sharples' office: 'I am the leader of the people I am following.'

I also know my place in my whakapapa. He iti taku iti.

One of the greatest things that this has taught me, is that I can't do everything. All that I, or anyone for that matter, can ever hope to achieve in the span of a lifetime, is to contribute ...

In the meantime, I have my wife to be with, our child to nurture, and a whānau and friends to love and enjoy. That is more important than anything else. A life is a mere blip in time. Gotta get on with it. Be gone soon.

Ko Whangatauatia te pae maunga
Ko Kariri Kura te tai mihi tangata
Ko Ahipara kāmehameha te marae
Ko Te Ōhākī te tūrangawaewae
Ko Te Rarawa te iwi
Ko Ngāti Moetonga rāua ko Te Rokekā ngā hapū
Tihewa Mauriora!

An Existence in History

IRIHAPETI RAMSDEN

Irihapeti Ramsden was born in 1946 and is of Ngāi Tahupōtiki and Rangitāne descent. She was brought up in Wellington by her Pākehā father as well as by the people of her mother, Ngāti Irakehu of Horomaka. She is a member of the Haeata Women's Collective and was a member of the Spiral Collective which published the bone people in 1984.

Irihapeti Ramsden is not unfamiliar with controversy. She is an architect of the educational process known as Cultural Safety which has now been adopted by most nursing schools in Aotearoa. Her current interests are in the urban experience of Māori people and the development of identity and confidence towards the achievement of sovereignty for Māori.

Like all young children, my brother and I had little insight into the context into which we were born and were to grow up. I had no idea that our mid-1940s and 50s childhood was unlike that of most other Māori children of our times. Now I see that there were consistent themes to our Māori-ness, and that the characters in our lives and their roles were largely managed by my Pākehā father, Eric Ramsden, and his involvement with Te Ao Māori. I discovered a telegram among his papers: COME TO NGARUAWAHIA ON FRIDAY....TE PUEA. I was born on Thursday night while he was on the overnight train. My mother, Merenia, left a cocktail party to go and give birth.

The earliest themes were based on my father's notions of noblesse oblige toward Māori (rangatira only) and the ideas which underpinned the liberal intellectual activities of his day. The Noble Savage was a constant looming shadow on our horizon and our father's heroes were the classical Greeks and Romans, Elsdon Best, Raymond Firth, Peter Buck, Apirana Ngata and Te Puea Herangi. He was also an admirer of

Samuel Marsden and James Busby, and became their biographer.

I think that I could say quite neutrally that growing up Māori in 1940s Wellington among the Diplomatic Corps, government circles, lunching at Government House, as well as frequently travelling to my old family in Ngāi Tahu, had a bell-jar feel to it. Life was and still is, a constant series of borders and frontier crossings.

Our mother, Merenia, was a mokopuna of Rangitāne. Ngāti Mairehau, Ngāti Aranaki, Te Rangi Te Paia and Te Rangi o Tū are her hapū. Ngāti Irakehu and Ngāi Tūāhuriri of Canterbury and Horomaka, and all Ngāi Tahu, are her whanaunga of the south.

Looking back on the lives of the people in Merenia's family provides a surprisingly neat vignette of New Zealand history since colonisation. The histories of Ngāi Tahu migration from the North Island, conflict and later intermarriage with local people, settlement, and population growth, followed their human courses and are known through the mechanism of whakapapa.

Then contact in 1769. Civil wars, evangelisation, massive ruptures in land ownership, disease, unkept government promises, marginalisation and poverty, required swift reform of every aspect of people's lives.

Our tipuna Tikao signed the Treaty of Waitangi at Onuku as 'John Love'. Under his name on the Treaty document it says: 'a most intelligent native ...'. Having lived in England and France, Tikao spoke and wrote English competently. Later, after his sturdy opposition to the land purchases in our area, George Grey referred to him as 'an insolent and turbulent native ...'. After spending time in Europe in the 1820s he warned his people of the price of land in England and of the dire consequences of colonisation. There was little they could do at the time. Decimated by civil war and disease, they signed the New Zealand Company and government deeds in order to retain the mana whenua status of Ngāi Tahu, frequently under protest.

Because Tikao resurveyed and corrected the boundaries of the land sales in our area, our families still have some land. Marginal economically though it is, we have land upon which we can stand, and an identity, however fragmented, which we can call our own and upon which we are sturdily rebuilding. We have a lot to live up to.

Great-great-grandmother Mata Repeka Score married a Jewish-American whaler. Their eight children established well-known families in the south. Manawatu, Tikao, Nihoniho, Te Aika, Tirikatene, Solomon and Pitama are all names connected to this marriage. Repeka lived 102 years. Born in 1824, there was nothing in her life which would not have been profoundly reshaped by the time she died in 1926, from the language of her birth to what she had for breakfast.

I think of her often and reflect that the pace of change has always been as speedy in each generation. But these ancestors of ours are freeze-framed. We colour them in colonial tones, romanticise them, render them humourless, apolitical, almost asexual and often very boring. Then we set them up as unreal role models for our young. Aided by the colonial education system, we refashion them according to our perceptions of their times and finally we come to believe the stories we have woven about them. Thus we are left with stereotypical images of gods, warriors, maidens and cute piccaninnies, bereft of real power.

Demythologising the stories of our country or teasing out the truth from these colonial constructs is a task we must face if we are to understand the passion and richness of being here. Then the tīpuna must be reinstated in their full humanity, strength, and frailty, so that their contribution to the human story might be truly understood.

Every child in this country should know of the magnificence of the achievements of the East Polynesians who arrived here in orderly migrations. And every child descended from them should come to know deeply that within their DNA resides the possibility to replicate the vision, courage, personality and intellect of those real family members. They should understand that we do indeed come from the deep end of the gene pool.

Our great-grandfather Teone Taare Tikao became the first Chair of the Federated Assembly of the Kotahitanga which met at Papawai, Wairarapa, in 1893, in an attempt to form a pan-tribal opposition movement to the Westminster-type parliamentary system in Wellington. His wife, Mata Hana Toko Solomon, often travelled with him and their babies were given names to commemorate those momentous times.

Life for their mokopuna Merenia Manawatu was transitional in every way. No Māori person could avoid the cultural chaos of colonisation in 1920s New Zealand. Merenia refused the traditional marriage which awaited people of her generation and status, eventually living in Wellington with my father at the time of my birth in 1946. They married several years later.

Merenia's names came from her Rangitāne and Ngāi Tahu families and her mother's name was given to me. The first Irihapeti in our whakapapa appears in 1842.

Throughout my life my grandmother's name has been reshaped and reinterpreted according to the power of those who have been able to redefine it to suit their comfort and their norms. When my parents separated my father immediately ceased calling me Irihapeti. I became Elizabeth at school and later, in the whizzy sixties, Liz. I knew my names but did not have the confidence or the power to restore them to myself. When I was finally able to do that in the early 1980s, I felt at peace with my whakapapa and strong enough to take on the political world around me.

There was never a time when I was not conscious of being Māori because nobody allowed me to forget it. Mine was a surprisingly nourishing Māori experience. The clear favourite of our Manawatu grandfather who often lived with us, I was dandled and indulged. I was also the rare child available to the young rural-urban migrants of the 1940s. Even today I have multiple grandparents from all over the country who cared for us as babies. From Ngāti Porou kōkā to Ngāi Tahu tāua and poua.

They came to Wellington and the Ngāti Pōneke Young Māori Club, as government-sponsored trade training schemes were short-sightedly located in the cities. Māori young people, educationally underserved, were the semi-skilled workforce as the post-war economic policies required the assembly of heavy machinery inside New Zealand. They were moved rapidly to town. The urban drift was a massive, orchestrated population shift.

At Ngāti Pōneke, Bishop Frederick Bennett baptised my cousin and I as Christians. Young women from the club made my gown and petticoats; they are still the aunts. Now, with the knowledge of the way Christianity was manipulated to become a deadly player in the colonial games, I cannot be a part of the praying and singing of hymns and Christian procedure which has become such a part of some Māori ritual. It always seemed to me that if our collective prayers had been

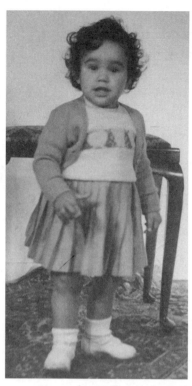

Snapped in Wellington in 1948 at almost three years old.

effective, we would be the healthiest, happiest and wealthiest people on the Earth. So far, no good.

In our own corner of the Ngāti Pōneke hall the tiny community of Māori children were taught waiata and haka. Among them were the family of Jacquie Sturm and James K Baxter.

The great throbbing haka, 'Poropeihana' and 'Ka Panapana', exercised by those migrant teenagers will always belong to my babyhood, along with the songs taught by nostalgic post-war aunts who looked very far away as they sang 'From the halls of Montezuma to the shores of Tripoli', 'The Marine Hymn', and 'Bueno Notte Signorina'. The American marines were well remembered by the aunts who stayed at home. So were the Italians remembered by the 28th Battalion uncles.

They taught me the raunchy songs in Māori and I piped them back again on cue, much to their delight. I remember kuia at Ngāti Pōneke instructing and counter-instructing me about how to sit on the lavatory without touching it or falling in, my short, fat, brown legs unable to reach the floor.Very confusing for a toddler. My father's diary at the end of my first year records: 'Baby took her first steps to her kuia from Rangitāne, Pirihira Heketa.'

Now those same trade trainees are in their sixties, contributing to urban Māori organisations, and continuing the emotional and political links with home. I have recently seen some taking their places as composers and judges at the huge Aotearoa Māori Cultural Festival.

On Sunday nights we solemnly listened to Bill Parker of Ngāti Porou reading the Māori news on 2YA. My father talked of the hard work to get a Māori-speaking voice on national radio. Later I saw some of the battle which Eric fronted to get the new English Queen to Tūrangawaewae for a few minutes of her post-Coronation tour.

Māori politics of the pragmatic kind were the issues of our

household. Our home was constantly filled with Māori shakers and movers, politicians (mostly conservative), artists, those who made music (serious only), and those few who were able to negotiate their way safely through the academic system. Inia Te Wiata, Maharaia Winiata, the multi-talented Bennetts, the Mitchell sisters from Te Arawa, and Te Mauri Meihana, and many, many more, vigorous, electric people. Some kuia had moko, which seemed normal then. The discussion was of legislation, housing, health status, getting representation, raising funds. Then, it seemed to me, they went out and did it. An early lesson in locating the focus of power and doing something about relocating it.

Early memories are of staying at Waiomatatini, riding with Apirana Ngata on his horse over land schemes. I remember Te Rangihiroa, who became godfather to my brother and gave him his name. Te Puea Herangi and Eric last met at Parliament one freezing day. In the shelter of the wooden wing they huddled together, she small and coughing and he anxious and frustrated at the independence many Māori were beginning to seek from his involvement in their affairs. As a small girl I sensed their mutual sadness rather than understood it. They had been close friends since the 1920s.

Because we were motherless, Eric took one or both of us everywhere with him, to the huge tangihanga of Te Rangihiroa, Te Puea, Te Kani Te Ua, hui and strategising meetings all over the country. In a time when people looked up to point out aircraft to each other and there were few cars, everybody travelled by train. People met at the station clutching pillows for a shilling and rocked through the night to their destinations.

One day when I was eight our sister came to live with us. We did not know that she existed, although she knew of us. From birth she had lived at Ngāruawāhia and now she and her whāngai mother were with us. Raised in the political environment of Tūrangawaewae, this child had little exposure to the Pākehā education system and as a result spoke pure Tainui dialect and was secure in her Māoritanga and confident of it. The process she endured to be socialised as Pākehā still wrings my puku. At the time I was more concerned about having to share my bedroom.

My grooming to be the new Te Rangihiroa continued. Thrice-weekly my father took me to the public library (bless Peter Fraser) and carefully selected my books, something for which I am still grateful. I was introduced to the Pākehā classics, history, geography and biography, and still have a taste for them all.

School had its moments. My first school was a private Anglican one in Wellington. Religiously, each afternoon, I was stoned as I left the school gates, for being Chinese. 'Ching chong Chinaman' still rings in my ears along with the thump of stone on my head and body.

Later, as part of the only Māori family in a very cosmopolitan school, I happily colluded with the museum view of Māori and the complete dislocation between myself and the rest of East Polynesia. I gave morning talks about the korowai which hung on our walls and covered our sofas at home and hauled those korowai and other taonga backward and forward to school. I did exactly the same with the first published copy of the *Evening Post* carefully obtained by my papa. That was the subject of equally little interest on the part of my fellow students.

Regularly, after our non-sectarian school day, the Roman Catholic girls from the convent next door were stoned as they tried to pass our school gates. How did all those New Zealand children learn those hateful lessons so early and so well?

What was important in hindsight was the almost complete success of the assimilationist policies which deliberately sought to sever Māori children from their Polynesian selves. I did not associate my grandparents, our pā or the way in which we did things with the school or museum view of Māori. Nor do I believe the education system of today serves our children any better. The waiata ā ringa, kapahaka, pōwhiri and attenuated and patronising rituals which the system tells us are Māori do not prepare our children for their economic and political future. Nor does it prepare them to transform their world. The continued manipulation and sanitisation of history sustains the void in identity. Swinging a poi or waving a taiaha at a prospective employer will not guarantee tino rangatiratanga.

Somehow I was able to make my intellectual and emotional way through my childhood and select my own heroes. She was a young Māori woman who captured my teenage imagination, who infuriated my father because she consistently refused to stay in her allotted place and keep deferentially quiet. She stood up to Eric and, worse, ignored him. Mira Petricivic (Szaszy) was and is a gracious, intelligent and beautiful woman. Her role modelling as a university student and activist gave me one of the the links I needed to find my place in the border countries and taught me how to make the bridges between all my worlds more solid and real.

From watching Mira and many others I knew that it was decent and proper to be Māori, that there was much work to be done, and that we would survive and grow. Later I learned that we exist in history and that whoever writes the story controls it. Like bell hooks, I thirsted for theory, thirsted to understand. Still do.

I understand that we must cease to believe the colonial stories we repeat to ourselves about ourselves. One of the most destructive is that we are a simple, oral, warrior culture. We are doubled in skill and power by our command of language through the written medium as well as oral communication. The facts are clear that our past family members voraciously sought the power of literacy. The early publishing of many Māori newspapers has helped lead to the generation of a political and creative literature recognised around the world; all this has somehow been kept from most of our people.

A literature of historical truth is a dangerous thing in a colonial environment and it will not be found in the systems set up for the future of the new people. The pen is mightier than the sword and writing endures if it has meaning for the world. We must continue to write our versions of the truth so that the people of this country can make informed decisions about our futures.

Even now that I am in my fifties the sound of a keyboard is still very comforting to me. I suppose I heard my journalist father tapping away at his Remmington typewriter all the time I was growing in my mother's womb. It is certainly a sound which can still send me very securely to sleep. My daughter tells me the same thing, as she sleeps in the room where I write.

There are so many questions to be asked about growing up Māori. First we should ask them of ourselves. What will happen to the fair generations of our mokopuna, the wellspring of our people? When will we revalue those of us who carry the āhua of their tīpuna inside them? When will whakapapa become more important than appearance or the possession of a Māori language often almost devoid of meaning because the old truths have been leached out of it and replaced with colonial constructs? How will our revamped identity affect those of the future? How can we make our children truly confident and powerful enough to take control of our destiny? There is so much still to write and learn.

I have had a wonderful life in many ways. The circularity of it has intrigued me. On the hill beside us is the site of Tūāhuriri's pā in the sixteenth century – we dug through their middens as we established our first garden. Down the road the now 'reclaimed' estuary which fed generations of our people has been turned into a playing field. The house where we live is two doors away from the one in which I was born. It is situated on the hill where our family of pre-contact times did their bird-hunting. In the garden lies my breast, and its cancer, buried by the women of my whānau, not to mention my mother's brother's teeth, found in his mug after his tangi.

The powerful Waitoa stream, known well to our ancestors, has shaped the street system in this Wellington suburb. Every now and then it breaks free of its piped constriction and erupts through the tarsealing. I mihi to it and know that we are indeed humble creatures in the face of nature, and reflect with a tad of satisfaction on my father's adage that everything which goes up must come down. This country will change to accommodate its first peoples in ways that will be of real benefit to us. I believe that we have a right and a duty to take part in the transformation of our society for the betterment of all our futures. How we do it is the issue.

WAKA 46 (From STAR WAKA)

it is feasible that we will enter space
colonise planets call our spacecraft waka
as well

perhaps we will name them after the first fleet
erect marae transport carvers renew stories
with celestial import

establish new forms of verse
free ourselves of the need for politics
and concentrate on beauty

like the release from gravity
orbit an image until it is absorbed
through the layers of skin

spin it
sniff and stroke the object
become poetic

oh to be in that generation
to write in freefall picking up the tools
our culture has given us

and to let them go again
knowing they won't hit anyone
just stay up there

no longer subject to peculiarities
of climate the political economies
of powers and powerless

a space waka
rocketing to another orb
singing waiata to the spheres

Robert Sullivan

E tamariki mā – study your whakapapa, and learn to trace your descent lines to all your ancestors, so you can join yourselves together. Do not use these treasures to raise yourself above others – ko mea, ko mea, ko hau! But if you are challenged, or somebody throws words at you on the marae, then it is proper to stand up and reply. The old people said to us, be humble; work amongst the people and they will learn to praise you. That was the wisdom of our ancestors, brought from the ancient houses of learning in Hawaiki. The old men told us, study your descent lines, as numerous as the hairs upon your head. When you have gathered them together as a treasure for your mind, you may wear the three plumes, 'te iho makawerau', 'te pareraukura' and 'te raukura' on your head. The men of learning said, understand the learning of your ancestors, so you can talk in the gatherings of the people. Hold fast to the knowledge of your kinship, and unite in the knot of mankind.

– ERUERA STIRLING (FROM *ERUERA: THE TEACHINGS OF A MĀORI ELDER*, REED, 1980)